# Poetry and a Principle

# Poetry and a Principle

Gene Montague

*J. B. Lippincott Company*
PHILADELPHIA NEW YORK TORONTO

ISBN-0-397-47216-1

Library of Congress Catalog
Card Number: 76-37397

Printed in the United States of America

# *Contents*

***For Study***

### *For Study*

# *Introduction*

If you came across a poem beginning

Because I could not stop for . . .

and you were asked to supply the last word in that line, you would probably supply something like "lunch"; for the same reason, in a sentence like "I went to the zoo yesterday and saw ______" you would supply "lions" or "bears" or "penguins." If somebody else supplied "God" as the last word in that sentence, you would stop and consider, just as you would if the last word in our first incomplete line were "Death"—as it is in the Emily Dickinson poem:

Because I could not stop for Death.

In both cases the writer traded on a pattern of expectation that you and he shared, and then he broke the pattern, shattering the expectation. When two people—or 200 million people—share the same language, they expect certain things of each other in the use of their common language. Among those are things as various as

(1) subjects having a certain relationship with verbs.
(2) busy people occasionally not stopping for lunch but always stopping for death.
(3) sonnets having 14 lines.
(4) a story that begins "Once upon a time, a beautiful princess..." probably including a Prince Charming but no motorcycles.

If a subject had no proper relationship with a verb, if busy people were said not to stop for death, if a sonnet had 18 lines, and if the princess sped away from her Prince Charming on a motorcycle, we would pay particular attention.

Another way to say the same thing at a more generalized level is that meaning in writing, particularly in poems, proceeds from patterns of expectation that are built into the poem and equally into the reader, and from sudden interruptions of the patterns. Meaning results from a juxtaposition of the expected with the unexpected.

That is the *principle* in the title of this book.

# 1

# *Poetry and a Principle*

*If any one reader says of a piece of writing "this is poetry," we are obliged to admit that it may be so for him, though it need not be for us. Thus the concept "poètry" is, ultimately, many-faceted, manipulatable, and definable only in terms of established practices which it is the chief endeavour of every poet to oppose, alter, and transform. Moreover, it is also clear that, from another point of view, and in the last resort, poetry is a quality, not of the thing written, but of the reader.*

—ROBIN SKELTON

A poem is something that somebody made, in the same sense that a painting or a birdhouse or a sculpture or a mud pie is. A painting is an arrangement of color that has behind it an idea or an impulse and an understanding of line and proportion and perspective. A mud pie is an arrangement of earth and water that has behind it some idea of what a pie looks like and a desire to make something and to have fun doing it. A poem is an arrangement of words and phrases that has behind it an idea or an impulse, some knowledge of how language works, and a need for expression. A poem is an object, made out of something for some purpose, containing meaning for someone.

In any creative act, the raw material is made to do what it cannot naturally do. As mud is not the same as a mud pie and color not the same as a painting, language is not poetry. It's the raw material. A mud pie is not a pie, nor is it simply mud anymore. It is an illusion of a pie. Nobody would care to eat it. It is what it is: a mud pie, neither pie nor mud and yet both. One admires a well-made mud pie or painting or poem without being fooled by it, and what he admires is the shape and the energy and imagination that went into it. It's a work of art—an illusion of reality—but only an illusion, and nobody who has his wits about him will bite into it or mistake it for the subject that it both copies and changes.

What we say of mud pies is true of any art object. One of the best-known art objects is Rodin's sculptured figure *The Thinker*. It is a hunched figure of a man, seated on a rock. Or is it? Practically speaking, it is bronze. Moreover, it was first clay and wax. Furthermore, it was at first not a single figure but a part of a larger sculpture, *The Gates of Hell*, in which it brooded over, and yet was a part of, Dante's damned and bedeviled creatures. In addition, it was briefly a gravestone: Rodin wanted it to be his epitaph and his headstone; when he was buried in Meudon in November 1917, the statue was moved to the head of his still-empty grave, where it towered over both the grave and the mourners. Add to this the fact that the figure is not manlike: the skin is rough textured, the hair is an undefined mass, the torso is top heavy, and the whole figure is more than life size.

What, then, is this thing? Suppose we ask the artist:

*Nature gives me my model, life and thought; the nostrils breathe, the heart beats, the lungs inhale, the being thinks, and feels, has pains and joys, ambitions, passions and emotions. These I must express. What makes my* Thinker *think is that he thinks not only with his brain, with his knitted brow, his distended nostrils and compressed lips, but with every muscle of his arms, back and legs, with his clenched fist and gripping toes.*

No man thinks with brow, nostrils, lips, muscles, clenched fist, and gripping toes. It is a man in the *act of thinking* that Rodin is rendering by repetition of the tension that the brain experiences in its own fashion—here extended to brow, nostrils, lips, etc. No man ever looked like this; no man ever thought like this. No clay, wax, or bronze ever looked like this before. *The Thinker* is an art object, a concrete representation of a creative insight. Easily within Rodin's capabilities was the creation of a smooth-skinned, life-size, exactly proportioned human figure. Instead he took the image of the human form and varied its attributes. What the statue *means* is a combination of what the viewer gathers from his own expectation of reality—the life-sized copy—and the variations, the breaking of that expectation.

The primary fact of art is that it makes things out of impossible materials. Pies cannot be made from mud. Experience cannot be made from language. Men cannot be made of clay. But mud can record someone's impression of a pie—a real or a possible pie—and language can record someone's impression of an experience. Mud can represent what mud cannot be, and language can communicate what language cannot say.

It is, for example, nearly impossible to convey emotion directly. If you say, "I am sad," one simply notes the fact that you say that you are sad but he himself feels no sadness. A good poem, however, never trying to state emotion directly, can so use language as to make the reader either feel sad or examine the nature of sadness.

As an illustration, look at one stanza of an old folk poem that exists in a dozen versions in several languages:

I gave my love a cherry that had no stone;
I gave my love a chicken that had no bone;
I sent my love a ring with no binding,
Then gave my love a baby with no crying.

What is the *subject* of the poem? Love. How do you know? Because it is the most-repeated noun in the poem. Is there a general statement about love made in the poem? Not on the surface, because the words *I* and *my* are repeated: this is a personal expression of the kind of love the speaker has had for his/her lover. (What in the poem would lead you to think that the speaker is a woman?)

What kind of love is it? Examine the language. In the statements made, the predicates repeat the same structure:

a cherry that had no stone
a chicken that had no bone
a ring with no binding
a baby with no crying

These are all paradoxes, seeming contradictions that state truths. A cherry without a stone must be a cherry in blossom. A chicken without a bone must be a chicken in the egg. A ring without binding must be a ring before it is put on or before it means something, i.e., engagement or marriage. A baby with no crying may mean a baby asleep or dead or in the womb. Which is the preferred meaning? Because of the previous meaning of cherry without a stone, chicken without a bone, ring without binding, the baby, in parallel fashion, must be a baby before it is born. What, then, did the speaker give as love tokens to her lover? What does this imply about the nature and intensity of her love?

The stanza has implied an emotional attachment that cannot be stated exactly. How did it manage that? By *repetition*. By repetition of word or phrase or syntax—by frequency or emphasis.

Poetry is communication that is highly personal, either to the poet or to the fictive speaker he creates, which must, nevertheless, be made clear to the reader who may or may not have shared his real or imagined experience. The method of communicating to the reader must therefore be through some body of shared signals, through what the reader expects to find or through what the reader does *not* expect to find. *What the reader expects to find is largely established by repetition. What the reader does not expect to find—and what, therefore, arrests his attention—is established by breaking a pattern of expectation.*

Meaning in any piece of writing is therefore created by the expected and the unexpected. What is expected because of repetition creates a form; what is unexpected creates emphasis. Both the form and the emphasis create *meaning.*

## Patterns

(1) Repetition creates patterns. If we repeat levels of *diction* (word choice), we create patterns of

| | |
|---|---|
| voice[1] | metaphor* |
| tone* | simile* |
| irony* | analogy* |
| paradox* | |

If we repeat the familiar *word order* of English, we produce patterns of

syntax*

If we repeat *sounds,* we produce patterns of

| | |
|---|---|
| rhythm* | alliteration* |
| meter* | consonance* |
| rhyme* | stanza* |
| assonance* | |

If we repeat an *expression* or an *event* that is familiar to the reader, we produce

allusion*
quotation*
paraphrase*

[1] Any term with an asterisk is defined in the glossary, pages 288-298.

And we may also again create

paradox*
parody*
irony*

(2) Variation on any pattern calls attention to itself and therefore creates emphasis.

To illustrate the two principles, let's take examples of some of these patterns and variations on them. Suppose we begin with the way a poet works both with and against a pattern of diction.

## Diction

As soon as any writer has set down more than four or five words, he has committed himself to a pattern of diction. He has set up an expectation in the reader's mind that amounts to setting limits to the poet's vocabulary *in that one poem.* A poem, for example, that begins

It was many and many a year ago
In a kingdom by the sea . . .

has shut out of its pattern of expectation thousands of English words, e.g., *hamburger*, *astronaut*, *barbershop*, *nitty-gritty*. But suppose one of these words did occur in the poem. What would become the most emphatic word in the poem?

A poem by e. e. cummings begins

The Cambridge ladies who live in furnished souls . . . .

What word breaks the pattern of diction? Obviously *souls.* One expects Cambridge ladies to live in furnished *rooms* or *houses,* but not in furnished *souls.* The most important word is the one that breaks the pattern. Predictably, the poem goes on to display the squalor of the moral opinions of the Cambridge ladies.

Theodore Roethke begins a poem with

> I have known the inexorable sadness of pencils.

What word breaks the pattern of expectation? *Pencils* stands out because it is not usually associated with sadness. Predictably, the poem goes on to illustrate the sadness of a life spent in the "tedium" of "pencils," "pad and paper-weight," "mucilage," "multigraph, paper-clip"—"Endless duplication of lives and objects."

## Syntax

Variation on normal English syntax produces equally important effects. In a poem that details the stupidity of erecting statues of generals in public parks (and lampoons the impulse behind this kind of hero worship), e. e. cummings pictures at the end of the poem one such statue standing "in real the rain." What word is out of its normal syntactical order? Obviously *real.* It is the unreality of the statue and the warped impulse that generates it that lies at the heart of the poem.

Dylan Thomas, in a poem lamenting the tendency of the modern world to divide all subjects into fact and fable, writes

> The insect certain is the plague of fables.

(*Insect* here preserves its root meaning of "divided," as well as suggesting "small" and "negligible.")

What word is out of its normal syntactical position? Obviously *certain.* One may in English say normally

Certainly the insect . . .
A certain insect . . .
The insect certainly . . .
The insect is the certain plague . . .
The insect is the plague of certain fables.

But one cannot normally say "The insect certain is the plague of fables." Thus *certain* must modify every important word in the sentence, justifying all the normal usages just listed.

## Grammatical Function

Allied to this practice is the technique of using a word in an unusual grammatical function. A classic example is Shakespeare's

Bare ruin'd choirs, where late the sweet birds sang. . . .

The unusual word, because of its position and function, is *sweet.* The song of the birds, not the birds themselves, was sweet (i.e., "where late the birds sang sweetly"). But by transferring the word, Shakespeare gets two effects: the reader will supply the normal reading anyway, and the poet is able to suggest how precious to him was the presence of those "sweet birds."

## Expression/Event

Repetition of expression or event works by comparison and contrast, as do the other practices. A repetition of expression may be a simple allusion, as when Milton, in a sonnet on his dead wife, speaks of her coming to him in a dream "like Alcestis from the grave." Milton, of course, was blind. The legendary Alcestis, who offered her own life to save her husband's and was rescued by Hercules, came from the grave hooded and veiled, as Milton's wife would have had to come, since he never saw her. By using one allusive word, *Alcestis,* Milton suggests several things about his condition and his view of his wife's death.

A slightly more complex example is Milton's reference in the poem "On His Blindness" to

> ... that one Talent which is death to hide,
> Lodg'd with me useless....

*Talent* recalls the parable of the talents (MATTHEW 25:24–30). The moral of the parable deepens the distress of the speaker in the poem, who went blind at age 42, when he was coming to the height of his powers.

*Talent* in both the parable and the poem has two meanings: the modern meaning of "natural ability for a specific pursuit" and the older meaning, "a large coin of great value." In the parable, the servant who was given one talent in trust by the master hid his talent in the ground and was subsequently thrown into the dark at the command of the master for not using that talent to produce more.

These examples, however, do not begin to plumb the possibilities of repetition of expression and event. We cited earlier a Dylan Thomas poem lamenting the modern tendency to divide all thought and feeling into fact and fable, into what is "true" and what is "visionary." The first line of that poem is

> To-day, this insect, and the world I breathe.

Thomas is speaking of his own verse. His first line echoes, sarcastically, the first line of a much more famous poem out of the age of fable, Virgil's *Aeneid*: "Of arms and the man, I sing." By this repetition and variation of expression, the sophisticated reader sees immediately the difference between the heroic poet and the contemporary poet, as Thomas conceives it.

Repetition of expression and event has been exploited by twentieth-century poets such as T. S. Eliot and Ezra Pound. The most celebrated and controversial poem of our century is surely *The Waste Land.* In it Eliot suggests the desolation of our civilization, in which faith, hope, and love have been replaced by sterility, indifference, and lust. Eliot makes his point by means of repetition of expression in which "The Way It Was" is contrasted with "The Way It Is." Situations out of older literature and tradition are juxtaposed with modern situations. Thus, in one passage:

> But at my back from time to time I hear
> The sound of horns and motors, which shall bring
> Sweeney to Mrs. Porter in the spring.
> O the moon shone bright on Mrs. Porter
> And on her daughter,
> They wash their feet in soda water.

The sarcastic *tone** of the passage can perhaps be sensed at first reading. But what Eliot is saying more precisely depends on recognizing the expressions he is paraphrasing:

(1) "But at my back I always hear/ time's winged chariot hurrying near;/ And yonder all before us lie/ Deserts of vast eternity." From Andrew Marvell's "To His Coy Mistress," a famous love poem in which the poet urges a lady to come to him now to make the most of the golden days of their youth.

(2) "You shall hear,/ A noise of horns and hunting, which shall bring/ Actaeon to Diana in the spring." From Day's *The Parliament of Bees,* which alludes to the tragic story of the goddess Diana and her admirer, Actaeon, killed by his own dogs for looking upon the goddess naked.

(3) "The moon shone bright on pretty Red Wing." From an American ballad about an Indian princess and her lover that has spawned several obscene versions.

(4) "The moon shone bright on Mrs. Porter/ And on her daughter;/ They wash their_______[1] in soda water/ And so they oughter,/ To keep 'em clean." From an Australian barracks ballad, familiar to veterans of two World Wars, in which Mrs. Porter is the madam of a brothel and her daughter is her chief employee. Sweeney ("ape-necked Sweeney") is a kind of modern Neanderthal that Eliot introduces into several poems as the prototype of contemporary animalism.

What is the purpose of these repetitions? They implicitly contrast epochs when love was more than sensuality with a time that, according to Eliot, has reduced love to lust. No reader need recognize all of the repetitions to see the contrast, but they all reinforce the contrast.

## Sounds

Repetition of sounds creates a wealth of patterns. For brief illustration, we limit ourselves to one example of repetition and two examples of variation.

A poet who wishes to appeal strongly to the ear of the reader can create intricate patterns of repetition that approximate music. John Keats, for example, in "The Eve of St. Agnes," occasionally duplicates exactly stressed vowel sounds in paired lines:

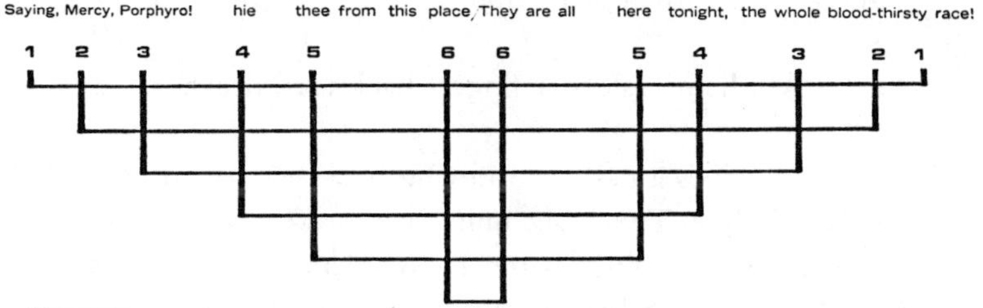


[1]Omitted not out of delicacy, but because of the multitude of colloquial synonyms for the female genitals.

The two lines are similar to singing the scales, up and then down.

Part of sound is *stress,** the relative weight that is put on a syllable. In English, two kinds of stress pattern are most common: rising stress, in which the stress appears after unstressed syllables ( ∪ | ) and falling stress, in which the stress precedes unstressed syllables ( | ∪ ). Perfectly regular lines can be, and often have been, written in either pattern. A poet may, however, achieve emphasis by substituting one unit of one pattern for another unit of the other pattern.

Thus, in Shakespeare's

> A kingdom for a stage, Princes to act . . .

the pattern is rising, but one falling unit has been substituted and the word that contains that substituted unit stands out as the most important word in the line. What word is it? Trust your ear:

> ∪ | ∪ | ∪ | | ∪ ∪ |
> A kingdom for a stage, Princes to act. . . .

The word is *Princes,* and that emphasis is justified in the lines that follow.

Occasionally a poet may want to build interest into a line that has little. Thus, a poet like the young Tennyson may try to spruce up an otherwise flat and uninteresting line by giving it a formal attraction:

> With rosy slender fingers backward drew.

The line describes a goddess drawing back her hair. It *sounds* attractive. Why? The basic units that make up the line are separate units in falling meter (rosy, slender, fingers, backward), but the poet has put an extra unstressed word at the beginning of the line (With) and a stressed word at the end (drew). The natural rhythm of the line is falling, but the meter is rising—not |∪|∪|∪|∪|∪ but ∪|∪|∪|∪|∪| —and the ear hears the two playing off against each other. One pattern rides over another, and what would have been a dull line suddenly sounds interesting.

In each of these examples, the poet has established some kind of pattern. The reader discerns the pattern and expects more of the same. The poet then breaks the pattern; and the reader, realizing the break, concentrates on the unit that broke the pattern.

It follows that the first task of the reader of poetry is to see patterns; that means only that he must be aware of language and its possibilities for forming patterns. The reader of poetry must take language seriously—not solemnly, but seriously. Every word in the language has meaning. It has meaning because:

(1) A word has a history. Through the years it may have taken on meanings other than its original meaning. Moreover, at a minimum, a word has a referent—something it points to. It has also an overtone—a connotation,* an emotional coloring that prevents any word in the language from being an exact synonym for any other word: a *snake* is not exactly a *serpent*, just as a *house* is not a *home*.

(2) A word has a sound. Words contain natural stresses and quantities that make them fit neatly into sound patterns or interrupt sound patterns.

(3) A word has a position. English is a distributive language; it indicates meaning primarily by the position of words in a sentence. Thus, "The boy bit the dog" does not mean the same as "The dog bit the boy," although the individual words are identical. Only their positions are different. Change the order and meaning changes. Change the order, and the reader will notice.

(4) A word has a function. English has grammatical patterns which dictate that, ordinarily, words have certain allowable grammatical functions. Thus, the word *how* is ordinarily adverbial. Change the function, and the reader will notice. What is the function of *how* in the following line?

anyone lived in a pretty how town....

What, for that matter, is the function of *anyone*, usually a pronoun?

The reader of poetry must take language seriously because the poet does. Much of what we read in day-to-day prose is, if taken seriously, nonsense. We take a sentence from a Sunday supplement with a circulation of millions:

> In our situation presently, we must hone our social consciousness in order to respond concretely and viably to the demands of our black citizens.

If you take language seriously, you cannot read that passage and gather what it has to say without giggling or swearing. What it says is logically absurd. *Presently* means "in the near future," not "now." How can you "hone" a "consciousness"? One hones a knife in order to use it to cut or slash—exactly the opposite of what the passage intends. What is "concrete" is solid. What is "viable" is capable of growth and expansion. How can a response be sharpened to cut, be solid and monolithic and yet be capable of growth and expansion? Moreover, a citizen is someone who owes allegiance to a government and is at the same time entitled to its protection. If a man is a citizen, he does not require someone who belongs ("we") to prepare himself to consider whatever the other demands, because the other is already part of *we*.

What the passage *intends* is probably something like: "We ought to put aside our usual prejudices and listen to the black American." What it *says*, if one takes language seriously, is something like "Sometime in the indefinable future, we ought to do something or other that I don't quite understand to show the black in America, who is not really a citizen, that he belongs here, but I don't know what that will be, although I hope it will improve things, sometime, somewhere, but deep down (*hone*) I still don't like the whole idea."

Words do have meaning. And men mean what they say and write, even though they sometimes do not say what they mean. In the beginning was the word, in more senses than one.

Nobody has yet built, nor is anybody ever likely to build, a cage that will confine, explain, or categorize all the operations of language. Probably nobody will ever cage and confine the possibilities of poetry. A mathematician might object to trying to construct a single theory of poetry by saying that there are too many variables to be taken into account; a dedicated critic would object by saying, "Thank God, there are too many variables." They are both right, thank God. A study of repetition and variation in poems is simply a way of entering poems, not a way of exhausting them. And enter we must—not skirt or glide over them, lest we lose the half of the poetic experience Robin Skelton points to in the epigraph to this chapter: ". . . in the last resort, poetry is a quality, not of the thing written, but of the reader."

# 2

# Discussion, Interpretation, Evaluation, and a Principle

The most difficult aspect of reading and discussing poetry is evaluation.

We are all judgmental; we can't wait to say good, bad, or indifferent about any object thrust in front of us. There's nothing sinful about that, but it does make a difference *on what basis and in what fashion we are judgmental.* It makes a difference because if we assume, for example, that a poem is a form of communication, and that discussion of a poem is a form of communication, communication would seem to have to rest on understood procedures. A discussion is not a discussion when everyone talks at once—that's just noise. A discussion is not a discussion if a series of people state, one by one, their set-in-concrete opinions and then sit, waiting to be challenged, impregnable in their opinions. A discussion will never be a discussion until the *roots* of opinion are exposed.

What often passes for discussion between and among governments as well as in college classrooms is really a confrontation, which may range in its absurdities from "I have this directly from God, and here I stand" to "I don't know much about poetry, but I know what I like." There was a time when it was more dangerous to challenge what one man got directly from God than what another man just liked, but that situation may be reversed today. In any event, neither position communicates much that is worthwhile unless the basic assumptions are investigated.

It would seem more profitable to propose, first, some method by which discussion can proceed and, second, some method by which evaluation can be attempted.

(1) It is ultimately unrewarding to argue over what one or another person "likes." What one likes is conditioned by a lifetime of experience that varies astronomically from person to person. In 1814 Samuel Taylor Coleridge set out a very useful distinction between the "agreeable" and the "beautiful." We find something agreeable, he said, because of the associations it has for us. But what is beautiful shows a harmonious organization, regardless of the associations it has. Many people call a thing beautiful when they mean only that they find it agreeable. What is agreeable may be good, bad, or indifferent; it may be beautiful or ugly. But what is beautiful is good, esthetically; it is a harmonious pattern created from disparate elements.

(2) Since this stated difference between the beautiful and the agreeable makes no distinctions about the beautiful in terms of subject matter but requires only that a harmonious organization be shown, it is doubtful that evaluation can profitably begin from preconceptions about what a poet must deal with or how he must deal with it. The criterion is harmonious organization. It is reasonable, then, to make two assumptions, one about the poem and the other about interpreting the poem:

a. *A good poem is one that is compatible with its own logic.* That is, the reader does not presume to require of the poet that he write on some topics and not on others, nor to dictate that he must not write on any given subject in a certain way. The poet chooses his own material and his own pattern; so long as the two are compatible—and *consistently* compatible—a harmonious organization develops. The poet determines, so to speak, the rules of the word game he is about to play. So long as he plays by those rules, he is safe from adverse judgments.

b. *The best interpretation of a poem is the one that takes into account the greatest number of elements ("facts") in the poem.* That is, the standard of excellence among interpretations is the fullest demonstration of "harmonious organization" in the poem. Again, this avoids the agreeable in favor of the beautiful. The interpretation that unites harmoniously the greatest number of elements in the poem is the best interpretation.

Teaching and learning would be much simpler if in the beginning we were to interest ourselves solely in *describing* rather than evaluating a poem (or painting, statue, film, novel, etc.). But it is futile to think that we can ever wholly separate those two processes. We judge as part of our initial response. What is important is that we reserve final judgment until we can state exactly the grounds of our judgment.

# 3

# *Patterns of Diction I*

We spoke in the first chapter of patterns of diction and how the poet either borrows an accepted pattern or creates his own and then breaks the pattern in order to create emphasis and meaning (pp. 7-17).

In this chapter we will investigate different ways in which poets build and break the pattern, without suggesting that these are the only ways.

Here is a single word cast as a poem:

> 1
> one
> 1
> y

*1.* The poem consists of four units, three identical in the statement they make. The last unit, *y*, is the stranger. What does the suffix *y* mean in English? (Compare *fun* > *funny*, *stink* > *stinky*.)

*2.* What is the subject matter of the poem? What is the theme*?

Here is a pattern of words making a complete statement:

THE RED WHEELBARROW

so much depends
upon

a red wheel
barrow

glazed with rain
water

beside the white
chickens

—WILLIAM CARLOS WILLIAMS

*1.* A statement is here fashioned into a poem consisting of four units shaped, measured, and spaced the same. Which one of the units is unlike the other three? In what way does that unit pose the only question in the poem?

*2.* When the last three units are taken together they make a picture. Why are the words *red*, *glazed*, and *white* important to that picture?

*3.* The last three units separately and collectively are simple yet precise and the details are carefully arranged. "So much depends/ upon" something there, says the poem. Remembering that the units make a detailed, vivid picture, what is it that "so much depends / upon"? Barnyards? This barnyard? The way this barnyard is seen? Is the poem about things or about a way of seeing things?

Here again is a single statement as a poem:

BOY AND TOP

Each time he spins it,
it lands, precisely,
at the center of the world.

—OCTAVIO PAZ

(translated by Muriel Rukeyser)

*1.* What single word stands out, both by its belonging to a different kind of diction and by its being separated visually from the other words?

*2.* What phrase stands out as being unexpected in a poem dealing with a boy and a top?

*3.* On the basis of your answers to questions 1 and 2, account for the tone of wonder in the poem.

Here is a poem in which the pattern is broken quickly:

## I HEARD A FLY BUZZ WHEN I DIED

I heard a fly buzz when I died;
The stillness in the room
Was like the stillness in the air
Between the heaves of storm.

The eyes around had wrung them dry,
And breaths were gathering firm
For that last onset when the king
Be witnessed in the room.

I willed my keepsakes, signed away
What portion of me be
Assignable—and then it was
There interposed a fly,

With blue, uncertain, stumbling buzz
Between the light and me;
And then the windows failed, and then
I could not see to see.

—EMILY DICKINSON

*1.* What word breaks the diction in the first line?

*2.* How does that break in the diction set up the contrast that continues through the rest of the poem? Imagine that this is a traditional deathbed scene with relatives, religion, relinquishment and bequests, and a sudden stranger, a blowfly, whose eggs make maggots, who carries quick decay and corruption.

*3.* The speaker says she is caught between the "heaves of storm." What does the poem imply about the realities of both "storms," given the contrasts in the poem?

Read the following poem by John Donne:

## A HYMN TO GOD THE FATHER

I

Wilt Thou forgive that sin where I begun,
  Which is my sin, though it were done before?
Wilt Thou forgive those sins, through which I run,
  And do run still, though still I do deplore?
  When Thou hast done, Thous hast not done,
    For I have more.

II

Wilt Thou forgive that sin by which I have won
  Others to sin, and made my sin their door?
Wilt Thou forgive that sin which I did shun
  A year or two, but wallowed in a score?
  When Thou hast done, Thou hast not done,
    For I have more.

III

I have a sin of fear, that when I have spun
  My last thread, I shall perish on the shore;
Swear by Thyself, that at my death Thy Son
  Shall shine as he shines now, and heretofore;
   And, having done that, Thou hast done:
    I fear no more.

*1.* The pattern of this ostensibly serious poem is broken by two puns* and a hidden quotation. That is, three phrases used in the poem have two meanings. (If it's not clear how a pun can break the diction, consider that in most but not all ages the pun has been considered a very low form of humor.) What are the two puns, based on homonyms* (words with different meanings, spelled differently but sounding alike)?

*2.* What two different meanings do the punning words have? Are the meanings compatible, given what the poem is talking of?

*3.* The poet lists a series of sins—original sin, habitual and willful sin, the sin of corrupting others, and the greatest sin of all in orthodox Christian doctrine, the "sin of fear," i.e., despair. Following that, the speaker says that he will be saved from this and the other sins if God will swear by himself that his Son (sun) will shine forever. Given the fact that in Genesis 22:16 God is said to have said to Abraham, "By myself have I sworn, for because thou hast done this thing, and hast not withheld thy son, thine only son, that in blessing I will bless thee . . . ," in what danger of damnation is the speaker in [Christian] actuality? How does this help to justify the use of puns in a seemingly serious poem?

*4.* How does the reader's view of the speaker's actual danger of damnation help to explain the title of the poem? It is called a hymn, which is a song of praise, not a prayer or petition as the poem on its surface would suggest.

In the following poem two voices share many of the same phrases but mean different things by them:

## SONNET FOR A PHILOSOPHER

"In categorical syllogisms," my logic professor said,
"Universal affirmatives distribute their subject terms only;
Thus," he said, "If 'All men are mortal,' the statement
Applies to all men but does not encompass mortality.
Or take another case: Sherman said 'War is Hell.'
The statement applies to all wars, but does not exhaust
The possibilities of Hell. Thus, Hell is not War."
He may be right. But I wanted to ask how many
Wars he'd been to and how many other possibilities
Of Hell he could conceive. I didn't ask.

It would have been something less than
A universal affirmative. "All men are
Mortal" is a safe example, well distributed.
Only the logical mind escapes mortality and the
predicated Hell that is War.

*1.* Who are the two speakers in the poem?
*2.* What is the difference between the two speakers in terms of what they assume and the way they view reality?
*3.* What is a "universal affirmative" in logic? What does the second speaker mean by that phrase in line 12?
*4.* What does the term *distributed* mean in logic? What does the second speaker mean by it in line 13?
*5.* What are the two meanings of *predicate*[*d*] in the poem?
*6.* What happens to the two voices in the last line? The content clearly belongs to the second speaker. But what of the style of utterance?
7. Explain the odd diction of the title: sonnets are not generally written by or for philosophers.

In the following poem an unusual and idiosyncratic diction is broken repeatedly by three other patterns, so much so that four patterns may be said to exist together.

### i sing of Olaf

i sing of Olaf glad and big
whose warmest heart recoiled at war:
a conscientious object-or

his wellbelovéd colonel(trig
westpointer most succinctly bred)
took erring Olaf soon in hand;
but–though an host of overjoyed
noncoms(first knocking on the head
him)do through icy waters roll
that helplessness which others stroke

with brushes recently employed
anent this muddy toiletbowl,
while kindred intellects evoke
allegiance per blunt instruments–
Olaf(being to all intents
a corpse and wanting any rag
upon what God unto him gave)
responds,without getting annoyed
"I will not kiss your f.ing flag"
straightway the silver bird looked grave
(departing hurriedly to shave)

but–though all kinds of officers
(a yearning nation's blueeyed pride)
their passive prey did kick and curse
until for wear their clarion
voices and boots were much the worse,
and egged the firstclassprivates on
his rectum wickedly to tease
by means of skilfully applied
bayonets roasted hot with heat–
Olaf(upon what were once knees)
does almost ceaselessly repeat
"there is some s. I will not eat"

our president,being of which
assertions duly notified
threw the yellowsonofabitch
into a dungeon,where he died

Christ(of His mercy infinite)
i pray to see;and Olaf,too

preponderatingly because
unless statistics lie he was
more brave than me:more blond than you.

–e. e. cummings

*1.* From what period of history and what cultural level are the following phrases drawn?

"I will not kiss your f.ing flag"
"there is some s. I will not eat"
"the yellowsonofabitch"

*2.* From what period of history and what cultural level are the following phrases drawn?

"but–though an host of overjoyed"
"first knocking on the head him"
"upon what God unto him gave"
"their passive prey did kick and curse"
"Christ(of His mercy infinite) i pray to see"

*3.* From what period of history and what activities or occupations are the following phrases drawn?

"recently employed/ anent"
"allegiance per blunt instruments"
"being to all intents"
"being of which/ assertions duly notified"
"unless statistics lie"

*4.* Is the poet suggesting a parallel between Olaf and a historical figure when he describes Olaf being tortured by the soldiers and dying at their hands? What other elements in the poem would you have to consider before answering?

*5.* Bearing in mind the answers to questions 1–4, what is the reason for the odd mingling of dictions?

*6.* "Olaf" suggests somebody blond and blue eyed. The soldiers are said to be "a yearning nation's blueeyed pride" and Olaf is said to be "more brave than me: more blond than you." What does this suggest about the nation's chosen heroes and its real heroes?

7. Notice that only Olaf is named in the poem; the soldiers have been reduced to their ranks (colonel, noncoms, officers, firstclass-privates) and even, in one instance, to the symbol of his rank, "the silver bird." Olaf is dehumanized in the poem, even though he is given a name. What does the trick of diction suggest about the effects of war on soldiers?

In the following poem, one pattern of diction has been deliberately and systematically altered. The ultimate variation of diction displaces entirely the reader's expectation by turning the poem into an anagram requiring the reader to reconstruct the underlying diction. But even that can be done according to a strict pattern of repetition.

when muckers pimps and tratesmen

when muckers pimps and tratesmen
delivered are of vicians
and all the world howls stadesmen
beware of politisions

beware of folks with missians
to turn us into rissions
and blokes with ammunicions
who tend to make incitions

and pity the fool who cright
god help me it aint no ews
eye like the steak all ried
but eye certainly hate the juse

—e. e. cummings

*1.* In the first and third stanzas,* the final syllables of the final words of the second and fourth lines have been interchanged, as have those of the first and third lines. In the second stanza, the first and second and the third and fourth exchange their final syllables. But to what purpose? None is perceptible in the first stanza, beyond establishing the pattern, unless one associates freely and perhaps wildly (i.e., tratesmen > trait-men, vician > vicious one, stadesmen > staid-men). But by this time a pattern of reference is emerging: muckers, pimps, and tradesmen were delivered of visions during the life of Christ, when he met all of them. In the second stanza, "blokes with ammunicions" are probably soldiers, and "blokes with ammunicions/ who tend to make incisions" must refer to the Roman soldiers who crucified Christ and pierced his side. On the other hand, "folks with missians/ to turn us into rissions" has to refer to Christ himself if "rission" is "medieval" English for "those who rise."

All of this, however, is simply preparation for the final stanza in which these word games are suddenly justified. In the last two lines, the speaker abruptly varies the normal spelling of important words; this means that homonyms reign. The last two lines, therefore, can be read in at least three ways:

(1) I like the steak all right
but I certainly hate the juice.

(2) I like the stake all right
but I certainly hate the juice.

(3) I like the stake all right
but I certainly hate the Jews.

The poem in its odd and deliberate misspellings, its repetition and variations, reproduces the dilemma of the Messianic experience. Consider the range of possibilities, using only the possible readings of the last two lines. The first is the remark of a down-to-earth, meat-and-potatoes creature. The second is the statement of a criminal—in one line ancient, in the next contemporary. The third is the statement of a historical, meat-and-potatoes but still Messianic Christ. Even this reading oversimplifies the possibilities since *stake* has been historically a metaphor for whatever death Christian martyrs meet, including the cross, the stake, and the sword; and *stake* also means the thing gambled and the thing gambled for.

2. In what way does the transposition and "confusion" of diction represent faithfully the confusion that surrounds Messiahs?

Here is a poem in which the words that break the diction almost leap out at the reader:

## CARELESS LOVE

Who have been lonely once
Are comforted by their guns.
Affectionately they speak
To the dark beauty, whose cheek
Beside their own cheek glows.

They are calmed by such repose,
Such power held in hand:
Their young bones understand
The shudder in that frame.
Without nation, without name,
They give the load of love,
And it's returned, to prove
How much the husband heart
Can hold of it: for what
This nymphomaniac enjoys
Inexhaustibly is boys.

—STANLEY KUNITZ

*1.* The two words that break the diction are *nymphomaniac* and *Inexhaustibly*. What is the relation between the two words? Is nymphomania normal or pathological?

*2.* Is the gun seen as male or female? Does it mate with male or female? Does it mate at all? What does the gun symbolize to the young man? What is the equivalent of "power held in the hand" and the "shudder in that frame"?

*3.* How is the meaning of *nymphomania* and *Inexhaustibly* prepared for in lines like "Without nation, without name,/ They give the load of love"?

*4.* The word *prove* means "to demonstrate or to test." What does "And it's returned, to prove/ How much the husband heart can hold of it" mean?

*5.* The poem is built on metaphors* of loveless sexuality (masturbation, nymphomania). What is said to be the result of those abnormalities?

*6.* What does the title of the poem mean?

7. Is it significant that the nymphomaniac enjoys not men but boys?

*8.* Assuming that the sexual drive is necessary and normal, what do the words *nymphomaniac* and *Inexhaustibly* imply about the basis and extent of the drive spoken of in the poem? Is it the sexual drive or another related drive that is the subject of the poem?

## The Refrain

Repetitive diction becomes most obviously fixed in a refrain,* which is a repetition of a set phrase. So-called "nonsense refrains" abound in songs and ballads: "Hey nonny nonny," "Fa la la la la la la," "Hi lily, hi lily, hi lo." They aren't nonsensical: *nonsense* means only that they contain no statement. These refrains may stand for understood phrases that the listeners supplied; they may be signals for the reforming of a dance group when the song was designed or adapted to a performance; they may signal intervals when the performing group could break and perform dance movements. They break the diction, but they always break it regularly and to some purpose.

More interesting and more predictable are the *incremental refrains* in which a set phrase is repeated; and each time, because of what has happened in the interval in the poem itself, the phrase takes on an added meaning, an increment, as in the refrain of "Billy Boy": "She's a young thing/ And cannot leave her mother."

Here is a ballad with incremental repetition in the refrain:

LORD RANDAL

*1*

"O where ha' you been, Lord Randal, my son?
And where ha' you been, my handsome young man?"
"I ha' been at the greenwood; mother, mak my bed soon,
For I'm wearied wi' huntin', and fain wad lie down."

2

"And wha met ye there, Lord Randal, my son?
And wha met you there, my handsome young man?"
"O I met wi' my true-love; mother, mak my bed soon,
For I'm wearied wi' huntin', and fain wad lie down."

*3*

"And what did she give you, Lord Randal, my son?
And what did she give you, my handsome young man?"
"Eels fried in a pan; mother, mak my bed soon,
For I'm wearied wi' huntin', and fain wad lie down."

*4*

"And wha gat your leavin's, Lord Randal, my son?
And wha gat your leavin's, my handsome young man?"
"My hawks and my hounds; mother, mak my bed soon,
For I'm wearied wi' huntin', and fain wad lie down."

*5*

"And what becam of them, Lord Randal, my son?
And what becam of them, my handsome young man?"
"They stretched their legs out and died; mother, mak my
bed soon,
For I'm wearied wi' huntin', and fain wad lie down."

*6*

"O I fear you are poisoned, Lord Randal, my son!
I fear you are poisoned, my handsome young man!"
"O yes, I am poisoned; mother, mak my bed soon,
For I'm sick at the heart, and I fain wad lie down."

*7*

"What d' ye leave to your mother, Lord Randal, my son?
What d' ye leave to your mother, my handsome young man?"
"Four and twenty milk kye; mother, mak my bed soon,
For I'm sick at the heart, and I fain wad lie down."

*8*

"What d' ye leave to your sister, Lord Randal, my son?
What d' ye leave to your sister, my handsome young man?"
"My gold and my silver; mother, mak my bed soon,
For I'm sick at the heart, and I fain wad lie down."

*9*

"What d' ye leave to your brother, Lord Randal, my son?
What d' ye leave to your brother, my handsome young man?"
"My houses and my lands; mother, mak my bed soon,
For I'm sick at the heart, and I fain wad lie down."

*10*

"What d' ye leave to your true-love, Lord Randal, my son?
What d' ye leave to your true-love, my handsome young man?"
"I leave her hell and fire; mother, mak my bed soon,
For I'm sick at the heart, and I fain wad lie down."

*1.* Say what the increment is in each stanza.

*2.* Is there a final and crucial increment reserved for the final stanza?

Here is a poem with a refrain that changes slightly each time it appears.

## TEARS, IDLE TEARS

Tears, idle tears, I know not what they mean,
Tears from the depth of some divine despair
Rise in the heart, and gather to the eyes,
In looking on the happy autumn-fields,
And thinking of the days that are no more.

Fresh as the first beam glittering on a sail,
That brings our friends up from the underworld,
Sad as the last which reddens over one
That sinks with all we love below the verge;
So sad, so fresh, the days that are no more.

Ah, sad and strange as in dark summer dawns
The earliest pipe of half-awaken'd birds
To dying ears, when unto dying eyes

The casement slowly grows a glimmering square;
So sad, so strange, the days that are no more.

Dear as remember'd kisses after death,
And sweet as those by hopeless fancy feign'd
On lips that are for others; deep as love,
Deep as first love, and wild with all regret;
O Death in Life, the days that are no more!

—ALFRED, LORD TENNYSON

*1.* The refrain in this poem is incremental. In fact, it is almost a progress report on the deepening despair of the speaker. What is the occasion for the despair? What in the last line keeps you from answering that the speaker is literally dying?

*2.* Does it alter your reading of the poem to know that the speaker is a young girl who with others has been living a cloistered life? (This is one of the songs from Tennyson's *The Princess.*)

## Juxtaposition

A poet may juxtapose words in an unusual fashion. If he does it consistently, the unusual becomes the usual in the pattern, as in the following poem:

### DELIGHT IN DISORDER

A sweet disorder in the dress
Kindles in clothes a wantonness:
A lawn about the shoulders thrown
Into a fine distraction,
An erring lace, which here and there
Enthralls the crimson stomacher,
A cuff neglectful, and thereby
Ribbands to flow confusedly,
A winning wave (deserving note)

In the tempestuous petticoat,
A careless shoe-string, in whose tie
I see a wild civility,
Do more bewitch me, than when art
Is too precise in every part.

—ROBERT HERRICK

*1.* Notice that the descriptive words don't match the nouns; that is, the descriptive words name characteristics of humans, not of clothes: *sweet, wantonness, distraction, erring, etc.* Why?

*2.* The speaker doesn't say he wants his lady artless. What adjective in the last line says what kind of art he is objecting to?

When in *The Rape of the Lock* Alexander Pope speaks of Queen Anne and breaks the diction with obvious ironies like "Here thou, Great Anna! whom three realms obey,/ Dost sometimes counsel take—and sometimes Tea," few can misunderstand. The shock comes not from the juxtaposition of *counsel* and *Tea* but from the fact that Pope would dare to speak of his queen in this fashion. When the cultural shock is gone, the irony* becomes less obvious, but the method remains. What is being juxtaposed in the following poem?

## IN WESTMINSTER ABBEY

Let me take this other glove off
  As the *vox humana* swells,
And the beauteous fields of Eden
  Bask beneath the Abbey bells.
Here, where England's statesmen lie,
Listen to a lady's cry.

Gracious Lord, oh bomb the Germans.
  Spare their women for Thy Sake,
And if that is not too easy
  We will pardon Thy Mistake.

But, gracious Lord, whate'er shall be,
Don't let anyone bomb me.

Keep our Empire undismembered,
  Guide our Forces by Thy Hand,
Gallant blacks from far Jamaica,
  Honduras and Togoland;
Protect them Lord in all their fights,
And, even more, protect the whites.

Think of what our Nation stands for:
  Books from Boots' and country lanes,
Free speech, free passes, class distinction,
  Democracy and proper drains.
Lord, put beneath Thy special care
One-eighty-nine Cadogan Square.

Although dear Lord I am a sinner,
  I have done no major crime;
Now I'll come to Evening Service
  Whensoever I have the time.
So, Lord, reserve for me a crown,
And do not let my shares go down.

I will labor for Thy Kingdom,
  Help our lads to win the war,
Send white feathers to the cowards,
  Join the Women's Army Corps,
Then wash the Steps around Thy Throne
In the Eternal Safety Zone.

Now I feel a little better,
  What a treat to hear Thy Word,
Where the bones of leading statesmen,
  Have so often been interred.
And now, dear Lord, I cannot wait
Because I have a luncheon date.

—JOHN BETJEMAN

*1.* What two dictions run through the poem?
*2.* What is the basic difference in the two dictions? Their concreteness? Their abstraction?

A word that dominates a poem by its repetition may, like an extended pun, ask the reader to call up all possible meanings of the word, or to examine the base of meaning of the word. One of the least definite words in the language, for example, is *etc.* (an abbreviation of a word that isn't English). Watch it work in this poem:

my sweet old etcetera

my sweet old etcetera
aunt lucy during the recent

war could and what
is more did tell you just
what everybody was fighting

for,
my sister
isabel created hundreds
(and
hundreds)of socks not to
mention shirts fleaproof earwarmers

etcetera wristers etcetera, my
mother hoped that

i would die etcetera
bravely of course my father used
to become hoarse talking about how it was
a privilege and if only he
could meanwhile my

self etcetera lay quietly
in the deep mud et

cetera
(dreaming,
et
  cetera, of
Your smile
eyes knees and of your Etcetera)

—e. e. cummings

*1.* When someone uses *etc.*, he assumes that everyone understands the possibilities implied in the term because there is an accepted extension of what came before *etc.* State the difference between the accepted extensions of what went before *etc.* in

*a.* my sweet old etcetera/ aunt lucy
*b.* earwarmers/ etcetera wristers etcetera
*c.* i would die etcetera/ bravely
*d.* while my/ self etcetera lay quietly
*e.* your Etcetera

*2.* Is there an implied difference between lumping things into etceteras and lumping human life, feelings, and desires into etceteras?

*3.* Why is the final *etc.* capitalized?

In the following poem words are strictly repeated or cast into cognates. In each case the original is said *not* to be whatever is repeated or cognate:

## SONNET 116

Let me not to the marriage of true minds
Admit impediments. Love is not love
Which alters when it alteration finds,
Or bends with the remover to remove:
O, no! it is an ever-fixèd mark,
That looks on tempests and is never shakèn;
It is the star to every wand'ring bark,
Whose worth's unknown, although his height be taken.

Love's not Time's fool, though rosy lips and cheeks
Within his bending sickle's compass come;
Love alters not with his brief hours and weeks,
But bears it out even to the edge of doom:—
  If this be error and upon me proved,
  I never writ, nor no man ever loved.

—WILLIAM SHAKESPEARE

*1.* Distinguish the difference between *Love* and *love* in terms of the difference between *alters/ alteration, remover/ remove.*

*2.* The poem is built on negatives: notice how all the major statements are *nots* or *nevers.* How does this harmonize with the contrasts set up in the first four lines?

*3.* Is there a plus or a positive in the poem?

## Semantic Change

What words break a diction is, of course, dependent on the meaning of the words in a given vocabulary. Instructors are forever pointing out to students, for example, that *fond* (as in *fond hope*) in the sixteenth and seventeenth centuries did not mean "lovingly" but "foolish." True enough. Language changes. But the fact remains that the meanings of English words and the shape of English syntax have been remarkably uniform for the past four centuries—the centuries in which the bulk of English and American verse was written. An occasional word requires a gloss. But the twentieth-century reader can still read earlier verse with little more use of a dictionary than his attentive reading of contemporary verse would require. Here, for example, is a seventeenth-century poem with several verbal cruxes:

### TO HIS COY MISTRESS

Had we but world enough, and time,
This coyness, lady, were no crime.

We would sit down, and think which way
To walk, and pass our long love's day.
Thou by the Indian Ganges' side
Shoudst rubies find; I by the tide
Of Humber would complain. I would
Love you ten years before the flood,
And you should, if you please, refuse
Till the conversion of the Jews.
My vegetable love should grow
Vaster than empires and more slow;
An hundred years should go to praise
Thine eyes, and on thy forehead gaze;
Two hundred to adore each breast,
But thirty thousand to the rest;
An age at least to every part,
And the last age should show your heart.
For, lady, you deserve this state,
Nor would I love at lower rate.
  But at my back I always hear
Time's wingéd chariot hurrying near;
And yonder all before us lie
Deserts of vast eternity.
Thy beauty shall no more be found;
Nor, in thy marble vault, shall sound
My echoing song; then worms shall try
That long-preserved virginity,
And your quaint honor turn to dust,
And into ashes all my lust:
The grave's a fine and private place,
But none, I think, do there embrace.
  Now therefore, while the youthful hue
Sits on thy skin like morning dew,
And while thy willing soul transpires
At every pore with instant fires,
Now let us sport us while we may,

And now, like amorous birds of prey,
Rather at once our time devour
Than languish in his slow-chapped power.
Let us roll all our strength and all
Our sweetness up into one ball,
And tear our pleasures with rough strife
Thorough the iron gates of life:
Thus, though we cannot make our sun
Stand still, yet we will make him run.

—ANDREW MARVELL

An anxious anthologist will gloss the title by pointing out that *coy* in the seventeenth century meant "quiet" and "disdainful" and that *mistress* meant "beloved." It is hard to see how those differ essentially from twentieth-century meanings, especially given what this poem is doing. The odd words (as opposed to the allusions) are three:

1. My *vegetable* Love should grow
2. And your *quaint* honor turn to dust
3. Than languish in his *slow-chapped* power

(1) *Vegetable* is here a reference to Renaissance theory that placed the vegetable faculty as the lowest on the scale of rational, sensitive, and vegetable faculties; the vegetable faculty had the ability to grow and decay and to reproduce itself asexually. That is esoteric information, but the point is that the phrase "vegetable love" would arrest attention in the seventeenth as well as the twentieth century; the difference is that it sends us scurrying to our dictionaries whereas it would make the seventeenth-century reader stop and reflect. Those two things amount to the same action.

(2) *Quaint*, in the seventeenth century, besides meaning "oddly old-fashioned," referred to the female sexual organs when used as a noun. The twentieth-century reader may miss the pun, but he can hardly miss the point being made:

...Then worms shall try
That long-preserved virginity:
And your quaint honor turn to dust,
And into ashes all my lust . . .

(3) *Slow-chapped* is an image, not a word to be found in a dictionary. It would puzzle the seventeenth-century reader as much as the twentieth-century reader, provided that the twentieth-century reader saw "chops" (jaws and jowls) in *chapped*. It probably means "ground slowly in the jaws," but we don't know that any more exactly than a seventeenth-century reader could have.

In other words, the signs that tell a reader that a word ought to be inspected closely have not really changed. *Any word that breaks what the reader understands as a diction ought to be looked up.* This is the first and great commandment.

*FOR DISCUSSION.*

I TASTE A LIQUOR NEVER BREWED

I taste a liquor never brewed–
From Tankards scooped in Pearl–
Not all the Frankfort Berries
Yield such an Alcohol!

Inebriate of Air–am I–
And Debauchee of Dew–
Reeling–thro endless summer days–
From inns of Molten Blue–

When "Landlords" turn the drunken Bee
Out of the Foxglove's door–
When Butterflies–renounce their "drams"–
I shall but drink the more!

Till Seraphs swing their snowy Hats—
And Saints—to windows run—
To see the little Tippler
From Manzanilla come!

—EMILY DICKINSON

*1.* There are several versions of this poem. Consider the pattern of diction; then say why these two revisions of the diction make it a better poem:

line 3: "Not all the Vats upon the Rhine"
line 16: "Leaning against the—Sun—"

*2.* In discussing line 16, consider that the speaker says she tastes "a liquor never brewed." Manzanilla in Cuba is the place where a very good rum is made. Can "Manzanilla" and "liquor never brewed" coexist?

*3.* In discussing both lines note that the verb in the first line is *brewed*. What liquor is brewed? Can one brew *berries* or from brewing produce rum?

## SPRING AND FALL : TO A YOUNG CHILD

Márgarét, are you gríeving
Over Goldengrove unleaving?
Leáves, líke the things of man, you
With your fresh thoughts care for, can you?
Ah! ás the heart grows older
It will come to such sights colder
By and by, nor spare a sigh
Though worlds of wanwood leafmeal lie;
And yet you wíll weep and know why.
Now no matter, child, the name:
Sórrow's spríngs áre the same.
Nor mouth had, no nor mind, expressed
What heart heard of, ghost guessed:
It ís the blight man was born for,
It is Margaret you mourn for.

—GERARD MANLEY HOPKINS

*1.* Unusual breaks in diction have to be weighed against strong patterns. In this poem the following stand out:

Goldengrove unleaving . . .
worlds of wanwood leafmeal lie . . .

Those phrases should pose no problem to anyone. "Goldengrove unleaving" means the leaves falling in a forest, orchard, or grove; "worlds of wanwood leafmeal lie" means the pale leaves of the world falling one by one, by analogy with *piecemeal.* A reader who can assimilate *telecaster* will surely have no problem with *leafmeal.* The real interpretive problem lies in the ordinary pattern.

*a.* What, for example, are the possible meanings of *fall,* if not only a season and the descent of leaves but "the blight man was born for" appear in the poem?

*b.* What are the different meanings of *spring* in the title and in line 11? Are they really different? Does the title mean what we take it to mean at first glance?

*2.* A quick reading of the poem will usually yield some equally quick generalization such as "We all die." But trees don't die when leaves fall. And Margaret isn't dying or, by analogy, even foreseeing her own death or the death of others. Even the "ghost" isn't dead, if it is something that the mouth and mind never expressed but the heart guessed. What is this "ghost"?

*3.* Summarize the statement made in the last two lines.

## FOR ANNE GREGORY

"Never shall a young man,
Thrown into despair
By those great honey-coloured
Ramparts at your ear,
Love you for yourself alone
And not your yellow hair."

"But I can get a hair-dye
And set such colour there,
Brown, or black, or carrot,
That young men in despair
May love me for myself alone
And not my yellow hair."

"I heard an old religious man
But yesternight declare
That he had found a text to prove
That only God, my dear,
Could love you for yourself alone
And not your yellow hair."

—W. B. YEATS

*1.* What word first breaks the diction by introducing the military into a discussion of love?

*2.* What does *Ramparts* imply? Offensive forces attack ramparts, but defenders also hide behind ramparts. If you assume that just before this poem begins, the young woman has uttered the cliché "Why can't they love me for myself alone and not my beauty (yellow hair)," what assumption about herself, contained in the cliché, is she probably hiding behind?

*3.* Is there a break in the diction when she lists the possibilities of hair color as "Brown, or black, or carrot"? What is the difference between being auburn-haired, red-headed, and carrot-topped?

*4.* Given your answers to questions 1–3, what are the possible meanings of "only God, my dear,/ Could love you for yourself alone/ And not your yellow hair"?

*5.* Is there an increment in the refrain?

Western wind, when wilt thou blow,
The small rain down can rain?
Christ, if my love were in my arms,
And I in my bed again!

*1.* We have modernized the spelling in this very old poem to avoid distractions. What word in the second line breaks the diction?

*2.* It is possible to be meteorological about the poem and suggest that the west wind will help the speaker to sail home, but the wind is asked to blow only so that the "small" rain can come down. Nothing in the poem says anything about returning anywhere. If the speaker would delight in the "small" rain, what has he apparently been going through?

## BLACK POET, WHITE CRITIC

A critic advises
not to write on controversial subjects
like freedom or murder,
but to treat universal themes
and timeless symbols
like the white unicorn.

A white unicorn?

—DUDLEY RANDALL

The poet, who is also president of the Broadside Press, one of the major publishing houses for new poets, especially Black poets, is quoting from a fictive review. The center of the poem is one word: *controversial.*

*1.* "Freedom" and "murder" are said by the reviewer to be "controversial." Are they?

*2.* Writing about "white unicorns" is said by the reviewer to be uncontroversial. Is it?

*3.* A white unicorn is said to be a "universal theme" and a "timeless symbol" by the reviewer. Is it?

*4.* Why is it appropriate that the poem ends with a question rather than a statement?

## HIGHWAY: MICHIGAN

Here from the field's edge we survey
The progress of the jaded. Mile
On mile of traffic from the town
Rides by, for at the end of day
The time of workers is their own.

They jockey for position on
The strip reserved for passing only.
The drivers from production lines
Hold to advantage dearly won.
They toy with death and traffic fines.

Acceleration is their need:
A mania keeps them on the move
Until the toughest nerves are frayed.
They are the prisoners of speed
Who flee in what their hands have made.

The pavement smokes when two cars meet
And steel rips through conflicting steel.
We shiver at the siren's blast.
One driver, pinned beneath the seat,
Escapes from the machine at last.

—THEODORE ROETHKE

*1.* Remember that the poem deals with production-line workers in automobile factories who must work at a set speed all day long. In what sense, then, is "The progress of the jaded" true? In what sense is it ironic?

*2.* Why would "drivers from production lines/ Hold to advantage dearly won"? What would have happened to them for the first time that day?

*3.* The level of diction is constant but several words and phrases stand out, especially as they relate to one another. What is the relationship of the following?

The progress of the jaded...
The time of workers is their own...
Acceleration is their need: ...
They are the prisoners of speed...

*4.* In what way and by what means do the prisoners escape "from the machine at last"?

## THE DEATH OF A TOAD

A toad the power mower caught,
Chewed and clipped of a leg, with a hobbling hop has got
To the garden verge, and sanctuaried him
Under the cineraria leaves, in the shade
Of the ashen heartshaped leaves, in a dim,
Low, and a final glade.

The rare original heartsblood goes,
Spends on the earthen hide, in the folds and wizenings, flows
In the gutters of the banked and staring eyes. He lies
As still as if he would return to stone,
And soundlessly attending, dies
Toward some deep monotone,

Toward misted and ebullient seas
And cooling shores, toward lost Amphibia's emperies.
Day dwindles, drowning, and at length is gone
In the wide and antique eyes, which still appear
To watch, across the castrate lawn,
The haggard daylight steer.

—RICHARD WILBUR

*1.* This is a complicated set of patterns of diction, because in the end the toad is being compared to something else, although the poet never mentions what that something else is. The "plot" of the poem is that the power mower mortally wounds a toad. Several odd things happen to the diction:

*a.* The toad is described in elevated terms: he is "sanctuaried," he is "soundlessly attending," he is associated with "ebullient seas" and a kingdom he once ruled, "lost Amphibia's emperies."

*b.* The scene is one of sudden and final desolation: the "ashen heartshaped leaves," the blood "on the earthen hide," the "deep monotone" toward which he dies, the "cooling shores," the day that "dwindles" and drowns, the "castrate lawn," the "haggard daylight," and the pun on "castrate . . . steer."

Something more than a toad has died in this poem. According to one theory, the first land animals–our ancestors–were the amphibians. According to another, that distinction ("The rare original heartsblood") belongs to another creature made of "earthen hide," who fled to the "garden verge," desperately hid among leaves after his wounding, and has ever since died "Toward some deep monotone."

Relate the one theory to the other and then say what the poem is saying, including what the "power mower" is.

## BECAUSE I COULD NOT STOP FOR DEATH

Because I could not stop for Death–
He kindly stopped for me–
The Carriage held but just Ourselves–
And Immortality.

We slowly drove–He knew no haste
And I had put away
My labor and my leisure too,
For His Civility–

We passed the School, where Children strove
At Recess–in the Ring–
We passed the Fields of Gazing Grain–
We passed the Setting Sun–

Or rather–He passed Us–
The Dews drew quivering and chill–
For only Gossamer, my Gown–
My Tippet–only Tulle–

We paused before a House that seemed
A Swelling of the Ground–
The Roof was scarcely visible–
The Cornice–in the Ground–

Since then–'tis Centuries–and yet
Feels shorter than the Day
I first surmised the Horses Heads
Were toward Eternity–

—EMILY DICKINSON

*1.* What word in the first line breaks the diction?

*2.* What several meanings of *stop* and *stopped* are implied in the first stanza?

*3.* What is the meaning of *Civility* in the second stanza?

*4.* In what way, given the earlier lines, is "We passed the Setting Sun–/ Or rather–He passed Us" not a contradiction?

*5.* A house is something someone lives in. Yet the "House" in the poem is a grave. Justify the paradox* by pointing to corroborating details in the poem.

## LONDON

I wander thro' each charter'd street,
Near where the charter'd Thames does flow,
And mark in every face I meet
Marks of weakness, marks of woe.

In every cry of every Man,
In every Infant's cry of fear,
In every voice, in every ban,
The mind-forg'd manacles I hear.

How the Chimney-sweeper's cry
Every black'ning Church appalls;
And the hapless Soldier's sigh
Runs in blood down Palace walls.

But most thro' midnight streets I hear
How the youthful Harlot's curse
Blasts the new born Infant's tear,
And blights with plagues the Marriage hearse.

—WILLIAM BLAKE

*1.* *Chartered* breaks the diction: it means "leased out" or "hired," therefore to be bought and sold. What things are implied to be chartered beyond the streets and the river?

*2.* In an earlier version of this poem Blake had used the word *dirty* in place of *chartered* in lines 1 and 2. Why is the change an improvement?

*3.* In the earlier version line 10 read:

Blackens o'er the church's walls

Is the present reading an improvement? Why?

*4.* In the earlier version the last stanza read:

But most the midnight harlot's curse
From every dismal street I hear
Weaves around the marriage hearse
And blasts the newborn infant's ear.

Is the present reading an improvement?

*5.* What is the double meaning of "harlot's curse"? What is the connection of that curse with Blake's view of London as "chartered"?

*FOR STUDY.*

## BELLS FOR JOHN WHITESIDE'S DAUGHTER

There was such speed in her little body,
And such lightness in her footfall,
It is no wonder that her brown study
Astonishes us all.

Her wars were bruited in our high window.
We looked among orchard trees and beyond,
Where she took arms against her shadow,
Or harried unto the pond

The lazy geese, like a snow cloud
Dripping their snow on the green grass,
Tricking and stopping, sleepy and proud,
Who cried in goose, Alas,

For the tireless heart within the little
Lady with rod that made them rise
From their noon apple-dreams, and scuttle
Goose-fashion under the skies!

But now go the bells, and we are ready;
In one house we are sternly stopped
To say we are vexed at her brown study,
Lying so primly propped.

—JOHN CROWE RANSOM

## LOVE POEM

My clumsiest dear, whose hands shipwreck vases,
At whose quick touch all glasses chip and ring,
Whose palms are bulls in china, burs in linen,
And have no cunning with any soft thing

Except all ill-at-ease fidgeting people:
The refugee uncertain at the door
You make at home; deftly you steady
The drunk clambering on his undulant floor.

Unpredictable dear, the taxi drivers' terror,
Shrinking from far headlights pale as a dime
Yet leaping before red apoplectic streetcars—
Misfit in any space. And never on time.

A wrench in clocks and the solar system. Only
With words and people and love you move at ease.
In traffic of wit expertly manoeuvre
And keep us, all devotion, at your knees.

Forgetting your coffee spreading on our flannel,
Your lipstick grinning on our coat,
So gayly in love's unbreakable heaven
Our souls on glory of spilt bourbon float.

Be with me, darling, early and late. Smash glasses—
I will study wry music for your sake.
For should your hands drop white and empty
All the toys of the world would break.

—JOHN FREDERICK NIMS

## IS MY TEAM PLOUGHING

"Is my team ploughing,
That I was used to drive

And hear the harness jingle
  When I was man alive?"

Ay, the horses trample,
  The harness jingles now;
No change though you lie under
  The land you used to plough.

"Is football playing
  Along the river shore,
With lads to chase the leather,
  Now I stand up no more?"

Ay, the ball is flying,
  The lads play heart and soul;
The goal stands up, the keeper
  Stands up to keep the goal.

"Is my girl happy,
  That I thought hard to leave,
And has she tired of weeping
  As she lies down at eve?"

Ay, she lies down lightly,
  She lies not down to weep:
Your girl is well-contented.
  Be still, my lad, and sleep.

"Is my friend hearty,
  Now I am thin and pine,
And has he found to sleep in
  A better bed than mine?"

Yes, lad, I lie easy,
  I lie as lads would choose;
I cheer a dead man's sweetheart,
  Never ask me whose.

—A. E. HOUSMAN

## VIRTUE

Sweet day, so cool, so calm, so bright,
The bridal of the earth and sky;
The dew shall weep thy fall to night,
For thou must die.

Sweet rose, whose hue, angry and brave,
Bids the rash gazer wipe his eye;
Thy root is ever in its grave,
And thou must die.

Sweet spring, full of sweet days and roses,
A box where sweets compacted lie;
My music shows ye have your closes,
And all must die.

Only a sweet and virtuous soul,
Like seasoned timber, never gives;
But though the whole world turn to coal,
Then chiefly lives.

—GEORGE HERBERT

## IT IS NOT GROWING LIKE A TREE

It is not growing like a tree
In bulk, doth make man better be;
Or standing long an oak, three hundred year,
To fall a log at last, dry, bald, and sere:
A lily of a day
Is fairer far in May,
Although it fall and die that night;
It was the plant and flower of light.
In small proportions we just beauties see;
And in short measures, life may perfect be.

—BEN JONSON

## KUBLA KHAN

In Xanadu did Kubla Khan
A stately pleasure-dome decree;
Where Alph, the sacred river, ran
Through caverns measureless to man
Down to a sunless sea.

So twice five miles of fertile ground
With walls and towers were girdled round:
And here were gardens bright with sinuous rills,
Where blossomed many an incense-bearing tree;
And here were forests ancient as the hills
Enfolding sunny spots of greenery.

But oh! that deep romantic chasm which slanted
Down the green hill athwart a cedarn cover!
A savage place! as holy and enchanted
As e'er beneath a waning moon was haunted
By woman wailing for her demon-lover!
And from this chasm, with ceaseless turmoil seething,
As if this earth in fast thick pants were breathing
A mighty fountain momently was forced:
Amid whose swift half-intermitted burst
Huge fragments vaulted like rebounding hail,
Or chaffy grain beneath the thresher's flail:
And 'mid these dancing rocks at once and ever
It flung up momently the sacred river.
Five miles meandering with a mazy motion
Through wood and dale the sacred river ran,
Then reached the caverns measureless to man,
And sank in tumult to a lifeless ocean:
And 'mid this tumult Kubla heard from far
Ancestral voices prophesying war!

The shadow of the dome of pleasure
Floated midway on the waves;

Where was heard the mingled measure
From the fountain and the caves.
It was a miracle of rare device,
A sunny pleasure-dome with caves of ice!

A damsel with a dulcimer
In a vision once I saw:
It was an Abyssinian maid,
And on her dulcimer she played,
Singing of Mount Abora.
Could I revive within me
Her symphony and song,
To such a deep delight 'twould win me,
That with music loud and long,
I would build that dome in air,
That sunny dome! those caves of ice!
And all who heard should see them there,—
And all should cry, Beware! Beware!—
His flashing eyes, his floating hair!
Weave a circle round him thrice,
And close your eyes with holy dread,
For he on honey-dew hath fed,
And drunk the milk of Paradise.

—SAMUEL TAYLOR COLERIDGE

## TIME OF DISTURBANCE

The best is, in war or faction or ordinary vindictive life, not to take sides.
Leave it for children, and the emotional rabble of the streets, to back their horse or support a brawler.

But if you are forced into it: remember that good and evil are as common as air, and like air shared

By the panting belligerents; the moral indignation that hoarsens orators is mostly a fool.

Hold your nose and compromise; keep a cold mind. Fight, if needs must; hate no one. Do as God does,
Or the tragic poets: they crush their man without hating him, their Lear or Hitler, and often save without love.

As for these quarrels, they are like the moon, recurrent and fantastic. They have their beauty but night's is better.
It is better to be silent than make a noise. It is better to strike dead than strike often. It is better not to strike.

—ROBINSON JEFFERS

*1.* If one says *better* and *best,* the progression the language forces on the reader is *good, better, best.* If *best* is "not to take sides" here, and *better* is "not to strike," what is *good?*

*2.* On another scale, the *good* is better than the best. Is that point of view supported in the poem?

*3.* What does it mean to "keep a cold mind"?

## THE PIONEERS

The Pioneers had
The best of this country
The boy said.
They grabbed all the
Adventure, Indian-fighting, danger.
Since, it's been Dullsville.
And he rushed out to his car
And tore down the road
Doing sixty, maybe
And came around a curve
Behind an old Pontiac
Carrying two Barona Indians
Slow-moving, twenty thereabouts.
Overloaded from a scavenging

Trip to the dump.
And the fine pipe for fences
They were taking to the reservation
Pierced the boy's skull,
Removing a scalp-lock, neatly
And they buried them both, the boy
Inside the stockaded Mem'ry Garden
And over the fence, in
Joe Booth's car dump
His faithful Mustang.

—CHARLOTTE MORTIMER

## THE CONVERGENCE OF THE TWAIN

(LINES ON THE LOSS OF THE TITANIC)

In a solitude of the sea
Deep from human vanity,
And the Pride of Life that planned her, stilly couches she.

Steel chambers, late the pyres
Of her salamandrine fires,
Cold currents thrid, and turn to rhythmic tidal lyres.

Over the mirrors meant
To glass the opulent
The sea-worm crawls—grotesque, slimed, dumb, indifferent.

Jewels in joy designed
To ravish the sensuous mind
Lie lightless, all their sparkles bleared and black and blind.

Dim moon-eyed fishes near
Gaze at the gilded gear
And query: "What does this vaingloriousness down here?" . . .

Well: while was fashioning
This creature of cleaving wing,
The Immanent Will that stirs and urges everything

Prepared a sinister mate
For her—so gaily great—
A Shape of Ice, for the time far and dissociate.

And as the smart ship grew
In stature, grace, and hue,
In shadowy silent distance grew the Iceberg too.

Alien they seemed to be:
No mortal eye could see
The intimate welding of their later history,

Or sign that they were bent
By paths coincident
On being anon twin halves of one august event,

Till the Spinner of the Years
Said "Now!" And each one hears,
And consummation comes, and jars two hemispheres.

—THOMAS HARDY

*1.* Consider the patterns of words in this poem that suggest a human problem, even though the things talked of are inanimate.

| (*a*) | (*b*) | (*c*) |
|---|---|---|
| human vanity | solitude | couches she |
| Pride of Life | Deep | mate |
| opulent | stilly | intimate welding |
| Jewels | late the pyres | twin halves |
| ravish | cold currents thrid | consummation |
| sensuous mind | | |
| sparkles | grotesque, slimed, dumb, indifferent | |
| gilded | lightless | |
| vaingloriousness | bleared and black and blind | |
| stature | | |
| grace | | |
| hue | | |

What is the common reference in each of those lists? How do those references relate to one another?

2. What bearing on your answer do the combinations of the dictions have? Look, for example, at stanza 2. "Pyres" are funeral fires that consume the body. "Salamandrine fires" refers to the legend that the salamander can run into a fire and hide there without being burnt. Here, however, it is not the salamander that is being burnt, but the fire itself. What "fires" are these?

## STOPPING BY WOODS ON A SNOWY EVENING

Whose woods these are I think I know.
His house is in the village though;
He will not see me stopping here
To watch his woods fill up with snow.

My little horse must think it queer
To stop without a farmhouse near
Between the woods and frozen lake
The darkest evening of the year.

He gives his harness bells a shake
To ask if there is some mistake.
The only other sound's the sweep
Of easy wind and downy flake.

The woods are lovely, dark and deep.
But I have promises to keep,
And miles to go before I sleep,
And miles to go before I sleep.

—ROBERT FROST

## MALCOLM X

*For Dudley Randall*

Original.
Ragged-round.
Rich-robust.

He had the hawk-man's eyes.
We gasped. We saw the maleness.
The maleness raking out and making guttural the air
and pushing us to walls.

And in a soft and fundamental hour
a sorcery devout and vertical
beguiled the world.

He opened us—
who was a key,

who was a man.

—GWENDOLYN BROOKS

## LESSONS OF THE WAR

To Alan Mitchell

Vixi duellis nuper idoneus Et militavi non sine gloria[1]

### I. NAMING OF PARTS

Today we have naming of parts. Yesterday,
We had daily cleaning. And tomorrow morning,
We shall have what to do after firing. But today,
Today we have naming of parts. Japonica
Glistens like coral in all the neighboring gardens,
        And today we have naming of parts.

This is the lower sling swivel. And this
Is the upper sling swivel, whose use you will see,
When you are given your slings. And this is the piling swivel,

[1]The epigraph of the poem is from Horace's *Odes*: "I have lived fit for the wars lately and acted like soldier not without glory." In some Horatian manuscripts, however, the word *duellis* (wars) appears as *puellis* (girls), yielding the reading, "I have lived fit for the girls lately and acted like a soldier not without glory." One therefore expects to find in the poem some opposition between seriousness and humor, war and love, rigidity and naturalness.

Which in your case you have not got. The branches
Hold in the gardens their silent, eloquent gestures,
Which in our case we have not got.

This is the safety-catch, which is always released
With an easy flick of the thumb. And please do not let me
See anyone using his finger. You can do it quite easy
If you have any strength in your thumb. The blossoms
Are fragile and motionless, never letting anyone see
Any of them using their finger.

And this you can see is the bolt. The purpose of this
Is to open the breech, as you see. We can slide it
Rapidly backwards and forwards: we call this
Easing the spring. And rapidly backwards and forwards
The early bees are assaulting and fumbling the flowers:
They call it easing the Spring.

They call it easing the Spring: it is perfectly easy
If you have any strength in your thumb: like the bolt,
And the breech, and the cocking-piece, and the point of balance,
Which in our case we have not got; and the almond-blossom
Silent in all of the gardens and the bees going backwards
and forwards,
For today we have naming of parts.

### II. Judging Distances

Not only how far away, but the way that you say it
Is very important. Perhaps you may never get
The knack of judging a distance, but at least you know
How to report on a landscape: the central sector,
The right of arc and that, which we had last Tuesday,
And at least you know

That maps are of time, not place, so far as the army
Happens to be concerned—the reason being,
Is one which need not delay us. Again, you know

There are three kinds of tree, three only, the fir and
the poplar,
And those which have bushy tops to; and lastly
That things only seem to be things.

A barn is not called a barn, to put it more plainly,
Or a field in the distance, where sheep may be safely grazing.
You must never be over-sure. You must say, when
reporting:
At five o'clock in the central sector is a dozen
Of what appear to be animals; whatever you do,
Don't call the bleeders sheep.

I am sure that's quite clear: and suppose, for the sake of
example,
The one at the end, asleep endeavors to tell us
What he sees over there to the west, and how far away,
After first having come to attention. There to the west,
On the fields of summer the sun and the shadows bestow
Vestments of purple and gold.

The still white dwellings are like a mirage in the heat,
And under the swaying elms a man and a woman
Lie gently together. Which is, perhaps, only to say
That there is a row of houses to the left of arc,
And that under some poplars a pair of what appear to
be humans
Appear to be loving.

Well that, for answer, is what we might rightly call
Moderately satisfactory only, the reason being,
Is that two things have been omitted, and those are important.
The human beings, now: in what direction are they,
And how far away, would you say? And do not forget
There may be dead ground in between.

There may be dead ground in between; and I may not have got
The knack of judging a distance; I will only venture
A guess that perhaps between me and the apparent lovers,

(Who, incidentally, appear by now to have finished,)
At seven o'clock from the houses, is roughly a distance
Of about one year and a half.

### III. Movement of Bodies

Those of you that have got through the rest, I am going to rapidly
Devote a little time to showing you, those that can master it,
A few ideas about tactics, which must not be confused
With what we call strategy. Tactics is merely
The mechanical movement of bodies, and that is what we mean by it.
Or perhaps I should say: by them.

Strategy, to be quite frank, you will have no hand in.
It is done by those up above, and it merely refers to
The larger movements over which we have no control.
But tactics are also important, together or single.
You must never forget that suddenly, in an engagement,
You may find yourself alone.

This brown clay model is a characteristic terrain
Of a simple and typical kind. Its general character
Should be taken in at a glance, and its general character
You can see at a glance it is somewhat hilly by nature,
With a fair amount of typical vegetation
Disposed at certain parts.

Here at the top of the tray, which we might call the northwards,
Is a wooded headland, with a crown of bushy-topped trees on;
And proceeding downwards or south we take in at a glance
A variety of gorges and knolls and plateaus and basins and saddles,
Somewhat symmetrically put, for easy identification.
And here is our point of attack.

But remember of course it will not be a tray you will
fight on,
Nor always by daylight. After a hot day, think of the night
Cooling the desert down, and you still moving over it:
Past a ruined tank or a gun, perhaps, or a dead friend,
Lying about somewhere: it might quite well be that.
It isn't always a tray.

And even this tray is different to what I had thought,
These models are somehow never always the same; the reason
I do not know how to explain quite. Just as I do know
Why there is always someone at this particular lesson
Who always starts crying. Now will you kindly
Empty those blinking eyes?

I thank you. I have no wish to seem impatient.
I know it is all very hard, but you would not like,
To take a simple example, to take for example,
This place we have thought of here, you would not like
To find yourself face to face with it, and you not knowing
What there might be inside?

Very well then: suppose this is what you must capture.
It will not be easy, not being very exposed,
Secluded away like it is, and somewhat protected
By a typical formation of what appear to be bushes,
So that you cannot see, as to what is concealed inside,
As to whether it is friend or foe.

And so, a strong feint will be necessary in this connection.
It will not be a tray, remember. It may be a desert stretch
With nothing in sight, to speak of. I have no wish to be
inconsiderate,
But I see there are two of you now, commencing to snivel,
I cannot think where such emotional privates can come from.
Try to behave like men.

I thank you. I was saying: a thoughtful deception
Is always somewhat essential in such a case. You can see
That if only the attacker can capture such an emplacement
The rest of the terrain is his: a key-position, and calling
For the most resourceful maneuvers. But that is what tactics is.
Or I should say rather: are.

Let us begin then and appreciate the situation.
I am thinking especially of the point we have been considering,
Though in a sense everything in the whole of the terrain
Must be appreciated. I do not know what I have said
To upset so many of you. I know it is a difficult lesson.
Yesterday a man was sick,

But I have never known as many as *five* in a single intake,
Unable to cope with this lesson. I think you had better
Fall out, all five, and sit at the back of the room,
Being careful not to talk. The rest will close up.
Perhaps it was me saying "a dead friend," earlier on?
Well, some of us live.

And I never know why, whenever we get to tactics,
Men either laugh or cry, though neither being strictly
called for.
But perhaps I have started too early with a difficult problem?
We will start again, further north, with a simpler assault.
Are you ready? Is everyone paying attention?
Very well then. Here are two hills.

## IV. UNARMED COMBAT

In due course of course you will all be issued with
Your proper issue; but until tomorrow,
You can hardly be said to need it; and until that time,
We shall have unarmed combat. I shall teach you
The various holds and rolls and throws and breakfalls
Which you may sometimes meet.

And the various holds and rolls and throws and breakfalls
Do not depend on any sort of weapon,
But only on what I might coin a phrase and call
The ever-important question of human balance,
And the ever-important need to be in a strong
        Position at the start.

There are many kinds of weakness about the body,
Where you would least expect, like the ball of the foot.
But the various holds and rolls and throws and breakfalls
Will always come in useful. And never be frightened
To tackle from behind: it may not be clean to do so,
        But this is global war.

So give them all you have, and always give them
As good as you get; it will always get you somewhere.
(You may not know it, but you can tie a Jerry
Up without rope: it is one of the things I shall teach you.)
Nothing will matter if only you are ready for him.
        The readiness is all.

*The readiness is all.* How can I help but feel
I have been here before? But somehow then,
I was the tied-up one. How to get out
Was always then my problem. And even if I had
A piece of rope I was always the sort of person
        Who threw the rope aside.

And in my time I have given them all I had,
Which was never as good as I got, and it got me nowhere.
And the various holds and rolls and throws and breakfalls
Somehow or other I always seemed to put
In the wrong place. And as for war, my wars
        Were global from the start.

Perhaps I was never in a strong position,
Or the ball of my foot got hurt, or I had some weakness

Where I had least expected. But I think I see your point.
While awaiting a proper issue, we must learn the lesson
Of the ever-important question of human balance.
It is courage that counts.

Things may be the same again; and we must fight
Not in the hope of winning but rather of keeping
Something alive; so that when we meet our end,
It may be said that we tackled wherever we could,
That battle-fit we lived, and though defeated;
Not without glory fought.

—HENRY REED

# 4

# *Patterns of Diction II*

So far we have been considering words largely as poetic diction. Words also make images,* metaphors,* similes,* analogies,* symbols,* and catalogs.*

## Image

An image is a word or phrase naming something that in the real world is apprehensible to one of the reader's five senses: touch, taste, sight, smell, hearing. An image, then, is a signal to the reader's nervous system. It asks him to reproduce the sensation embodied in the thing named.

Since the medium of poetry is language, it is not really possible to render in verse the sensation of touch, taste, and smell. And only in pattern poems (see pp. 279-281) can a poem actually make "pictures." With only one of the senses can language appeal directly by repeating with reasonable accuracy the sensation named: the sense of hearing. Thus we get onomatopoeic* words and phrases (those that reproduce the sound of the thing named) such as

I galloped, Dirck galloped, we galloped all three...

and

The moan of doves in immemorial elms
And the murmur of innumerable bees.

Less obvious effects may appear in patterns such as the following:

## THE EVE OF ST. AGNES

### I

St. Agnes' Eve–Ah, bitter chill it was!
The owl, for all his feathers, was a-cold;
The hare limped trembling through the frozen grass,
And silent was the flock in woolly fold:
Numb were the Beadsman's fingers, while he told
His rosary, and while his frosted breath,
Like pious incense from a censer old,
Seemed taking flight for Heaven, without a death,
Past the sweet Virgin's picture, while his prayer he saith.

—JOHN KEATS

How is the image of a frozen scene accomplished here?

*1.* What nouns and adjectives that are images in themselves suggest "cold"?

*2.* What is frozen is static, by definition. Look at the verb forms. What about them reinforces the frozen aspect?

*3.* Notice how many times the word *while* is repeated in the stanza. What does that repetition do for the images? In what sense is "frozen" true not only to the temperature of the scene but the way in which the reader perceives the scene?

Images relay not only sensation but information and connotation.* Since an image may have any of several denotations* and connotations associated with it by the reader, the poet often arranges his images in groups or patterns that channel and validate the meaning of the individual images. At the same time, a grouping of images can suggest new overtones to a reader—can, in effect, open up the individual image. In either case it is the relationship of one image to another that determines its proper meaning in a poem. Here is an example:

### NOTHING GOLD CAN STAY

Nature's first green is gold,
Her hardest hue to hold.
Her early leaf's a flower;
But only so an hour.

Then leaf subsides to leaf.
So Eden sank to grief,
So dawn goes down to day.
Nothing gold can stay.

—ROBERT FROST

The visual images—green, gold, leaf, flower, Eden, dawn, day—take their meaning partly from each other. Notice that "green" is "gold," "leaf" is "flower." Furthermore, *flower* is to *leaf* as *dawn* is to *day*. And as *early leaf* (*flower*) is to *leaf*, *Eden* is to *grief*.

| | | |
|---|---|---|
| *green* | | |
| *gold* | | *leaf* |
| *flower* | are opposed to | *grief* |
| *Eden* | | *day* |
| *dawn* | | |

The first line can be read accurately by consulting the images that follow it. What is "Nature's first green" if it is "gold"? A tree or bush as seen in the early, golden light of dawn? A golden flower? Something larger than a tree or flower? Another way to ask the same questions is, is the period of *green/gold* a matter of hours? of seasons? of more than seasons?

The answer is that all three references and all three levels of time are suggested by

(1) So dawn goes down to day
(2) Her early leaf's a flower
(3) So Eden sank to grief.

Those three levels of time "prove" the concluding statement: "Nothing gold can stay."

The question remains: what are the proper overtones of *gold* here? If we look again at the three preceding statements and the equivalences and analogies we worked out, we see that *gold* suggests beauty and value—but a short-lived beauty and value, perhaps made precious by its rarity and promise of worse things to come.

Images rarely carry the whole burden of communication in a poem. They are, after all, connected by something and, therefore, are related to one another by something. In "Nothing Gold Can Stay" the images are related by simple logical patterns: one thing *is* another, and *as* one thing *is to* another, *so* another thing *is to* something else.

In the following two poems (originally written as one poem and then separated), the images themselves say something that is supplemented and reinforced by a repeated grammatical pattern:

## MEETING AT NIGHT

### I

The gray sea and the long black land;
And the yellow half-moon large and low;

And the startled little waves that leap
In fiery ringlets from their sleep,
As I gain the cove with pushing prow,
And quench its speed i' the slushy sand.

II

Then a mile of warm sea-scented beach;
Three fields to cross till a farm appears;
A tap at the pane, the quick sharp scratch
And blue spurt of a lighted match,
And a voice less loud, thro' its joys and fears,
Than the two hearts beating each to each!

—ROBERT BROWNING

## PARTING AT MORNING

Round the cape of a sudden came the sea,
And the sun looked over the mountain's rim:
And straight was a path of gold for him,
And the need of a world of men for me.

—ROBERT BROWNING

The images in the first stanza of "Meeting at Night" are widely assorted; they have in common overtones of separateness, perhaps even opposition when they are taken together (the gray sea, the black land, the yellow half-moon), and, added to these, the human qualities of impatience and irritation (the startled little waves leaping from sleep and the pushing prow of the boat quenching its speed in the slushy sand). The impatience carries over into the second stanza in the hurried gestures of *tap*, *quick sharp scratch*, and *blue spurt* but dissolves into the regular beating of "two hearts each to each." Notice that the two stanzas are constructed of phrases and dependent clauses. No action is completed because no statement is completed.

In "Parting at Morning," four lines make four complete statements in which occur three images, each almost as much a matter of fact as the statements themselves: the tide came in, the sun came up, the sun's reflection made a path on the sea. In these two poems the images are supported by the grammatical patterns.

### SO WE'LL GO NO MORE A-ROVING

So, we'll go no more a-roving
  So late into the night,
Though the heart be still as loving,
  And the moon be still as bright.

For the sword outwears its sheath,
  And the soul wears out the breast,
And the heart must pause to breathe,
  And love itself have rest.

Though the night was made for loving,
  And the day returns too soon,
Yet we'll go no more a-roving
  By the light of the moon.

—LORD BYRON

*1.* Compare this poem with "Parting at Morning" above. What images and grammatical structure do the two poems share? What meaning do they share? It may be helpful to point out that *a-roving* is a form of the verb *to reeve,* as well as of *to rove.*

*2.* How, incidentally, is that distinction borne out by the images in lines 5 and 6?

## Metaphor

Words also create metaphors. A metaphor is a small art object in which something is compared with another thing in the imaginative sense, not in the realistic sense.

Metaphor is repetition with variation. The usual distinction between metaphor and simile is that while they are both comparative, metaphor implies that one thing *is* another, whereas a simile asserts that one thing is *like* another. Thus, "He fought like a tiger" is a simile; "He was a tiger in the ring" is a metaphor.

A metaphor does not, in fact, imply that one thing is another. One man shouting at another, "You rat!" (a metaphor) does not imply that the other is a rat but that he finds the other repulsive, sneaky, dangerous. The basis of the comparison is selected qualities of "ratness" and of the other person. In the end, as in a simile, a metaphor simply asserts that one thing is like another, not identical to it. The difference is basically grammatical and syntactical.

The important difference in the *use* of metaphor and simile lies in the number of *repeated* characteristics one finds in the two things being compared and the number of significant characteristics one finds *varying* between the two things. *The greater the number of repeated characteristics, the greater the probability that the poet will use a metaphor; the greater the number of variations, the greater the probability that the poet will use a simile.* Why? Because the simile, by using *as*, *like*, or *seems*, calls attention to the fact that a comparison is being made and, therefore, normalizes unusual comparisons. Strong emphasis, of course, can be achieved by reversing that practice—by asserting in metaphor that two radically dissimilar things are similar, as when Theodore Roethke speaks of a young wife:

My lizard, my lively writher.

The most far-fetched simile is less arresting than that:

As a bathtub lined with white porcelain,
When the hot water gives out or goes tepid,

So is the slow cooling of our chivalrous passion,
O my much praised but not-altogether-satisfactory
    lady.

—EZRA POUND

## Analogy

Metaphor becomes analogy either by multiplying the number of resemblances in the objects being compared or by applying the comparison made to a similar (i.e., analogous) event or situation. Consider, for example, this couplet from a Ghazal (a five-couplet Indian poem) by Adrienne Rich:

If the mind of the teacher is not in love with
    the mind of the student,
he is simply practicising rape, and deserves our
    pity.

An analogy can be sudden and startling, and the subject matter in the compared events quite different on the surface. Thus this poem:

TERRIBLE BEAUTY

Hearing how tourists, dazed with reverence,
Looked through sun-glasses at the Parthenon,
I thought of that cold night outside the Gents
When Dai touched Gwyneth up with his gloves on.

—KINGSLEY AMIS

What are the similarities between looking at the Parthenon through sunglasses and, on a cold night, caressing a girl with your gloves on?

Metaphors, converted into analogies, can structure longer poems:

## ON FIRST LOOKING INTO CHAPMAN'S HOMER

Much have I travell'd in the realms of gold,
And many goodly states and kingdoms seen;
Round many western islands have I been
Which bards in fealty to Apollo hold.
Oft of one wide expanse had I been told
That deep-brow'd Homer ruled as his demesne;
Yet did I never breathe its pure serene
Till I heard Chapman speak out loud and bold:
Then felt I like some watcher of the skies
When a new planet swims into his ken;
Or like stout Cortez when with eagle eyes
He star'd at the Pacific—and all his men
Look'd at each other with a wild surmise—
Silent, upon a peak in Darien.

—JOHN KEATS

Keats could not read Greek; a friend introduced him to George Chapman's translation of the *Iliad;* that is the occasion of the poem.

*1.* Notice that the sonnet is split exactly into octave (the first eight lines) and sestet (the final six lines). Is there a difference between the subject matter of the octave and that of the sestet?

*2.* Is there a difference between the metaphor used in the octave and that in the sestet? (For example "I" in the octave = the reader/speaker seen metaphorically as an explorer). Is he more than an explorer in the sestet?

*3.* Why is it appropriate to use the figure of an explorer/traveller when speaking of Homer?

*4.* The explorer/traveller metaphor is developed into an analogy in the octave. Work out the progression that follows by filling in the blanks:

explorer/traveller = reader
goodly states and kingdoms = exceptionally good literature
western islands = ____________________

in fealty to Apollo = poetry (Apollo, the God of poetry)
one wide expanse [Homer rules] = ________________

Homer = one epic poet
Chapman speak out = ________________

5. Refer to your answer for question 2. Many readers are bothered by Keats' "mistake" of citing Cortez instead of Balboa, who was the first European to see the Pacific from Darien in Panama. Consider, however, the integrity of the metaphor. If Keats says "like stout Balboa," then he is saying "I am the first to discover the beauty of Chapman's translation of Homer." If he uses *Cortez*, what is he saying instead?

Of course, our answer does not solve the problem of Cortez's probably never having been in Panama. It may even raise the question of whether consistency of metaphor can be more important than fact.

### DEATH IS A DIALOGUE

Death is a Dialogue between
The Spirit and the Dust.
"Dissolve" says Death–The Spirit "Sir
I have another Trust["]–

Death doubts it–Argues from the Ground–
The Spirit turns away
Just laying off for evidence
An Overcoat of Clay.

—EMILY DICKINSON

*1.* Something goes wrong with the analogy in this poem. Say what it is.
*2.* Can you repair the analogy?

## Catalogs

In catalog* poems, the repetitive series is a list of images, metaphors, similes, or allusions* bound together by a common idea or feeling. Sometimes the items in the list are similar. Sometimes they seem to have no relation to one another. What the poem is "about" is the common denominator.

The repeated element may be easily apparent, as in Elizabeth Barrett Browning's best-known sonnet. She asks, as if she herself had been asked, "How do I love thee?" She then says, "Let me count the ways" and proceeds to count them: 1, 2, 3, etc.

## SONNET 43

How do I love thee? Let me count the ways.
I love thee to the depth and breadth and height
My soul can reach, when feeling out of sight
For the ends of Being and ideal Grace.
I love thee to the level of everyday's
Most quiet need, by sun and candle-light.
I love thee freely, as men strive for Right;
I love thee purely, as they turn from Praise.
I love thee with the passion put to use
In my old griefs, and with my childhood's faith.
I love thee with a love I seemed to lose
With my lost saints,–I love thee with the breath,
Smiles, tears, of all my life!–and, if God choose,
I shall but love thee better after death.

*1.* Although there is a list here, there are also pairs within the list. Summarize the list and then group the pairs. What common element does the list of single statements show? What common element does the list of pairs show?

*2.* What point is being made when one contrasts the statement made in lines 2–4 with that made in lines 13–14? What does that point do to the common elements arrived at in question 1?

Sometimes the repeated element is not immediately apparent and has to be deduced from the catalog.

## TO A SKYLARK

Hail to thee, blithe Spirit!
Bird thou never wert,
That from Heaven, or near it,
Pourest thy full heart
In profuse strains of unpremeditated art.

Higher still and higher
From the earth thou springest
Like a cloud of fire;
The blue deep thou wingest,
And singing still dost soar, and soaring ever singest.

In the golden lightning
Of the sunken sun,
O'er which clouds are bright'ning,
Thou dost float and run;
Like an unbodied joy whose race is just begun.

The pale purple even
Melts around thy flight;
Like a star of Heaven,
In the broad daylight
Thou art unseen, but yet I hear thy shrill delight,

Keen as are the arrows
Of that silver sphere,
[5] Whose intense lamp narrows
In the white dawn clear
Until we hardly see—we feel that it is there.

All the earth and air
With thy voice is loud,
As, when night is bare,
From one lonely cloud
The moon rains out her beams, and Heaven is overflowed.

What thou art we know not;
  What is most like thee?
From rainbow clouds there flow not
  Drops so bright to see
As from thy presence showers a rain of melody.

Like a Poet hidden
  In the light of thought,
Singing hymns unbidden,
  Till the world is wrought
To sympathy with hopes and fears it heeded not:

Like a high-born maiden
  In a palace tower,
Soothing her love-laden
  Soul in secret hour
With music sweet as love, which overflows her bower:

Like a glowworm golden
  In a dell of dew,
[10] Scattering unbeholden
  Its aërial hue
Among the flowers and grass, which screen it from the view!

Like a rose embowered
  In its own green leaves,
By warm winds deflowered,
  Till the scent it gives
Makes faint with too much sweet those heavy-wingéd thieves:

Sound of vernal showers
  On the twinkling grass,
Rain-awakened flowers,
  All that ever was
Joyous, and clear, and fresh, thy music doth surpass:

Teach us, Sprite or Bird,
What sweet thoughts are thine:
I have never heard
Praise of love or wine
That panted forth a flood of rapture so divine.

Chorus Hymeneal,
Or triumphal chant,
Matched with thine would be all
But an empty vaunt,
A thing wherein we feel there is some hidden want.

What objects are the fountains
Of thy happy strain?
[15] What fields, or waves, or mountains?
What shapes of sky or plain?
What love of thine own kind? What ignorance of pain?

With thy clear keen joyance
Languor cannot be:
Shadow of annoyance
Never came near thee:
Thou lovest–but ne'er knew love's sad satiety.

Waking or asleep,
Thou of death must deem
Things more true and deep
Than we mortals dream,
Or how could thy notes flow in such a crystal stream?

We look before and after,
And pine for what is not:
Our sincerest laughter
With some pain is fraught;
Our sweetest songs are those that tell of saddest thought.

Yet if we could scorn
  Hate, and pride, and fear;
If we were things born
  Not to shed a tear,
I know not how thy joy we ever should come near.

Better than all measures
  Of delightful sound,
[20] Better than all treasures
  That in books are found,
Thy skill to poet were, thou scorner of the ground!

Teach me half the gladness
  That thy brain must know,
Such harmonious madness
  From my lips would flow
The world should listen then—as I am listening now.

—P. B. SHELLEY

*1.* Shelley is obviously not talking about a bird, but about a bird as a symbol, as something else. What that something else is has to be deduced from the catalog. There are three catalogs in the poem—one encompassing stanzas 1–6; another, stanzas 8–12; and a third, stanzas 14–17. They all deal with the same thing. Make a list of the characteristics set out in stanzas 1–6. Then say what it is, besides a bird, that has these characteristics.

*2.* Stanzas 8–12 try to define more exactly the thing portrayed in stanzas 1–6 by a series of similes ("What is most like thee?"). Make a list of the qualities listed, and then say what is the common element in all the items.

*3.* Now look at the negative catalog, so to speak, that is presented in stanzas 14–17. What is the common element there?

*4.* From our grouping, it is apparent that the stanzas that break the catalog pattern are 7, 13, 18–21. Now say what the function of those stanzas is. In what way does stanza 21 validate the answers you have made to questions 1, 2, and 3?

Different catalogs dealing with the same subject matter often produce quite different effects. Here are two examples:

## THE UNKNOWN CITIZEN

(TO JS/07/M/378
THIS MARBLE MONUMENT
IS ERECTED BY THE STATE)

He was found by the Bureau of Statistics to be
One against whom there was no official complaint,
And all the reports on his conduct agree
That, in the modern sense of an old-fashioned word, he
was a saint,
For in everything he did he served the Greater Community.
Except for the War till the day he retired
He worked in a factory and never got fired,
But satisfied his employers, Fudge Motors Inc.
Yet he wasn't a scab or odd in his views,
For his Union reports that he paid his dues,
(Our report on his Union shows it was sound)
And our Social Psychology workers found
That he was popular with his mates and liked a drink.
The Press are convinced that he bought a paper every day
And that his reactions to advertisements were normal in
every way.
Policies taken out in his name prove that he was fully
insured,
And his Health-card shows he was once in hospital but
left it cured.
Both Producers Research and High-Grade Living declare
He was fully sensible to the advantages of the Installment
Plan
And had everything necessary to the Modern Man,
A phonograph, a radio, a car and a frigidaire.

Our researchers into Public Opinion are content
That he held the proper opinions for the time of year;
When there was peace, he was for peace; when there was
war, he went.
He was married and added five children to the population,
Which our Eugenist says was the right number for a
parent of his generation,
And our teachers report that he never interfered with their
education.
Was he free? Was he happy? The question is absurd:
Had anything been wrong, we should certainly have
heard.

—W. H. AUDEN

*1.* The irony of the catalog rests on the fact that in this poem *saint* means "conformist," which belies the older definition of the word; in this poem the "saint" conforms to the special interests of corporations and agencies. Is the ending surprising, or has it been anticipated in the body of the poem itself?

*2.* Where is the catalog interrupted? How is the interrupting element different from the catalog in tone and structure?

## LIFE CYCLE OF A COMMON MAN

Roughly figured, this man of moderate habits,
This average consumer of the middle class,
Consumed in the course of his average life span
Just under half a million cigarettes,
Four thousand fifths of gin and about
A quarter as much vermouth; he drank
Maybe a hundred thousand cups of coffee,
And counting his parents' share it cost
Something like half a million dollars
To put him through life. How many beasts
Died to provide him with meat, belt and shoes
Cannot be certainly said.
But anyhow,

It is in this way that a man travels through time,
Leaving behind him a lengthening trail
Of empty bottles and bones, of broken shoes,
Frayed collars and worn out or outgrown
Diapers and dinnerjackets, silk ties and slickers.

Given the energy and security thus achieved,
He did . . . ? What? The usual things, of course,
The eating, dreaming, drinking and begetting,
And he worked for the money which was to pay
For the eating, et cetera, which were necessary
If he were to go on working for the money, et cetera,
But chiefly he talked. As the bottles and bones
Accumulated behind him, the words proceeded
Steadily from the front of his face as he
Advanced into the silence and made it verbal.
Who can tally the tale of his words? A lifetime
Would barely suffice for their repetition;
If you merely printed all his commas the result
Would be a very large volume, and the number of times
He said "thank you" or "very little sugar, please,"
Would stagger the imagination. There were also
Witticisms, platitudes, and statements beginning
"It seems to me" or "As I always say."

Consider the courage in all that, and behold the man
Walking into deep silence, with the ectoplastic
Cartoon's balloon of speech proceeding
Steadily out of the front of his face, the words
Borne along on the breath which is his spirit
Telling the numberless tale of his untold Word
Which makes the world his apple, and forces him to eat.

—HOWARD NEMEROV

*1.* If the central figure of Auden's poem is pathetic, what do you think of the central figure of Nemerov's poem? Answering the following questions will help to answer this one.

*2.* This poem begins, like Auden's, with a catalog of statistical horrors; yet the first two words of the poem are "Roughly figured." Is that compatible with the list? What are the overtones of "Roughly figured"?

*3.* At line 25 the diction and focus break. The catalog is interrupted by

> But chiefly he talked. As the bottles and bones
> Accumulated behind him, the words proceeded
> Steadily from the front of his face as he
> Advanced into the silence and made it verbal.

It is true that most of the verbalizing consists of "Thank you" and "It seems to me" and "As I always say," but the verbalizing is said to contain "courage." How so?

*4.* The diction is broken again with the word *ectoplastic*. What does that mean?

*5.* A pattern contrary to the statistical analysis emerges with the phrases

> "behold the man"
> "the breath which is his spirit"
> "his untold Word"
> "the world his apple, and forces him to eat."

What do those phrases have in common? What are they drawn from? What do they say about the nature of man?

*6.* If God is said to have made the world out of nothing, how does that relate to man making words out of silence?

7. Auden concentrates on the modern tendency to reduce man to his statistical measurements. What does Nemerov say about the relationship of man to statistical measurement?

## ON THE LIFE OF MAN

What is our life? a play of passion,
Our mirth the musicke of division,
Our mothers wombes the tyring houses be,
Where we are drest for this short Comedy,
Heaven the Judicious sharpe spectator is,
That sits and markes still who doth act amisse,
The graves that hide us from the searching Sun,
Are like drawne curtaynes when the play is done,

Thus march we playing to our latest rest,
Onely we dye in earnest, that's no Jest.

—SIR WALTER RALEIGH

*1.* Poem as analogy. Life is being compared to what? (Don't say a *play*: what kind of play?)

2. What are the characteristics of this life? Consider these glosses:

*a. passion* = strong feeling, not necessarily love or lust
*b. musicke of division* = scene and act divisions, therefore infrequent
*c. tyring houses* = dressing rooms, but also resting rooms
*d. Judicious sharpe spectator* = the one who decides whether you played poorly. (Any sign that he applauds?)
*e. searching Sun* = apparently the sun does not shine easily or frequently

*3.* What happens to the way the analogy is handled at line 7? The pattern is broken. How? Why?

## A BIRTHDAY

My heart is like a singing bird
  Whose nest is in a watered shoot;
My heart is like an apple-tree
  Whose boughs are bent with thickset fruit;
My heart is like a rainbow shell
  That paddles in a halcyon sea;
My heart is gladder than all these
  Because my love is come to me.

Raise me a dais of silk and down;
  Hang it with vair and purple dyes;
Carve it in doves and pomegranates,
  And peacocks with a hundred eyes;
Work it in gold and silver grapes.
  In leaves and silver fleur-de-lys:

Because the birthday of my life
Is come, my love is come to me.

—CHRISTINA ROSETTI

*1.* Here are two catalogs within a single poem, with a radical difference between them. What is the basic difference between the two catalogs?

*2.* How is the speaker seen in the catalog in the first stanza? How is she seen in the catalog in the second stanza?

*3.* Resolve the paradox you stated in your answer to question 2.

## Symbol

Symbols* are deeply buried metaphors. In a metaphor, one thing is named as itself and implied to be similar to something else. In a symbol, one thing is named as itself and implied *repeatedly* (but without expansion, as in analogy) to be something else. Here is an example:

### YOUNG WATERS

About Yule, when the winds blew cule,
And the round tables began,
A there is cum to our king's court
Mony a well-favored man.

The queen luikt owre the castle-wa,
Beheld baith dale and down,
And there she saw Young Waters
Cum riding to the town.

His footmen they did rin before,
His horsemen rade behind;
And mantel of the burning gowd
Did keep him frae the wind.

Gowden-graithed his horse before,
And siller-shod behind;
The horse Young Waters rade upon
Was fleeter than the wind.

Out then spack a wylie lord,
Unto the queen said he,
"O tell me wha's the fairest face
Rides in the company?

"I've sene lord, and I've sene laird,
And knights of high degree,
Bot a fairer face than Young Waters
Min eyne did never see."

Out then spack the jealous king,
And an angry man was he;
"O if he had bin twice as fair,
You micht have excepted me."

"You're neither laird nor lord," she says,
"Bot the king that wears the crown;
There is not a knight in fair Scotland
Bot to these maun bow down."

For a' that she could do or say,
Appeased he wad nae bee,
Bot for the words which she had said,
Young Waters he maun die.

They hae taen Young Waters,
And put fetters to his feet;
They hae taen Young Waters,
And thrown him in dungeon deep.

"Aft I have ridden thro Stirling town
In the wind bot and the weit;
Bot I neir rade thro Stirling town
Wi fetters at my feet.

"Aft I have ridden thro Stirling town
In the wind bot and the weit;
Bot I neir rade thro Stirling town
Neir to return again."

They hae taen to the heiding-hill
His young son in his craddle,
And they hae taen to the heiding-hill
His horse bot and his saddle.

They hae taken to the heiding-hill
His lady fair to see,
And for the words the queen had spoken
Young Waters he did die.

You will have noticed in this folk ballad the reappearance of the "wind." Young Waters (i.e., Walter) comes to court when the winds blow cool; he has been through Stirling town before when it was raining and blowing, but he never came to harm. Why? Because his horse could outrun the wind and his golden mantle kept out both the wind and the wet.

No horse can outrun the wind, and a mantle is no guarantee against a drenching. Only noblemen, at the time this ballad was current, rode fine horses and wore golden mantles. What has protected Young Waters in the past is his rank as a noble. But when his enemy becomes the king, rank is no protection. The wind is a symbol, not just of danger but of the kind of danger that can outrun any horse, pierce any garment, humble any rank. Thus *wind, horse*, and *golden mantle* are all three symbols in the poem.

There are no universal symbols, although some metaphors have been used as symbols so frequently as to become almost automatically associated with a symbolic meaning: the rose, for example, is a symbol of love and innocence with overtones of fragility and transience. What a repeated metaphor that refuses to become an analogy stands for has to be determined from the specific poem. In Poe's poem "The Raven," for example, a raven (which "traditionally" symbolizes death, melancholy, etc.) flies in and alights on a bust of Pallas Athene. The raven can speak one word, *Nevermore*. The speaker of the poem deliberately but perhaps unconsciously asks the raven questions that, when answered with the one word the raven knows, lead to melancholy and despair. Whatever the raven "symbolizes" is in the speaker, not in the bird. Poe trades on the traditional symbol, but it is only validated by the *questions*, not by the answer.

Here is a poem by D. H. Lawrence:

## SNAKE

A snake came to my water-trough
On a hot, hot day, and I in pyjamas for the heat,
To drink there.

In the deep, strange-scented shade of the great dark
    carob-tree
I came down the steps with my pitcher
And must wait, must stand and wait, for there he was at
    the trough before me.

He reached down from a fissure in the earth-wall in the
    gloom
And trailed his yellow-brown slackness soft-bellied down,
    over the edge of the stone trough
And rested his throat upon the stone bottom,
And where the water had dripped from the tap, in a small
    clearness,
He sipped with his straight mouth,
Softly drank through his straight gums, into his slack long
    body,
Silently.

Someone was before me at my water-trough,
And I, like a second comer, waiting.

He lifted his head from his drinking, as cattle do,
And looked at me vaguely, as drinking cattle do,

And flickered his two-forked tongue from his lips, and
mused a moment,
And stooped and drank a little more,
Being earth-brown, earth-golden from the burning
bowels of the earth
On the day of Sicilian July, with Etna smoking.

The voice of my education said to me
He must be killed,
For in Sicily the black, black snakes are innocent, the gold
are venomous.

And voices in me said, If you were a man
You would take a stick and break him now, and finish
him off.

But must I confess how I liked him,
How glad I was he had come like a guest in quiet, to drink
at my water-trough
And depart peaceful, pacified, and thankless,
Into the burning bowels of this earth?

Was it cowardice, that I dared not kill him?
Was it perversity, that I longed to talk to him?
Was it humility, to feel so honoured?
I felt so honoured.

And yet those voices:
*If you were not afraid, you would kill him!*

And truly I was afraid, I was most afraid,
But even so, honoured still more
That he should seek my hospitality
From out the dark door of the secret earth.

He drank enough
And lifted his head, dreamily, as one who has drunken,
And flickered his tongue like a forked night on the air, so
black,

Seeming to lick his lips,
And looked around like a god, unseeing, into the air,
And slowly turned his head.
And slowly, very slowly, as if thrice adream,
Proceeded to draw his slow length curving round
And climb again the broken bank of my wall-face.

And as he put his head into that dreadful hole,
And as he slowly drew up, snake-easing his shoulders, and entered farther,
A sort of horror, a sort of protest against his withdrawing into that horrid black hole,
Deliberately going into the blackness, and slowly drawing himself after,
Overcame me now his back was turned.

I looked round, I put down my pitcher,
I picked up a clumsy log
And threw it at the water-trough with a clatter.

I think it did not hit him,
But suddenly that part of him that was left behind convulsed in undignified haste,
Writhed like lightning, and was gone
Into the black hole, the earth-lipped fissure in the wallfront,
At which, in the intense still noon, I stared with fascination.

And immediately I regretted it.
I thought how paltry, how vulgar, what a mean act!
I despised myself and the voices of my accursed human education.

And I thought of the albatross,
And I wished he would come back, my snake.

For he seemed to me again like a king,
Like a king in exile, uncrowned in the underworld,
Now due to be crowned again.

And so, I missed my chance with one of the lords
Of life.
And I have something to expiate;
A pettiness.

*1.* Look carefully at all the characteristics of the snake as seen by the narrator; then say what the snake symbolizes in the poem.

*2.* The snake is said by some to be an archetype of evil; by others, a phallic symbol. Do either of those things fit what the snake symbolizes in this poem?

*FOR DISCUSSION.*

## UPON WESTMINSTER BRIDGE

Earth has not anything to show more fair:
Dull would he be of soul who could pass by
A sight so touching in its majesty:
This City now doth, like a garment, wear
The beauty of the morning; silent, bare,
Ships, towers, domes, theatres, and temples lie
Open unto the fields, and to the sky;
All bright and glittering in the smokeless air.
Never did sun more beautifully steep
In his first splendour valley, rock, or hill;
Ne'er saw I, never felt, a calm so deep!
The river glideth at his own sweet will:
Dear God! the very houses seem asleep;
And all that mighty heart is lying still!

—WILLIAM WORDSWORTH

*1.* A simile and a metaphor lie at the heart of the poem. What is the City being compared with?

*2.* What is implied about the character of the City that is being praised when the simile "This City now doth, like a garment, wear" appears?

*3.* Does the comparison break down at the word *bare?* Given the metaphor, how can the sleeping city wear beauty and yet be "bare"?

## A SORT OF A SONG

Let the snake wait under
his weed
and the writing
be of words, slow and quick, sharp
to strike, quiet to wait,
sleepless.

—through metaphor to reconcile
the people and the stones.

Compose. (No ideas
but in things) Invent!
Saxifrage is my flower that splits
the rocks.

—WILLIAM CARLOS WILLIAMS

*1.* This is a poem about metaphors in poems. The snake under the weed is probably a reference to Lady Macbeth's advice to Macbeth when they are plotting the murder of Duncan:

> . . . . To beguile the time,
> Look like the time; bear welcome in your eye,
> Your hand, your tongue: look like the innocent flower,
> But be the serpent under 't.

How does that relate to what the poet is saying?

*2.* How can metaphor "reconcile/ the people and the stones"?

*3.* *Compose* means literally "to place together." Is the word itself a buried metaphor in this poem?

4. *Invent* means literally "to bring in" or "to come upon" or "to find." Is the word a buried metaphor?

5. Saxifrage is a small flower that grows in cracks in rocks and does, indeed, split those rocks. The word itself, *saxifrage*, means literally "to split rocks." Is that a buried metaphor? Consider the last statement in the poem as a summary of what the poem is saying.

## DOVER BEACH

The sea is calm to-night.
The tide is full, the moon lies fair
Upon the straits;—on the French coast the light
Gleams and is gone; the cliffs of England stand,
Glimmering and vast, out in the tranquil bay.
Come to the window, sweet is the night air!
Only, from the long line of spray
Where the sea meets the moon-blanched land,
Listen! you hear the grating roar
Of pebbles which the waves draw back, and fling,
At their return, up the high strand,
Begin, and cease, and then again begin,
With tremulous cadence slow, and bring
The eternal note of sadness in.

Sophocles long ago
Heard it on the Ægean, and it brought
Into his mind the turbid ebb and flow
Of human misery; we
Find also in the sound a thought,
Hearing it by this distant northern sea.
The Sea of Faith
Was once, too, at the full, and round earth's shore
Lay like the folds of a bright girdle furled.
But now I only hear
Its melancholy, long, withdrawing roar,
Retreating, to the breath

Of the night wind, down the vast edges drear
And naked shingles of the world.

Ah, love, let us be true
To one another! for the world, which seems
To lie before us like a land of dreams,
So various, so beautiful, so new,
Hath really neither joy, nor love, nor light,
Nor certitude, nor peace, nor help for pain;
And we are here as on a darkling plain
Swept with confused alarms of struggle and flight
Where ignorant armies clash by night.

—MATTHEW ARNOLD

*1.* A pattern of repetition is established in the images in this poem. Make a list of the visual images. What do they all deal with?

*2.* Make a list of auditory images. What do they all deal with?

*3.* Do the two patterns come together in the final image of the darkling plain? How?

## REDEMPTION

Having been tenant long to a rich Lord,
    Not thriving, I resolved to be bold,
    And make a suit unto him, to afford
A new small-rented lease, and cancell th' old.

In heaven at his manour I him sought:
    They told me there, that he was lately gone
    About some land, which he had dearly bought
Long since on earth, to take possession.

I straight return'd, and knowing his great birth,
    Sought him accordingly in great resorts;
    In cities, theatres, gardens, parks, and courts:
At length I heard a ragged noise and mirth

Of thieves and murderers: there I him espied,
Who straight, *Your suit is granted*, said, & died.

—GEORGE HERBERT

*1.* What biblical phrase is the analogy built on?
*2.* Explain the odd typography of the final "and"—an ampersand (&). Does it fit the analogy?

## TERENCE, THIS IS STUPID STUFF

"Terence, this is stupid stuff;
You eat your victuals fast enough;
There can't be much amiss, 'tis clear,
To see the rate you drink your beer.
But oh, good Lord, the verse you make,
It gives a chap the belly-ache.
The cow, the old cow, she is dead;
It sleeps well, the horned head:
We poor lads, 'tis our turn now
To hear such tunes as killed the cow.
Pretty friendship 'tis to rhyme
Your friends to death before their time
Moping melancholy mad:
Come, pipe a tune to dance to, lad."
Why, if 'tis dancing you would be,
There's brisker pipes than poetry.
Say, for what were hop-yards meant,
Or why was Burton built on Trent?
Oh, many a peer of England brews
Livelier liquor than the Muse.
And malt does more than Milton can
To justify God's ways to man.
Ale, man, ale's the stuff to drink
For fellows whom it hurts to think:
Look into the pewter pot
To see the world as the world's not.

And faith, 'tis pleasant till 'tis past:
The mischief is that 'twill not last.
Oh, I have been to Ludlow fair
And left my necktie God knows where,
And carried half way home, or near,
Pints and quarts of Ludlow beer:
Then the world seemed none so bad,
And I myself a sterling lad;
And down in lovely muck I've lain,
Happy till I woke again,
Then I saw the morning sky:
Heigho, the tale was all a lie;
The world, it was the old world yet,
I was I, my things were wet.
And nothing now remained to do
But begin the game anew.

Therefore, since the world has still
Much good, but much less good than ill,
And while the sun and moon endure
Luck's a chance, but trouble's sure,
I'd face it as a wise man would.
And train for ill and not for good.
'Tis true, the stuff I bring for sale
Is not so brisk a brew as ale:
Out of a stem that scored the hand
I wrung it in a weary land.
But take it: if the smack is sour,
The better for the embittered hour:
It should do good to heart and head
When your soul is in my soul's stead;
And I will friend you, if I may,
In the dark and cloudy day.

There was a king reigned in the East:
There, when kings will sit to feast.
They get their fill before they think

With poisoned meat and poisoned drink.
He gathered all that springs to birth
From the many-venomed earth;
First a little, thence to more,
He sampled all her killing store;
And easy, smiling, seasoned sound,
Sate the king when healths went round.
They put arsenic in his meat
And stared aghast to watch him eat;
They poured strychnine in his cup
And shook to see him drink it up:
They shook, they stared as white's their shirt:
Them it was their poison hurt.
–I tell the tale that I heard told.
Mithridates, he died old.

—A. E. HOUSMAN

*1.* Analogy can serve as argument. What is the analogy developed in the last stanza that supports the poet's argument for the kind of verse he writes?

2. Notice the repeated word *think*.

Ale, man, ale's the stuff to drink
For fellows whom it hurts to think: . . .

They get their fill before they think
With poisoned meat and poisoned drink.

In each case, *drink* is rhymed with and opposed to *think*. How does that bear out what is said in the poem?

## DIRGE

1-2-3 was the number he played but today the number came
3-2-1;
bought his Carbide at 30 and it went to 29; had the favorite
at Bowie but the track was slow—

O, executive type, would you like to drive a floating power, knee-action, silk-upholstered six? Wed a Hollywood star? Shoot the course in 58? Draw to the ace, king, jack?
O, fellow with a will who won't take no, watch out for three cigarettes on the same, single match; O, democratic voter born in August under Mars, beware of liquidated rails—

Denoument to denoument, he took a personal pride in the certain, certain way he lived his own, private life,
but nevertheless, they shut off his gas; nevertheless, the bank foreclosed; nevertheless, the landlord called; nevertheless, the radio broke,

And twelve o'clock arrived just once too often,
just the same he wore one grey tweed suit, bought one straw hat, drank one straight Scotch, walked one short step, took one long look, drew one deep breath,
just one too many,

And wow he died as wow he lived,
going whop to the office and blooie home to sleep and biff got married and bam had children and oof got fired,
zowie did he live and zowie did he die,

With who the hell are you at the corner of his casket, and where the hell we going on the righthand silver knob, and who the hell cares walking second from the end with an American Beauty wreath from why the hell not,

Very much missed by the circulation staff of the *New York Evening Post;* deeply, deeply mourned by the B.M.T.,

Wham, Mr. Roosevelt; pow, Sears Roebuck; awk, big dipper; bop, summer rain;
bong, Mr., bong, Mr., bong, Mr., bong.

—KENNETH FEARING

*1.* Here is a catalog that, taken as a whole, defines the quality of a life. What is the quality of that life?

*2.* The images that conclude the poem are probably double edged, since they refer not only to the quality of the life but to what immediately precedes them: the funeral.

> *a.* The poem appeared at the height of the popularity of the pinball machine in the U.S.; *wham, pow, awk, bop, bong, bong, bong* reproduces the sound of the machine. What relevance has this to the man's life?
>
> *b.* If the "bongs" are bells, they might be funeral bells. A reader might hear behind the bongs John Donne's conclusion to a famous meditation in which he says that when any man dies Donne himself is the less for it because he is involved in mankind, and therefore none should "send to know for whom the bell tolls; it tolls for thee." Does that fit the poem? Or is that a forced connection? How do you know?

## FOR MY PEOPLE

For my people everywhere singing their slave songs repeatedly: their dirges and their ditties and their blues and jubilees, praying their prayers nightly to an unknown god, bending their knees humbly to an unseen power;

For my people lending their strength to the years, to the gone years and the now years and the maybe years, washing ironing cooking scrubbing sewing mending hoeing plowing digging planting pruning patching dragging along never gaining never reaping never knowing and never understanding;

For my playmates in the clay and dust and sand of Alabama backyards playing baptizing and preaching and doctor and jail and soldier and school and mama and cooking and playhouse and concert and store and hair and Miss Choomby and company;

For the cramped bewildered years we went to school to learn to know the reasons why and the answers to and the people who and the places where and the days when, in memory of the bitter hours when we discovered we were black and poor and small and different and nobody cared and nobody wondered and nobody understood;

For the boys and girls who grew in spite of these things to be man and woman, to laugh and dance and sing and play and drink their wine and religion and success, to marry their playmates and bear children and then die of consumption and anemia and lynching;

For my people thronging 47th Street in Chicago and Lenox Avenue in New York and Rampart Street in New Orleans, lost disinherited dispossessed and happy people filling the cabarets and taverns and other people's pockets needing bread and shoes and milk and land and money and something—something all our own;

For my people walking blindly spreading joy, losing time being lazy, sleeping when hungry, shouting when burdened, drinking when hopeless, tied and shackled and tangled among ourselves by the unseen creatures who tower over us omnisciently and laugh;

For my people blundering and groping and floundering in the dark of churches and schools and clubs and societies, associations and councils and committees and conventions, distressed and disturbed and deceived and devoured by money-hungry glory-craving leeches, preyed on by facile force of state and fad and novelty, by false prophet and holy believer;

For my people standing staring trying to fashion a better way from confusion, from hypocrisy and misunderstanding, trying to fashion a world that will hold all the people, all the faces, all the adams and eves and their countless generations;

Let a new earth rise. Let another world be born. Let a bloody peace be written in the sky. Let a second generation full of courage issue forth; let a people loving freedom come to growth. Let a beauty full of healing and a strength of final clenching be the pulsing in our spirits and our blood. Let the martial songs be written, let the dirges disappear. Let a race of men now rise and take control.

—MARGARET WALKER

Here, the catalog is prayer, manifesto, and diatribe. There is temporal order to the catalog.

*1.* What is the progression of time at the historical level in the poem? What are the "gone years," the "now years," and the "maybe years"?
*2.* Is there another level of time in the poem? Consider the "playmates," the "school" years, and so on.
*3.* Given the answers to questions 1 and 2, is the final plea based on a view of history or a view of an individual life, or both?

## FROM SONG OF MYSELF

1

I celebrate myself, and sing myself,
And what I assume you shall assume,
For every atom belonging to me as good belongs to you.

I loafe and invite my soul,
I lean and loafe at my ease observing a spear of summer grass.

My tongue, every atom of my blood, form'd from this soil, this air,
Born here of parents born here from parents the same, and their parents the same,
I, now thirty-seven years old in perfect health begin,
Hoping to cease not till death.

Creeds and schools in abeyance,
Retiring back a while sufficed at what they are, but never
forgotten,
I harbor for good or bad, I permit to speak at every hazard,
Nature without check with original energy.

2

Houses and rooms are full of perfumes, the shelves are crowded
with perfumes,
I breathe the fragrance myself and know it and like it,
The distillation would intoxicate me also, but I shall not let it.

The atmosphere is not a perfume, it has no taste of the
distillation, it is odorless,
It is for my mouth forever, I am in love with it,
I will go to the bank by the wood and become undisguised and
naked,
I am mad for it to be in contact with me.
The smoke of my own breath,
Echoes, ripples, buzz'd whispers, love-root, silk-thread, crotch
and vine,
My respiration and inspiration, the beating of my heart, the
passing of blood and air through my lungs,
The sniff of green leaves and dry leaves, and of the shore and
dark-color'd sea-rocks, and of hay in the barn,
The sound of the belch'd words of my voice loos'd to the
eddies of the wind,
A few light kisses, a few embraces, a reaching around of arms,
The play of shine and shade on the trees as the supple boughs
wag,
The delight alone or in the rush of the streets, or along the
fields and hill-sides,
The feeling of health, the full-noon trill, the song of me rising
from bed and meeting the sun.

Have you reckon'd a thousand acres much? have you reckon'd the earth much?
Have you practis'd so long to learn to read?
Have you felt so proud to get at the meaning of poems?

Stop this day and night with me and you shall possess the origin of all poems,
You shall possess the good of the earth and sun, (there are millions of suns left,)
You shall no longer take things at second or third hand, nor look through the eyes of the dead, nor feed on the spectres in books,
You shall not look through my eyes either, nor take things from me,
You shall listen to all sides and filter them from your self.

4

Trippers and askers surround me,
People I meet, the effect upon me of my early life or the ward and city I live in, or the nation,
The latest dates, discoveries, inventions, societies, authors old and new,
My dinner, dress, associates, looks, compliments, dues,
The real or fancied indifference of some man or woman I love,
The sickness of one of my folks or of myself, or ill-doing or loss or lack of money, or depressions or exaltations,
Battles, the horrors of fratricidal war, the fever of doubtful news, the fitful events;
These come to me days and nights and go from me again,
But they are not the Me myself.

Apart from the pulling and hauling stands what I am,
Stands amused, complacent, compassionating, idle, unitary,

Looks down, is erect, or bends an arm on an impalpable certain rest,
Looking with side-curved head curious what will come next,
Both in and out of the game and watching and wondering at it.

Backward I see in my own days where I sweated through fog with linguists and contenders,
I have no mockings or arguments, I witness and wait.
A word of the faith that never balks,
Here or henceforward it is all the same to me, I accept Time absolutely.
It alone is without flaw, it alone rounds and completes all,
That mystic baffling wonder alone completes all.

I accept Reality and dare not question it,
Materialism first and last imbuing.

Hurrah for positive science! long live exact demonstration!
Fetch stonecrop mixt with cedar and branches of lilac,
This is the lexicographer, this the chemist, this made a grammar of the old cartouches,
These mariners put the ship through dangerous unknown seas,
This is the geologist, this works with the scalpel, and this is a mathematician.

Gentlemen, to you the first honors always!
Your facts are useful, and yet they are not my dwelling,
I but enter by them to an area of my dwelling.

Less the reminders of properties told my words,
And more the reminders they of life untold, and of freedom and extrication,

And make short account of neuters and geldings, and favor men and women fully equipt,
And beat the gong of revolt, and stop with fugitives and them that plot and conspire.

24

Walt Whitman, a kosmos, of Manhattan the son,
Turbulent, fleshly, sensual, eating, drinking and breeding,
No sentimentalist, no stander above men and women or apart from them,
No more modest than immodest.

Unscrew the locks from the doors!
Unscrew the doors themselves from their jambs!

Whoever degrades another degrades me,
And whatever is done or said returns at last to me.

Through me the afflatus surging and surging, through me the current and index.
I speak the pass-word primeval, I give the sign of democracy,
By God! I will accept nothing which all cannot have their counterpart of on the same terms.

Through me many long dumb voices,
Voices of the interminable generations of prisoners and slaves,
Voices of the diseas'd and despairing and of thieves and dwarfs,
Voices of cycles of preparation and accretion,
And of the threads that connect the stars, and of wombs and of the father-stuff,
And of the rights of them the others are down upon,
Of the deform'd, trivial, flat, foolish, despised,
Fog in the air, beetles rolling balls of dung.

Through me forbidden voices,
Voices of sexes and lusts, voices veil'd and I remove the veil,
Voices indecent by me clarified and transfigur'd.

I do not press my fingers across my mouth,
I keep as delicate around the bowels as around the head and heart,
Copulation is no more rank to me than death is.

I believe in the flesh and the appetites,
Seeing, hearing, feeling, are miracles, and each part and tag of me is a miracle.

Divine am I inside and out, and I make holy whatever I touch or am touch'd from,
The scent of these arm-pits aroma finer than prayer,
This head more than churches, bibles, and all the creeds.

If I worship one thing more than another it shall be the spread of my own body, or any part of it,
Translucent mould of me it shall be you!
Shaded ledges and rests it shall be you!
Firm masculine colter it shall be you!
Whatever goes to the tilth of me it shall be you!
You my rich blood! your milky stream pale strippings of my life!
Breast that presses against other breasts it shall be you!
My brain it shall be your occult convolutions!
Root of wash'd sweet-flag! timorous pond-snipe! nest of guarded duplicate eggs! it shall be you!
Mix'd tussled hay of head, beard, brawn, it shall be you!
Trickling sap of maple, fibre of manly wheat, it shall be you!
Suns so generous it shall be you!
Vapors lighting and shading my face it shall be you!
You sweaty brooks and dews it shall be you!

Winds whose soft-tickling genitals rub against me it shall be you!
Broad muscular fields, branches of live oak, loving lounger in my winding paths, it shall be you!
Hands I have taken, face I have kiss'd, mortal I have ever touch'd, it shall be you.

I dote on myself, there is that lot of me and all so luscious,
Each moment and whatever happens thrills me with joy,
I cannot tell how my ankles bend, nor whence the cause of my faintest wish,
Nor the cause of the friendship I emit, nor the cause of the friendship I take again.

That I walk up my stoop, I pause to consider if it really be,
A morning-glory at my window satisfies me more than the metaphysics of books.

To behold the day-break!
The little light fades the immense and diaphanous shadows,
The air tastes good to my palate.

Hefts of the moving world at innocent gambols silently rising, freshly exuding,
Scooting obliquely high and low.

Something I cannot see puts upward libidinous prongs,
Seas of bright juice suffuse heaven.

The earth by the sky staid with, the daily close of their junction,
The heav'd challenge from the east that moment over my head,
The mocking taunt, See then whether you shall be master!

—WALT WHITMAN

*1.* This catalog moves through various stages. What are the stages?
2. What is the "Myself" that is being sung?

## AFTERNOON OF A PAWNBROKER

Still they bring me diamonds, diamonds, always diamonds,
Why don't they pledge something else for a change, if they must have loans, other than those diamond clasps and diamond rings,
Rubies, sapphires, emeralds, pearls,
Ermine wraps, silks and satins, solid gold watches and silver plate and violins two hundred years old,
And then again diamonds, diamonds, the neighborhood diamonds I have seen so many times before, and shall see so many times again?

Still I remember the strange afternoon (it was a season of extraordinary days and nights) when the first of the strange customers appeared,
And he waited, politely, while Mrs. Nunzio redeemed her furs, then he stepped to the counter and he laid down a thing that looked like a trumpet,
In fact, it was a trumpet, not mounted with diamonds, not plated with gold or even silver, and I started to say: "We can't use trumpets–"
But a light was in his eyes,
And after he was gone, I had the trumpet. And I stored it away. And the name on my books was Gabriel.
It should be made clear my accounts are always open to the police, I have nothing to conceal,
I belong, myself, to the Sounder Business Principles League,
Have two married daughters, one of them in Brooklyn, the other in Cleveland,
And nothing like this had ever happened before.

How can I account for my lapse of mind?
All I can say is, it did not seem strange. Not at the time. Not in that neighborhood. And not in that year.
And the next to appear was a man with a soft, persuasive voice,
And a kindly face, and the most honest eyes I have ever seen, and ears like arrows, and a pointed beard,
And what he said, after Mrs. Case had pledged her diamond ring and gone, I cannot now entirely recall,
But when he went away I found I had an apple. An apple, just an apple.
"It's been bitten," I remember that I tried to argue. But he smiled, and said in his quiet voice: "Yes, but only once."
And the strangest thing is, it did not seem strange. Not strange at all.

And still those names are on my books.
And still I see listed, side by side, those incongruous, and not very sound securities:
(1) Aladdin's lamp (I must have been mad), (1) Pandora's box, (1) Magic carpet,
(1) Fountain of youth (in good condition), (1) Holy Grail, (1) Invisible man (the only article never redeemed, and I cannot locate him), and others, others, many others.
And still I recall how my storage vaults hummed and crackled, from time to time, or sounded with music, or shot forth flame,
And I wonder, still, that the season did not seem one of unusual wonder, not even different—not at the time.
And still I think, at intervals, why didn't I, when the chance was mine, drink just once from that Fountain of youth?
Why didn't I open that box of Pandora?
And what if Mr. Gabriel, who redeemed his pledge and went away, should some day decide to blow on his trumpet?
Just one short blast, in the middle of some busy afternoon?

But here comes Mr. Barrington, to pawn his Stradivarius.
And here comes Mrs. Case, to redeem her diamond ring.

—KENNETH FEARING

*1.* This is a different kind of catalog, in that items are singled out and developed. What do all the items have in common, from the apple and trumpet through the violins and rings?

*FOR STUDY.*

## MY GALLEY CHARGED WITH FORGETFULNESS

My galley charged with forgetfulness
  Through sharp seas in winter nights doth pass
  'Tween rock and rock; and eke mine enemy, alas,
  That is my lord, steereth with cruelness;
And every oar a thought in readiness,
  As though that death were light in such a case.
  An endless wind doth tear the sail apace
  Of forced sighs, and trusty fearfulness.
A rain of tears, a cloud of dark disdain,
  Hath done the wearied cords great hinderance;
  Wreathed with error and eke with ignorance,
The stars be hid that led me to this pain;
  Drowned is reason that should me consort,
  And I remain despairing of the port.

—THOMAS WYATT

## SONNET 81

Fayre is my love, when her fayre golden heares,
With the loose wynd ye waving chance to marke:
Fayre when the rose in her red cheekes appeares,

Or in her eyes the fyre of love does sparke.
Fayre when her brest lyke a rich laden barke,
With pretious merchandize she forth doth lay:
Fayre when that cloud of pryde, which oft doth dark
Her goodly light with smiles she drives away.
But fayrest she, when so she doth display,
The gate with pearles and rubyes richly dight:
Throgh which her words so wise do make their way
To beare the message of her gentle spright.
The rest be works of natures wonderment,
But this the worke of harts astonishment.

—EDMUND SPENSER

## SONNET 18

Shall I compare thee to a summer's day?
Thou art more lovely and more temperate:
Rough winds do shake the darling buds of May,
And summer's lease hath all too short a date:
Sometimes too hot the eye of heaven shines,
And often is his gold complexion dimmed;
And every fair from fair sometimes declines,
By chance or nature's changing course untrimmed;
But thy eternal summer shall not fade,
Nor lose possession of that fair thou ow'st,
Nor shall death brag thou wander'st in his shade,
When in eternal lines to time thou grow'st:
So long as men can breathe, or eyes can see,
So long lives this, and this gives life to thee.

—WILLIAM SHAKESPEARE

## SONNET 30

When to the sessions of sweet silent thought
I summon up remembrance of things past,
I sigh the lack of many a thing I sought,
And with old woes new wail my dear time's waste:
Then can I drown an eye, unused to flow,
For precious friends hid in death's dateless night,
And weep afresh love's long since canceled woe,
And moan the expense of many a vanished sight:
Then can I grieve at grievances foregone,
And heavily from woe to woe tell o'er
The sad account of fore-bemoanéd moan,
Which I new pay as if not paid before.
But if the while I think on thee, dear friend,
All losses are restored and sorrows end.

—WILLIAM SHAKESPEARE

## RHINE BURIAL

*A brave man*
*Is one who can hide his fear—*
Those were the last words we heard you say.

It was near dusk
When we removed your body
(Your lashes fringed with blown snow,
Making you gray in the gray winter light);
We stood freezing on the white hill
Overlooking the swift Rhine,
Our hands stiff with remembrance of your body,
And Jim said, "Christ!"

That was all–
For pity or cold,
It did not matter.

We laid you in the trailer
Beside the German soldier
Cautiously,

Like a clump of earth holding a tender shoot;
Side by side we laid you, friend and foe,
Coeval in the Rhineland dusk,
Your love and his hatred grotesquely one,
Dissolved in an endless peace
You did not make,
Neither he nor you.

Now we recall your goodness,
Your simple way of saying
Just what you had to say
Even when it was the scraggly truth;

We remember you the falconer,
Tamer of hawks,
Lover of wild things misunderstood
And only by kindness won.

Though you are dead,
And the fear you hid so well
To make you brave
Is dead too,
Yet more sudden
Than ever bird to wrist
Your laughter's caught
In a vein of steel,
To gather root and stone
In earth that is not home.

—JOSEPH LEONARD GRUCCI

## A VALEDICTION FORBIDDING MOURNING

As virtuous men pass mildly away,
  And whisper to their souls to go,
Whilst some of their sad friends do say,
  "The breath goes now," and some say, "No,"

So let us melt and make no noise,
  No tear-floods nor sigh-tempests move;
'Twere profanation of our joys
  To tell the laity our love.

Moving of th' earth brings harms and fears;
  Men reckon what it did and meant,
But trepidation of the spheres,
  Though greater far, is innocent.

Dull sublunary lovers' love,
  Whose soul is sense, cannot admit
Absence, because it doth remove
  Those things which elemented it.

But we by a love so much refin'd
  That ourselves know not what it is,
Interassurèd of the mind,
  Care less eyes, lips, and hands to miss.

Our two souls, therefore, which are one,
  Though I must go, endure not yet
A breach, but an expansion,
  Like gold to airy thinness beat.

If they be two, they are two so
  As stiff twin compasses are two;
Thy soul, the fix'd foot, makes no show
  To move, but doth if th' other do.

And though it in the center sit,
  Yet when the other far doth roam,
It leans and hearkens after it,
  And grows erect as that comes home.

Such wilt thou be to me, who must,
  Like th' other foot, obliquely run;
Thy firmness makes my circle just,
  And makes me end where I begun.

—JOHN DONNE

## THE RETREAT

Happy those early days when I
Shined in my angel-infancy!
Before I understood this place
Appointed for my second race,
Or taught my soul to fancy aught
But a white celestial thought;
When yet I had not walked above
A mile or two from my first love,
And looking back at that short space.
Could see a glimpse of his bright face;
When on some gilded cloud or flower
My gazing soul would dwell an hour,
And in those weaker glories spy
Some shadows of eternity;
Before I taught my tongue to wound
My conscience with a sinful sound,
Or had the black art to dispense
A sev'ral sin to ev'ry sense;
But felt through all this fleshly dress

Bright shoots of everlastingness.
  Oh, how I long to travel back
And tread again that ancient track! –
That I might once more reach that plain
Where first I left my glorious train,
From whence th' enlightened spirit sees
That shady city of palm trees.
But, ah, my soul with too much stay
Is drunk, and staggers in the way.
Some men a forward motion love,
But I by backward steps would move,
And when this dust falls to the urn,
In that state I came, return.

—HENRY VAUGHAN

## THE WORLD IS TOO MUCH WITH US

The world is too much with us: late and soon,
Getting and spending, we lay waste our powers:
Little we see in Nature that is ours;
We have given our hearts away, a sordid boon!
This Sea that bares her bosom to the moon;
The winds that will be howling at all hours,
And are up-gathered now like sleeping flowers;
For this, for everything, we are out of tune;
It moves us not.–Great God! I'd rather be
A Pagan suckled in a creed outworn;
So might I, standing on this pleasant lea,
Have glimpses that would make me less forlorn;
Have sight of Proteus rising from the sea;
Or hear old Triton blow his wreathed horn.

—WILLIAM WORDSWORTH

## SONNET

I on my horse, and Love on me, doth try
Our horsemanships, while by strange work I prove
A horseman to my horse, a horse to Love,
And now man's wrongs in me, poor beast, descry.
The reins wherewith my rider doth me tie
Are humbled thoughts, which bit of reverence move,
Curbed in with fear, but with gilt boss above
Of hope, which makes it seem fair to the eye.
The wand is will; thou, fancy, saddle art,
Girt fast by memory; and while I spur
My horse, he spurs with sharp desire my heart;
He sits me fast, however I do stir;
And now hath made me to his hand so right
That in the manage myself takes delight.

—SIR PHILIP SIDNEY

## RÉSUMÉ

Razors pain you;
Rivers are damp;
Acids stain you;
And drugs cause cramp.
Guns aren't lawful;
Nooses give;
Gas smells awful;
You might as well live.

—DOROTHY PARKER

# 5

# *Patterns of World Order*

*Syntax** means the order of words in a sentence. Since each language has its own syntax, the normal syntactical patterns of English are patterns of expectation. In English, for example, the most basic sentence pattern is subject–verb–object; adjectives generally precede their nouns, and adverbs immediately precede or follow their verbs.

Any variation on the basic pattern produces emphasis. Variations are not uncommon; all of us produce them without conscious thought. It is immediately apparent, for example, that "Here I stand" is a more emphatic statement than the normal "I stand here." And it is more emphatic because of an inversion of syntax, however common that inversion may be. The point to be observed is that the more extreme the variation, the greater the emphasis that occurs.

Here is the first stanza of a poem, "The Carpenter's Son," by A. E. Housman:

> Here the hangman stops his cart:
> Now the best of friends must part.
> Fare you well, for ill fare I:
> Live, lads, and I will die.

There is a slight inversion of syntax in the first line (*Here* is moved from the end to the beginning) and an equally slight inversion in the second line (*Now* is moved from the end to the beginning).

The strongest inversion occurs in the third line: "Fare you well, for ill fare I." In the second clause, the emphasis falls on *I*, which is out of its normal position. (Compare "Fare you well, for I fare ill.")

"Fare you well" is an imperative; "for I fare ill" is declarative; "for ill fare I" is an altered declarative. Look now at the fourth line: "Live, lads, and I will die." As the first two lines are syntactically and grammatically similar (two declaratives with the same slight inversion), these last two have the same general syntax and grammar: imperative, then declarative. But why doesn't the last line repeat the strong inversion of the third, i.e., "Live, lads, and die I will"?

The answer cannot be "to get a rhyme." Poets without their wits about them will invert syntax simply to get a rhyme and therefore arrive at an emphasis they don't intend; but that can't be the case here, because the poet could still get his rhyme:

> Fare you well, for I fare ill
> Live, lads, and die I will.

From this example can you say what the limits of inversion are?

Syntax and grammar are intimately related, and deviations from normal grammatical relationships (i.e., the way in which one word or set of words affects another word or set of words) are probably inseparable from syntax. W. H. Auden begins a poem

> Lay your sleeping head, my love,
> Human on my faithless arm . . . .

Two words are strangers in those lines: *faithless*, because one does not normally think of arms as being either faithful or faithless, and *Human*. *Human*, which is normally either a noun or an adjective, seems to be used as an adverb here. Will you not then inevitably look to the rest of the poem to tell you what the unusual adjective and adverb mean?

The aspect of their own language that most readers find most "natural" is syntax, a notion that really comes down to "We say things *this* way." The point doesn't need elaboration or even much explanation. We are conditioned to our own syntactical patterns, in speech and writing. Any reader who sees, for example, this (expects later to see this). Punctuation is simply a method of rendering intonation and syntactical patterns on paper. Here is a poem that trades on that expectation:

kumrads die because they're told

kumrads die because they're told)
kumrads die before they're old
(kumrads aren't afraid to die
kumrads don't
and kumrads won't
believe in life)and death knows whie

(all good kumrads you can tell
by their altruistic smell
moscow pipes good kumrads dance)
kumrads enjoy
s.freud knows whoy
the hope that you may mess your pance

every kumrad is a bit
of quite unmitigated hate
(travelling in a futile groove

god knows why)
and so do i
(because they are afraid to love

—e. e. cummings

The last line of the poem is the first phrase of the theme, and the last phrase of the theme is the first line of the poem—*because of the reader's expectation, not about the poem, but about language.* The theme is exactly "(because they are afraid to love/ kumrads die because they're told)."

If expectations are to be taken seriously, they must be taken seriously consistently. A parenthesis is to be read consistently as parenthesis. Thus the last stanza of the poem does not say "God knows why, and so do I" but "every comrade is a bit of quite unmitigated hate, and so do [am] I," and second, "Every Comrade travels in a futile groove, and so do I" and third, and only third, "God knows why, and so do I."

*FOR DISCUSSION.*

Here are the first two stanzas of "To an Athlete Dying Young":

The time you won your town the race
We chaired you through the market-place;
Man and boy stood cheering by,
And home we brought you shoulder-high.

To-day, the road all runners come,
Shoulder-high we bring you home,
And set you at your threshold down,
Townsman of a stiller town.

*1.* What line is the stranger in the syntactical patterns?

*2.* Why is that one line important? Read the entire poem before you answer:

## TO AN ATHLETE DYING YOUNG

The time you won your town the race
We chaired you through the market-place;
Man and boy stood cheering by,
And home we brought you shoulder-high.

To-day, the road all runners come,
Shoulder-high we bring you home,
And set you at your threshold down,
Townsman of a stiller town.

Smart lad, to slip betimes away
From fields where glory does not stay
And early though the laurel grows
It withers quicker than the rose.

Eyes the shady night has shut
Cannot see the record cut,
And silence sounds no worse than cheers
After earth has stopped the ears:

Now you will not swell the rout
Of lads that wore their honours out,
Runners whom renown outran
And the name died before the man.

So set, before its echoes fade,
The fleet foot on the sill of shade,
And hold to the low lintel up
The still-defended challenge-cup.

And round that early-laurelled head
Will flock to gaze the strengthless dead,
And find unwithered on its curls
The garland briefer than a girl's.

—A. E. HOUSMAN

Here is a stanza from Thomas Hardy's "Neutral Tones":

Your eyes on me were as eyes that rove
Over tedious riddles of years ago;
And some words played between us to and fro
On which lost the more by our love.

*1.* Where does the syntax break?
*2.* What does the syntactically ambiguous unit say? Can you paraphrase it?
*3.* What bearing does the unit have on the preceding lines?

Here is a sonnet:

## THOU ART INDEED JUST, LORD

JUSTUS QUIDEM TU ES, DOMINE, SI DISPUTEM TECUM: VERUMTAMEN JUSTA LOQUAR AD TE: QUARE VIA IMPIORUM PROSPERATUR ? &C.[1]

Thou art indeed just, Lord, if I contend
With thee; but, sir, so what I plead is just.
Why do sinners' ways prosper? and why must
Disappointment all I endeavour end?
Wert thou my enemy, O thou my friend,
How wouldst thou worse, I wonder, than thou dost

[1]"Thou indeed, O Lord, art just, if I plead with thee, but yet I will speak what is just to thee: Why doth the way of the wicked prosper: Why is it well with all them that transgress, and do wickedly?" (JEREMIAS 12:1—Douay version)

Defeat, thwart me? Oh, the sots and thralls of lust
Do in spare hours more thrive than I that spend,
Sir, life upon thy cause. See, banks and brakes
Now, leavèd how thick! lacèd they are again
With fretty chervil, look, and fresh wind shakes
Them; birds build—but not I build; no, but strain,
Time's eunuch, and not breed one work that wakes.
Mine, O thou lord of life, send my roots rain.

—GERARD MANLEY HOPKINS

*1.* Cope with the broken syntax by paraphrasing lines 4, 6–7, and 12–14.

*2.* The last line is probably the most difficult to deal with. What is the reference of *Mine?* Is it *roots* or *lord of life?* or both?

Here is another sonnet by the same poet:

## CARRION COMFORT

Not, I'll not, carrion comfort, Despair, not feast on thee;
Not untwist—slack they may be—these last strands of man
In me ór, most weary, cry *I can no more*. I can;
Can something, hope, wish day come, not choose not to be.
But ah, but O thou terrible, why wouldst thou rude on me
Thy wring-world right foot rock? lay a lionlimb against me? scan
With darksome devouring eyes my bruisèd bones? and fan,
O in turns of tempest, me heaped there; me frantic to avoid thee and flee?

Why? That my chaff might fly; my grain lie, sheer and clear.
Nay in all that toil, that coil, since (seems) I kissed the rod,
Hand rather, my heart lo! lapped strength, stole joy, would laugh, chéer.

Cheer whom though? the hero whose heaven-handling flung
    me, fóot tród
Me? or me that fought him? O which one? is it each one?
    That night, that year
Of now done darkness I wretch lay wrestling with
    (my God!) my God.

*1.* Attempt a prose paraphrase of the poem by putting the statements into normal syntax.

*2.* Compare your paraphrase with the original. What does your version lose when it normalizes phrases like the following?

> Thy wring-world right foot rock....

> (my God!) my God.

Here is a poem in which the problem of interpretation is almost totally syntactical:

## SOME THINGS THAT FLY THERE BE

Some things that fly there be—
Birds—Hours—the Bumblebee—
Of these no Elegy.

Some things that stay there be—
Grief—Hills—Eternity—
Nor this behooveth me.

There are that resting, rise.
Can I expound the skies?
How still the Riddle lies!

—EMILY DICKINSON

*1.* Put each of the three stanzas in a prose statement that observes normal syntax. The first, for example, might look something like this: There are some things that fly—birds, hours, bumblebees—and of these no one sings or writes elegies.

*2.* Then put each of the prose statements into another expanded prose statement or series of statements that explain the metaphors and images. The first, for example, might look something like this: There are some things that pass by swiftly; these things are beautiful and short-lived, but no one seems to lament their passing.

*3.* In doing this, you will find the most difficult line to be the sixth. Why is that so?

*4.* The last two lines are the most normal lines syntactically. Are they also the easiest to paraphrase? to expand and explain?

Here is a poem in which the syntax has been dismembered:

go(perpe)go

go(perpe)go
(tu)to(al
adve

nturin
g p
article

s of s
ini
sterd
exte

ri)go to(ty)the(om
nivorou salways lugbrin
g ingseekfindlosin g
motilities
are)go to

the
ant
(al
ways

alingwaysing)
go to the ant thou go
(inging)

to the
ant,thou ant-

eater

—e. e. cummings

*1.* Reconstruct the statement made in the poem.

*2.* What cliché is the poet parodying and protesting?

*3.* If he deals with a cliché and protests it, does the complication of the form of the statement the poem makes seem justified?

Here is a poem in which syntax and grammar are disjointed regularly but slightly:

anyone lived in a pretty how town

anyone lived in a pretty how town
(with up so floating many bells down)
spring summer autumn winter
he sang his didn't he danced his did.

Women and men(both little and small)
cared for anyone not at all
they sowed their isn't they reaped their same
sun moon stars rain

children guessed(but only a few
and down they forgot as up they grew
autumn winter spring summer)
that noone loved him more by more

when by now and tree by leaf
she laughed his joy she cried his grief
bird by snow and stir by still
anyone's any was all to her

someones married their everyones
laughed their cryings and did their dance
(sleep wake hope and then)they
said their nevers they slept their dream

stars rain sun moon
(and only the snow can begin to explain
how children are apt to forget to remember
with up so floating many bells down)

one day anyone died i guess
(and noone stooped to kiss his face)
busy folk buried them side by side
little by little and was by was

all by all and deep by deep
and more by more they dream their sleep
noone and anyone earth by april
wish by spirit and if by yes.

Women and men(both dong and ding)
summer autumn winter spring
reaped their sowing and went their came
sun moon stars rain

—e. e. cummings

*1.* If the standard phrase is "how pretty a town," what is the obvious question posed by the phrase if you take it seriously? Is that question answered in the poem?

2. To say that something is "pretty this" or "that" is standard usage (i.e., pretty difficult, pretty expensive). If one said that a town was "pretty how," as opposed, for example, to "pretty why" or "pretty how-much," what would one be saying of it?

3. *Anyone* and *noone* are people in the poem. Describe the characteristics of these two.

4. *Someone* and *everyone* are people, but groups, not individuals. Describe their characteristics.

5. Comment on the double use of words like *anyone* and *noone* when they figure in phrases like:

anyone lived
noone stooped to kiss his face
Women and men . . . / cared for anyone not at all

6. Comment on the accuracy of this critical summary: "The poem deals with two subjects: it is a love story and it is a story about growing up and losing the qualities that can make life a love story."

## ON THIS ISLAND

Look, stranger, on this island now
The leaping light for your delight discovers,
Stand stable here
And silent be,
That through the channels of the ear
May wander like a river
The swaying sound of the sea.

Here at a small field's ending pause
When the chalk wall falls to the foam and its tall ledges
Oppose the pluck
And knock of the tide,
And the shingle scrambles after the suck-
-ing surf,
And a gull lodges
A moment on its sheer side.

Far off like floating seeds the ships
Diverge on urgent voluntary errands,
And this full view
Indeed may enter
And move in memory as now these clouds do,
That pass the harbor mirror
And all the summer through the water saunter.

—W. H. AUDEN

*1.* Examine the syntax of the first stanza. Write the statement it makes in prose and then explain the statement.

*2.* Examine the syntax of the last stanza. Write the statement it makes in prose and then explain the statement.

*3.* Examine the syntax of the second stanza. Write the statement it makes in prose and then explain the statement.

*4.* What is the difference between what you had to do with the first and third stanzas and what you had to do with the second stanza? Define the difference in syntactical problems.

*FOR STUDY.*

## ON DONNE'S POETRY

With Donne, whose muse on dromedary trots,
Wreathe iron pokers into true-love knots;
Rhyme's sturdy cripple, fancy's maze and clue,
Wit's forge and fire-blast, meaning's press and screw.

—SAMUEL TAYLOR COLERIDGE

*1.* Clarify the syntax of this poem, which is, appropriately, as involuted as Donne's own.

## SKERRYVORE: THE PARALLEL

Here all is sunny, and when the truant gull
Skims the green level of the lawn, his wing

Dispetals roses; here the house is framed
Of kneaded brick and the plumed mountain pine,
Such clay as artists fashion and such wood
As the tree-climbing urchin breaks. But there
Eternal granite hewn from the living isle
And dowelled with brute iron, rears a tower
That from its wet foundation to its crown
Of glittering glass, stands, in the sweep of winds,
Immovable, immortal, eminent.

—ROBERT LOUIS STEVENSON

*1.* Although the rhetoric of a sentence is not the same thing as the syntax of a sentence, rhetoric (which is, in this context, the placement of words in the most effective order) sometimes leans heavily on syntax. In this poem both the syntax and the rhetoric fail dismally at a crucial point. What is wrong with the last line?

*2.* What are the objects Stevenson is writing about? One is "here"; the other is "there." The thing "here" is a house, apparently a cottage, since it is flanked by roses and is built of pine and handmade brick. What is it that is made of granite, reinforced with iron, rises like a tower and has a glass top, while its foundation is always wet and it stands always exposed to the wind?

## OF MODERN POETRY

The poem of the mind in the act of finding
What will suffice. It has not always had
To find: the scene was set; it repeated what
Was in the script.
Then the theatre was changed
To something else. Its past was a souvenir.
It has to be living, to learn the speech of the place.
It has to face the men of the time and to meet
The women of the time. It has to think about war
And it has to find what will suffice. It has
To construct a new stage. It has to be on that stage

And, like an insatiable actor, slowly and
With meditation, speak words that in the ear,
In the delicatest ear of the mind, repeat,
Exactly, that which it wants to hear, at the sound
Of which, an invisible audience listens,
Not to the play, but to itself, expressed
In an emotion as of two people, as of two
Emotions becoming one. The actor is
A metaphysician in the dark, twanging
An instrument, twanging a wiry string that gives
Sounds passing through sudden rightnesses, wholly
Containing the mind, below which it cannot descend,
Beyond which it has no will to rise.
It must
Be the finding of a satisfaction, and may
Be of a man skating, a woman dancing, a woman
Combing. The poem of the act of the mind.

—WALLACE STEVENS

*1.* What is the relationship between the unusual syntax of the first and final "statements" and the thing named in those statements?

*2.* What is the relationship between the almost pedestrian syntax and rhetoric of the middle lines and the thing named and described there?

## LINES FOR A DEAD POET

Here lies the poet, deaf and dumb.
Into his ear no sound can come,

Into his eye no sight
Of life, or limb, or the marvelous light.

Ice are his eyes, that once were seas,
In which dwelt creatures more than these

He left us by his going there,
Into the earth, out of the air

Where verity did once reside,
Of the ear the grace, of the eye the pride.

The tongue lies useless now that was
The maker of such strange, sweet laws.

We were his citizens, and stayed
In a country that his poems made.

—DAVID FERRY

## THE DARK HILLS

Dark hills at evening in the west,
Where sunset hovers like a sound
Of golden horns that sang to rest
Old bones of warriors under ground,
Far now from all the bannered ways
Where flash the legions of the sun,
You fade—as if the last of days
Were fading and all wars were done.

—EDWIN ARLINGTON ROBINSON

## WHEN LILACS LAST IN THE DOORYARD BLOOM'D

1

When lilacs last in the dooryard bloom'd,
And the great star early droop'd in the western sky in the night,
I mourn'd, and yet shall mourn with ever-returning spring.

Ever-returning spring, trinity sure to me you bring,
Lilac blooming perennial and drooping star in the west,
And thought of him I love.

2

O powerful western fallen star!
O shades of night—O moody, tearful night!
O great star disappear'd—O the black murk that hides the star!
O cruel hands that hold me powerless—O helpless soul
of me!
O harsh surrounding cloud that will not free my soul.

3

In the dooryard fronting and old farm-house near the white-
wash'd palings,
Stands the lilac-bush tall-growing with heart-shaped leaves of
rich green,
With many a pointed blossom rising delicate, with the perfume
strong I love,
With every leaf a miracle—and from this bush in the
dooryard,
With delicate-color'd blossoms and heart-shaped leaves of
rich green,
A sprig with its flower I break.

4

In the swamp in secluded recesses,
A shy and hidden bird is warbling a song.

Solitary the thrush,
The hermit withdrawn to himself, avoiding the settlements,
Sings by himself a song.

Song of the bleeding throat,
Death's outlet song of life, (for well dear brother I know,
If you wast not granted to sing thou would'st surely die.)

5

Over the breast of the spring, the land, amid cities,
Amid lanes and through old woods, where lately the violets peep'd from the ground, spotting the gray debris,
Amid the grass in the fields each side of the lanes, passing the endless grass,
Passing the yellow-spear'd wheat, every grain from its shroud in the dark-brown fields uprisen,
Passing the apple-tree blows of white and pink in the orchards,
Carrying a corpse to where it shall rest in the grave,
Night and day journeys a coffin.

6

Coffin that passes through lanes and streets,
Through day and night with the great cloud darkening the land,
With the pomp of the inloop'd flags with the cities draped in black,
With the show of the States themselves as of crape-veil'd women standing,
With processions long and winding and the flambeaus of the night,
With the countless torches lit, with the silent sea of faces and the unbared heads,
With the waiting depot, the arriving coffin, and the sombre faces,
With dirges through the night, with the thousand voices rising strong and solemn,
With all the mournful voices of the dirges pour'd around the coffin,
The dim-lit churches and the shuddering organs—where amid these you journey,
With the tolling tolling bells' perpetual clang,
Here, coffin that slowly passes,
I give you my sprig of lilac.

7

(Nor for you, for one alone,
Blossoms and branches green to coffins all I bring,
For fresh as the morning, thus would I chant a song for you
O sane and sacred death.

All over bouquets of roses,
O death, I cover you over with roses and early lilies,
But mostly and now the lilac that blooms the first,
Copious I break, I break the sprigs from the bushes,
With loaded arms I come, pouring for you,
For you and the coffins all of you O death.)

8

O western orb sailing the heaven,
Now I know what you must have meant as a month since
I walk'd,
As I walk'd in silence the transparent shadowy night,
As I saw you had something to tell as you bent to me night
after night,
As you droop'd from the sky low down as if to my side,
(while the other stars all look'd on,)
As we wander'd together the solemn night, (for something I
know not what kept me from sleep,)
As the night advanced, and I saw on the rim of the west how
full you were of woe,
As I stood on the rising ground in the breeze in the cool
transparent night,
As I watch'd where you pass'd and was lost in the netherward
black of the night,
As my soul in its trouble dissatisfied sank, as where you sad orb,
Concluded, dropt in the night, and was gone.

9

Sing on there in the swamp,
O singer bashful and tender, I hear your notes, I hear your call,

I hear, I come presently, I understand you,
But a moment I linger, for the lustrous star has detain'd me,
The star my departing comrade holds and detains me.

10

O how shall I warble myself for the dead one there I loved?
And how shall I deck my song for the large sweet soul that
has gone?
And what shall my perfume be for the grave of him I love?
Sea-winds blown from east and west,
Blown from the Eastern sea and blown from the Western sea,
till there on the prairies meeting,
These and with these and the breath of my chant,
I'll perfume the grave of him I love.

11

O what shall I hang on the chamber walls?
And what shall the pictures be that I hang on the walls,
To adorn the burial-house of him I love?

Pictures of growing spring and farms and homes,
With the Fourth-month eve at sundown, and the gray smoke
lucid and bright,
With floods of the yellow gold of the gorgeous, indolent,
sinking sun, burning, expanding the air,
With the fresh sweet herbage under foot, and the pale green
leaves of the trees prolific,
In the distance the flowing glaze, the breast of the river, with
a wind-dapple here and there,
With ranging hills on the banks, with many a line against the
sky, and shadows,
And the city at hand with dwellings so dense, and stacks of
chimneys,
And all the scenes of life and the workshops, and the workmen
homeward returning.

12

Lo, body and soul—this land,
My own Manhattan with spires, and the sparkling and hurrying tides, and the ships,
The varied and ample land, the South and the North in the light, Ohio's shores and flashing Missouri,
And ever the far-spreading prairies cover'd with grass and corn.

Lo, the most excellent sun so calm and haughty,
The violet and purple morn with just-felt breezes,
The gentle soft-born measureless light,
The miracle spreading bathing all, the fulfill'd noon,
The coming eve delicious, the welcome night and the stars,
Over my cities shining all, enveloping man and land.

13

Sing on, sing on you gray-brown bird,
Sing from the swamps, the recesses, pour your chant from the bushes,
Limitless out of the dusk, out of the cedars and pines.

Sing on dearest brother, warble your reedy song,
Loud human song, with voice of uttermost woe.

O liquid and free and tender!
O wild and loose to my soul—O wondrous singer!
You only I hear—yet the star holds me, (but will soon depart,)
Yet the lilac with mastering odor holds me.

14

Now while I sat in the day and look'd forth,
In the close of the day with its light and the fields of spring, and the farmers preparing their crops,
In the large unconscious scenery of my land with its lakes and forests,

In the heavenly aerial beauty, (after the perturb'd winds and the storms,)
Under the arching heavens of the afternoon swift passing, and the voices of children and women.
The many-moving sea-tides, and I saw the ships how they sail'd,
And the summer approaching with richness, and the fields all busy with labor,
And the infinite separate houses, how they all went on, each with its meals and minutia of daily usages,
And the streets how their throbbings throbb'd, and the cities pent—lo, then and there,
Falling upon them all and among them all, enveloping me with the rest,
Appear'd the cloud, appear'd the long black trail,
And I knew death, its thought, and the sacred knowledge of death.

Then with the knowledge of death as walking one side of me,
And the thought of death close-walking the other side of me,
And I in the middle as with companions, and as holding the hands of companions,
I fled forth to the hiding receiving night that talks not,
Down to the shores of the water, the path by the swamp in the dimness,
To the solemn shadowy cedars and ghostly pines so still.

And the singer so shy to the rest receiv'd me,
The gray-brown bird I know receiv'd us comrades three,
And he sang the carol of death, and a verse for him I love.

From deep secluded recesses,
From the fragrant cedars and the ghostly pines so still,
Came the carol of the bird.

And the charm of the carol rapt me,
As I held as if by their hands my comrades in the night,
And the voice of my spirit tallied the song of the bird.

*Come lovely and soothing death,*
*Undulate round the world, serenely arriving, arriving,*
*In the day, in the night, to all, to each,*
*Sooner or later delicate death.*

*Prais'd be the fathomless universe,*
*For life and joy, and for objects and knowledge curious,*
*And for love, sweet love—but praise! praise! praise!*
*For the sure-enwinding arms of cool-enfolding death.*

*Dark mother always gliding near with soft feet,*
*Have none chanted for thee à chant of fullest welcome?*
*Then I chant it for thee, I glorify thee above all,*
*I bring thee a song that when thou must indeed come, come unfalteringly.*

*Approach strong deliveress,*
*When it is so, when thou hast taken them I joyously sing the dead,*
*Lost in the loving floating ocean of thee,*
*Laved in the flood of thy bliss O death.*

*From me to thee glad serenades,*
*Dances for thee I propose saluting thee, adornments and feastings for thee,*
*And the sights of the open landscape and the high-spread sky are fitting,*
*And life and the fields, and the huge and thoughtful night.*

*The night in silence under many a star,*
*The ocean shore and the husky whispering wave whose voice I know,*

*And the soul turning to thee O vast and well-veil'd death,*
*And the body gratefully nestling close to thee.*

*Over the tree-tops I float thee a song,*
*Over the rising and sinking waves, over the myriad fields and the prairies wide,*
*Over the dense-pack'd cities all and the teeming wharves and ways,*
*I float this carol with joy, with joy to thee O death.*

15

To the tally of my soul,
Loud and strong kept up the gray-brown bird,
With pure deliberate notes spreading filling the night.

Loud in the pines and cedars dim,
Clear in the freshness moist and the swamp-perfume,
And I wish my comrades there in the night.

While my sight that was bound in my eyes unclosed,
As to long panoramas of visions.

And I saw askant the armies,
I saw as in noiseless dreams hundreds of battle-flags,
Borne through the smoke of the battles and pierc'd with missiles I saw them,
And carried hither and yon through the smoke, and torn and bloody,
And at last but a few shreds left on the staffs, (and all in silence,)
And the staffs all splinter'd and broken.

I saw battle-corpses, myriads of them,
And the white skeletons of young men, I saw them,
I saw the debris and debris of all the slain soldiers of the war,
But I saw they were not as was thought,

They themselves were fully at rest, they suffer'd not,
The living remain'd and suffer'd, the mother suffer'd,
And the wife and the child and the musing comrade suffer'd,
And the armies that remain'd suffer'd.

16

Passing the visions, passing the night,
Passing, unloosing the hold of my comrades' hands,
Passing the song of the hermit bird and the tallying song of my soul,
Victorious song, death's outlet song, yet varying ever-altering song,
As low and wailing, yet clear the notes, rising and falling, flooding the night,
Sadly sinking and fainting, as warning and warning, and yet again bursting with joy,
Covering the earth and filling the spread of the heaven,
As that powerful psalm in the night I heard from recesses,
Passing, I leave thee lilac with heart-shaped leaves,
I leave thee there in the door-yard, blooming, returning with spring.

I cease from my song for thee,
From my gaze on thee in the west, fronting the west, communing with thee,
O comrade lustrous with silver face in the night.

Yet each to keep and all, retrievements out of the night,
The song, the wondrous chant of the gray-brown bird,
And the tallying chant, the echo arous'd in my soul,
With the lustrous and drooping star with the countenance full of woe,
With the holders holding my hand nearing the call of the bird,
Comrades mine and I in the midst, and their memory ever to keep, for the dead I loved so well,

For the sweetest, wisest soul of all my days and lands—and this for his dear sake,
Lilac and star and bird twined with the chant of my soul,
There in the fragrant pines and the cedars dusk and dim.

—WALT WHITMAN

This is Whitman's elegy for Abraham Lincoln. Notice that in each of the first five sections one statement occurs in strongly inverted syntax:

(1) trinity sure to me you bring
(2) O helpless soul of me!
(3) with the perfume strong I love
(*also*: A sprig with its flower I break)
(4) Sings by himself a song.
(5) Night and day journeys a coffin.

*1.* What is the function of those inverted constructions in each case? Do all of them have the same general function?

*2.* Do the other 11 sections of the poem share the characteristic just noted?

*3.* Although the poem is (or was, for its time) unconventional in its free verse, it does use conventions, including the traditional form of the lament, repeated in the "O" phrases, and some highly conventional symbols.

*a.* What does the lilac traditionally symbolize?

*b.* What does the fallen star traditionally symbolize?

*c.* What does the voice of a bird in the presence of death symbolize?

*4.* Another tradition of the elegy is that the poet must finally reconcile himself to the particular death by making sense of it. How does Whitman achieve that?

*5.* What is implied about Lincoln when Whitman sings of the best aspects of America as his funeral song and refers to Lincoln as a fallen star that has only "disappear'd" behind a "black murk"—and then converts that murk to a cloud surrounding the mind of the speaker?

## THE CONSTANT LOVER

Out upon it! I have lovéd
Three whole days together,
And am like to love three more—
If it prove fair weather.

Time shall moult away his wings
Ere he shall discover
In the whole wide world again
Such a constant lover.

But the spite on't is, no praise
Is due at all to me:
Love with me had made no stays,
Had it any been but she.

Had it any been but she,
And that very face,
There had been at least ere this
A dozen dozen in her place.

—SIR JOHN SUCKLING

## ON MY FIRST SON

Farewell, thou child of my right hand, and joy;
My sin was too much hope of thee, loved boy.
Seven years thou wert lent to me, and I thee pay,
Exacted by thy fate, on the just day.

O, could I lose all father now! For why
Will man lament the state he should envy?
To have so soon 'scaped world's and flesh's rage,
And, if no other misery, yet age!

Rest in soft peace and, asked, say: Here doth lie
  Ben Jonson his best piece of poetry.
For whose sake, henceforth, all his vows be such,
  As what he loves may never like too much.

—BEN JONSON

## YOU, ANDREW MARVELL

And here face down beneath the sun
And here upon earth's noonward height
To feel the always coming on
The always rising of the night:

To feel creep up the curving east
The earthly chill of dusk and slow
Upon those under lands the vast
And ever-climbing shadow grow

And strange at Ecbatan the trees
Take leaf by leaf the evening strange
The flooding dark about their knees
The mountains over Persia change

And now at Kermanshah the gate
Dark empty and the withered grass
And through the twilight now the late
Few travelers in the westward pass

And Baghdad darken and the bridge
Across the silent river gone
And through Arabia the edge
Of evening widen and steal on

And deepen on Palmyra's street
The wheel rut in the ruined stone
And Lebanon fade out and Crete
High through the clouds and overblown

And over Sicily the air
Still flashing with the landward gulls
And loom and slowly disappear
The sails above the shadowy hulls

And Spain go under and the shore
Of Africa the gilded sand
And evening vanish and no more
The low pale light across that land

Nor now the long light on the sea:
And here face downward in the sun
To feel how swift how secretly
The shadow of the night comes on . . .

—ARCHIBALD MACLEISH

## PORTRAIT OF THE ARTIST AS A PREMATURELY OLD MAN

It is common knowledge to every schoolboy and even every Bachelor of Arts,
That all sin is divided into two parts.
One kind of sin is called a sin of commission, and that is very important,
And it is what you are doing when you are doing something you ortant,

And the other kind of sin is just the opposite and is called a sin of omission and is equally bad in the eyes of all right-thinking people, from Billy Sunday to Buddha,
And it consists of not having done something you shudda.
I might as well give you my opinion of these two kinds of sin as long as, in a way, against each other we are pitting them,
And that is, don't bother your head about sins of commission because however sinful, they must at least be fun or else you wouldn't be committing them.
It is the sin of omission, the second kind of sin,
That lays eggs under your skin.
The way you get really painfully bitten
Is by the insurance you haven't taken out and the checks you haven't added up the stubs of and the appointments you haven't kept and the bills you haven't paid and the letters you haven't written.
Also, about sins of omission there is one particularly painful lack of beauty,
Namely, it isn't as though it had been a riotous red-letter day or night every time you neglected to do your duty;
You didn't get a wicked forbidden thrill
Every time you let a policy lapse or forgot to pay a bill;
You didn't slap the lads in the tavern on the back and loudly cry Whee,
Let's all fail to write just one more letter before we go home, and this round of unwritten letters is on me.
No, you never get any fun
Out of the things you haven't done,
But they are the things that I do not like to be amid,
Because the suitable things you didn't do give you a lot more trouble than the unsuitable things you did.
The moral is that it is probably better not to sin at all, but if some kind of sin you must be pursuing,
Well, remember to do it by doing rather than by not doing.

—OGDEN NASH

## UPON THE DEATH OF A RARE CHILD OF SIX YEARS OLD

Wit's perfection, Beauty's wonder,
Nature's pride, the Graces' treasure,
Virtue's hold, his friends' sole pleasure,
This small marble stone lies under,
Which is often moist with tears
For such loss in such young years.

—FRANCIS DAVISON

## THE PARTING

Since there's no help, come let us kiss and part—
Nay, I have done, you get no more of me;
And I am glad, yea, glad with all my heart,
That thus so cleanly I myself can free.
Shake hands for ever, cancel all our vows,
And when we meet at any time again,
Be it not seen in either of our brows
That we one jot of former love retain.
Now at the last gasp of Love's latest breath,
When, his pulse failing, Passion speechless lies,
When Faith is kneeling by his bed of death,
And Innocence is closing up his eyes,
Now if thou would'st, when all have given him over,
From death to life thou might'st him yet recover.

—MICHAEL DRAYTON

# 6

# *Patterns of Sound: Meter, Rhythm, Stanza, and the Forms*

*Prosody** is the study of patterned sound in poetry. Since a poet simultaneously works with and against any pattern in poetry, it is not surprising to find a prosodist peering at an oscilloscope to discover what an individual performance of a poem reveals, or muttering dum-de-dum-de-dum over the printed text of a poem.

The two terms that prosody hangs on are *rhythm** and *meter*.* There is an important and often confusing difference between them. Rhythm is "natural": it deals with repeated thumps, thrusts, beats, strokes, etc., recurring at varying paces. We breathe in rhythm, our hearts beat in rhythm, we brush our teeth and dance in rhythm. But rhythms differ: our hearts beat to different rhythms depending on whether we are sleeping or exercising; we dance to different rhythms. A prosodist who has gone through a printed poem, dum-de-dum, will discover a different pattern from that discovered by a prosodist watching a performance of the poem on an oscilloscope. Rhythms are refreshingly natural and different. Meter is regular, artificial, and theoretical. It is the pattern with and against which the poet works. A meter is an underlying pattern that the poet probably has in mind and that the reader discovers as the prosodic norm. Rhythm is what a performer puts into a poem.

And all of this talk of meter assumes that the poet is not writing in *free verse.** Free verse is unmetered; it establishes its own patterns. All poems have in common their adaptability to different rhythms. Some poems have meter.

The history of English meters is a history of the assimilation of radically different prosodic systems. For anyone who wants to learn about meters, there is no short-cut through history.

Four metrical systems have dominated poetry in English.

## Accentual-Alliterative Prosody

The oldest metrical system in English is sometimes called *accentual* (accent = stress, prominent relative loudness), sometimes *alliterative* (i.e., involving the repetition of initial consonants), and properly *accentual-alliterative.* Take two lines from the Anglo-Saxon (Old English) *Beowulf* as an example.

Wæs se grimma gæst      Grendel hāten
Mǣre mearcstapa      Sē pe mōras hēold

Loosely translated:

There was a terrible monster      named Grendel
A terrible marsh-walker      who ruled over the moors.

Even if you can't pronounce the Anglo-Saxon exactly—and who really knows if he can?—exaggerate your reading of the lines and answer these questions:

1. How many accents (stresses) are there in each line?
2. How many instances of alliteration are there in each line?
3. Is there some kind of division here except the full line?

Check your answers:

1. There are four stresses (accents) in each line.
2. Three of these stresses fall on alliterating consonants:
   grimma — gaest — Grendel
   mǣre — mearcstapa — mōras
3. Each line is divided into two half-lines.

The basic metrical principle of Anglo-Saxon (accentual-alliterative) verse is that in each full line there must be at least three stressed syllables that alliterate. The key stress is the first stressed syllable of the second half-line, which sets the alliterative pattern.

The accentual-alliterative system has not entirely disappeared. Here, for example, in our own day is W. H. Auden:

My deuce, my double, my dear image
Is it lively there, that land of glass
Where song is a grimace, sound logic
A suite of gestures? You seem amused.
How well and witty when you wake up,
How glad and good when you go to bed,
Do you feel, my friend? What flavor has
That liquor you lift with your left hand;
Is it cold by contrast, cool as this
For a soiled soul; does your self like mine
Taste of untruth?

Prosody would have been very simple and English poetry quite different if that system had prevailed. But Christianity and the Romans invaded England and brought Latin and Greek with them.

## Quantitative Prosody

Classical—that is to say, Latin and Greek—verse is not accentual-alliterative but *quantitative*. And it is so because of major characteristics of Latin and Greek that are minor in English. Syllables in Latin and Greek can be weak or strong, *weak* meaning of short duration and *strong* of longer duration. If this is confusing, notice the same characteristic in English: the vowel in *get* has shorter duration than the vowel in *go*. English pretty much buries that distinction, because it is such a heavily stressed language. Classical measures, however, were preserved in the minds of English poets and prosodists, to the extent that (1) in some contemporary studies of prosody syllables are still spoken of as *short* and *long* (although the prosodist usually means *unstressed* and *stressed*), (2) some English poets—e.g. Tennyson and Robert Bridges—have written quantitative verse, and (3), most important, English prosodists eventually borrowed the terminology of quantitative prosody to describe what went on in non-quantitative verse: *iamb*, *trochee*, *anapest*, for example, are terms from quantitative prosody, and they originally dealt with quantity, not stress. The confusion began to grow.

## Syllabic Prosody

In 1066 the Norman French invaded and conquered England. Although the Normans (i.e., Norsemen, Scandinavians) had been in France only a century and a half before they leaped the Channel, they brought with them the French language, and with it French poetry and French prosody.

French prosody, again because of the characteristics of the French language, was basically *syllabic*—the metrical system was based on counting syllables. And as English was to assimilate the vocabulary of a quantitative system to the practice of an accentual-alliterative system, it now assimilated a syllabic system. Or rather, it began to count syllables, along with everything else.

## Accentual-Syllabic Prosody

A system that emerged from this last marriage was *accentual-syllabic*. In it, from a reader's point of view, one described the meter of a line by

(1) determining the number of syllables in a line;
(2) determining the number of stressed syllables in the line;
(3) determining the number of units in a line when a unit was defined as any group containing one stressed syllable and any number of unstressed syllables (a foot);
(4) giving that line a name by reference to the number of stresses and the composition of the units.

That may be confusing, and it may encourage the notion that prosodists are simply people who can count and are on occasion capable of higher mathematics. The historical fact is that following the four rules above, and doing enough of the dum-de-dum thing, a line of Shakespeare may come out as "iambic pentameter." That definition is a result of counting stresses in the accentual fashion, counting syllables in the syllabic fashion, and then using quantitative terms for both.

Because the bulk of English poetry is accentual-syllabic, we furnish here the nomenclature of that prosody.

Accentual-syllabic scansion deliberately ignores quantity and the presence of four degrees of stress in English to concentrate on stress or no stress in each syllable. Stress means *relative stress*—i.e., stressed or not stressed by comparison with the syllable that precedes or (with a first syllable) follows it. The unit of measurement is the *foot*, a unit containing one stressed syllable and one or two unstressed syllables in one of the following four patterns:

∪| – the iambic foot
|∪ – the trochaic foot
∪∪| – the anapestic foot
|∪∪ – the dactylic foot

In scansion, one declares the *character* of the most frequent foot in the line and the *number* of feet in the line.

The length (number of feet) is indicated by these terms:

one foot – *monometer*
two feet – *dimeter*
three feet – *trimeter*
four feet – *tetrameter*
five feet – *pentameter*
six feet – *hexameter*
seven feet – *heptameter*
eight feet – *octameter*

It should be pointed out that since determining syllables can be done by the eye but determining stresses only by the ear, some attention has to be paid to what is not visible but only audible, despite ignoring quantity and half, quarter, and weak stresses. Take, for example, two lines that differ to the eye:

he bent the silken tent
he bent the silk    tent

The reader who is only counting what he sees will scan the first as consistently iambic ( ∪|∪| ), the second (at the end) as containing some exotic foot such as spondee ( || ) with an extra unaccented syllable added—for which there is also an exotic name. This is an illusion. If you will listen carefully to what you pronounce as you read the two lines, you will find they are metrically identical ( ∪|∪| ) because you have added a compensatory pause after *silk* and before *tent.* The isochronic principle is operating: intervals between major stresses tend to remain the same.

If one objects that the two lines don't "sound identical," the answer is, "Of course they don't; the rhythms are different. But the *meters* are identical."

There are other metrical systems in English, but most of them are not sound patterns but visual patterns. Here, for example, is Marianne Moore writing in an English version of syllabic verse:

WHAT ARE YEARS?

  What is our innocence,
what is our guilt? All are
  naked, none is safe. And whence
is courage: the unanswered question,
the resolute doubt—
dumbly calling, deafly listening—that
is misfortune, even death,
    encourages others
    and in its defeat, stirs

  the soul to be strong? He
sees deep and is glad, who
  accedes to mortality
and in his imprisonment rises
upon himself as
the sea in a chasm, struggling to be
free and unable to be,
    in its surrendering
    finds its continuing.

  So he who strongly feels,
behaves. The very bird,
  grown taller as he sings, steels

his form straight up. Though he is captive,
his mighty singing
says, satisfaction is a lowly
thing, how pure a thing is joy.
    This is mortality,
    this is eternity.

—MARIANNE MOORE

*1.* Establish the metrical pattern by counting the syllables in each line.

*2.* How does the pattern of the concluding two lines differ from that of earlier stanzas? What effect is achieved by the variation?

A variation on syllabics is this kind of poem:

## MESSAGE CLEAR

```
 am            i
                         if
i am                   he
      he r       o
      h    ur  t
     the re          and
      he      re     and
      he re
 a              n   d
     the r                e
i am    r                ife
               i n
          s    ion and
i                   d    i e
 am   e res   ect
 am   e res   ection
                o        f
     the                 life
```

                    o            f
    m    e           n
            sur e
      the             d      i e
i           s
            s   e t    and
i am  the   sur          d
  a   t   res     t
                    o          life
i am   he r                       e
i a             ct
i         r  u       n
i   m   e  e      t
i                 t             i e
i           s     t    and
i am  th            o      th
i am      r            a
i am  the   su       n
i am  the   s        on
i am  the  e  rect on       e  if
i am      re         n     t
i am        s          a        fe
i am        s   e    n     t
i      he  e             d
i     t e   s     t
i         re            a d
  a   th  re            a d
  a         s     t on        e
  a   t   re            a d
  a   th  r          on       e
i         resurrect
                       a       life
i am              i n          life
i am      resurrection
i am the resurrection and

i am
i am the resurrection and the life

—EDWIN MORGAN

*1.* Is the metrical pattern here purely visual?

*2.* What effect, once its novelty has worn off, does this plan have? Is it like a problem in addition? Or is there a sense of struggling toward a full statement?

Here is a similar example:

## I VOW

I vow perpetual chastity poverty and obedience.

I                                    a
        r e al
        per          s     o         n
  vow                                and     die
                     t     o                 i

I vow            chastity
I          al              o         n     e
                     i               n
        perpetu      ity
                     y       e t
I          l               ove

I vow                      poverty
I   ow   e e               ver y          o     n e.
I          l         i     ve
                 as                  n    o     n e.
                     y      e t
I                ha         ve
        pe      a  c        e

I vow                                        obedience.
I        r e a ch
  o        u        t                                 i n
            t    h           e
  vo                 i                        d    .
I      p r                                obe
         r e  al       ity                             .
I                     t      r y                    .
I                s                             e  e
            t    h           e
    w          a         y                              .
                l             ove
                          p   e     a            ce
            t    h           e
                l             o   r      d         .
I      p r      a        y         and      die
                      t      o                   i   .

I vow perpetual chastity poverty and obedience.

—FRANK WESCHLER

*1.* The poem was written by a Jesuit, using the Jesuit vow as the full statement. What is the difference in what a poem says if one begins with the full statement, as here, and deduces, so to speak, other statements from it, as opposed to beginning with pieces of a statement and working toward the full statement as in the previous poem?

Other metrical systems appear and vanish. Some years ago *Rundscheibe* was popular. *Rundscheibe* required a poem to be written in half-formed letters on a disk much like a phonograph record. The disk was then turned at a steady, slow speed. The eye supplied the remainder of the letters and the poem spun out before the reader.

Poems must be scanned according to the prosodic system that the poem used. It is useless to talk of iambs in a syllabic poem or tetrameters in accentual-alliterative verse.

And it is useless to talk of any of those things in free verse. Free verse creates its own patterns, sometimes by means of cadences* (i.e., a pattern of heavy stresses that appears sporadically for emphasis), sometimes by means that have nothing to do with metrical systems. Here is an example:

## THE ORANGE BEARS

The orange bears with soft friendly eyes
Who played with me when I was ten,
Christ, before I left home they'd had
Their paws smashed in the rolls, their backs
Seared by hot slag, their soft trusting
Bellies kicked in, their tongues ripped
Out, and I went down through the woods
To the smelly crick with Whitman
In the Haldeman-Julius edition,
And I just sat there worrying my thumbnail
Into the cover—What did he know about
Orange bears with their coats all stunk up with soft coal
And the National Guard coming over
From Wheeling to stand in front of the millgates
With drawn bayonets jeering at the strikers?

I remember you could put daisies
On the windowsill at night and in
The morning they'd be so covered with soot
You couldn't tell what they were anymore.

A hell of a fat chance my orange bears had!

—KENNETH PATCHEN

*1.* No meter, no cadence. What then holds the poem together? Not sound patterns but another kind of pattern. Consider the first two lines.

*a.* What is odd about an orange bear?

*b.* Do teddy bears really have soft, friendly eyes?

*c.* Do teddy bears play with children? What is being said in those first two lines?

2. Teddy bears don't go to work in coal mines or mills and there get "smashed," "seared," "kicked," "ripped." What does? Teddy bears *do* get "smashed," "seared," "kicked," "ripped," although not in mines or mills. What two things are being said here?

3. What is the connection between Walt Whitman's view of America and teddy bears?

4. What do daisies on a windowsill in a mining or mill town have in common with teddy bears?

5. What, essentially, is being compared with teddy bears, Walt Whitman, and daisies?

## Stress Prosody

Some poets have occasionally adopted a stress prosody,* distributing in a line a fixed number of stresses without considering the number of unstressed syllables. This metrical system has been used by poets as various as Coleridge ("Christabel"), W. H. Auden ("September 1, 1939"), and Gerard Manley Hopkins, for whom stress prosody was the basis of his theory of "sprung rhythm."

## Stress

These poets have tacitly acknowledged a fact: that stress is the overriding audible characteristic of English. If any generalization can be made about sound patterns in English poetry, it will have to deal with stress:

*Any repeated pattern of sound calls attention to itself. Any series of close-packed stresses calls attention to itself. Any pattern of stress that interrupts an established pattern calls strong attention to itself. Whenever two patterns coincide* (i.e., *rhyme and stress*), *strong emphasis results.*

## Rhyme

Aside from stress, probably the most obvious repetition of sound occurs in rhyme,* which is the identity or near-identity of vowel sounds and following consonant sounds. Prosodists distinguish various kinds of rhyme:

(1) by the position of the rhyme: end rhyme* (the most common), internal rhyme* (less common), head rhyme* ("The sunlight on the garden/ Hardens and grows cold"—least common of all).

(2) by the strength of the rhyme: full rhyme,* light rhyme,* slant rhyme,* eye rhyme* (i.e., by how nearly there is full identity of vowel and consonant sound).

(3) by the coincidence of rhyme and stress: masculine rhyme* (when the final syllable of rhymed words is stressed) and feminine rhyme* (when the final syllable is unstressed).

(4) by the number of rhyming syllables, the ultimate being something like Byron's rhyming *ladies intellectual* with *hen-peck'd you-all.*

These distinctions are doubtless useful for some purposes. For our purposes, however, two different things are important:

(1) When stress and rhyme coincide, strong emphasis is produced. Masculine rhyme, therefore, actually "says" something different from feminine rhyme. Masculine rhyme also inevitably stops the flow of a line in a way that feminine rhyme does not.

(2) End rhyme is the basis of stanza patterns.

## Stanza

Foot patterns, line lengths, and rhyme schemes create all sorts of fascinating stanzas. One of the simpler stanzas (simpler to identify, not to write) is the *heroic couplet*, which consists of two lines of iambic pentameter rhyming together and containing a single thought. One of the more complicated is the *Spenserian stanza*: nine lines, the first eight in iambic pentameter, the last in iambic hexameter, rhyming abab abcc.

Considerations such as this, however, are probably outside the scope of an introduction to poetry. The study of exotic forms is a matter of getting behind the scenes; it is a kind of shoptalk. It is, for example, all very well for W. H. Auden to say that his ideal reader is the one who can appreciate what he has done here and there with an amphibrach or a paeonic foot, but the fact is that the major difficulty posed for the reader by Auden's verse is wrapped up in his allusions, metaphors, and syntax, not in amphibrachs and paeonic feet. It is no triumph to spot a spondee in a passage that simply bewilders the spotter.

### Alliteration and Assonance

Many of the minor repetitive sound devices used by poets are incomplete rhymes and are therefore less noticeable, less emphatic. Alliteration,* for example, the repetition of consonant sounds, is a kind of half-rhyme. So is assonance,* the repetition of vowel sounds. If a given syllable alliterated and assonated with another syllable, the two would rhyme. Both alliteration and assonance create minor emphasis.

Individual sounds or repeated sounds, however, have little significance in themselves. They do not really produce predictable effects, except to call attention to themselves. (Look, for example, at the alliteration and assonance in the two sentences you have just read.) That some sounds are beautiful and others are ugly, or that certain combinations are invariably attractive or repulsive is pure myth, as the linguist Ralph Long once illustrated by arguing that if all that has been said about the inherent qualities of liquid and palatal sounds is true, the most beautiful word in English must be *syphilis*. Meaning overpowers sound.

For that reason, it is important in a poem to observe how sounds combine with denotation and connotation to produce effects, without assuming that any combination of sounds always produces the same effect. The classic illustration is a section from Pope's *Essay on Criticism,* in which he speaks of second-rate critics and poets and then illustrates the proper marriage of sound and sense:

But most by numbers judge a poet's song,
And smooth or rough with them is right or wrong.
In the bright Muse though thousand charms conspire,
Her voice is all these tuneful fools admire,
Who haunt Parnassus but to please their ear,
Not mend their minds; as some to church repair,
Not for the doctrine, but the music there.
These equal syllables alone require,
Though oft the ear the open vowels tire,
While expletives their feeble aid do join,
And ten low words oft creep in one dull line:
While they ring round the same unvaried chimes,
With sure returns of still expected rhymes;
Where'er you find the "cooling western breeze,"
In the next line, it "whispers through the trees";
If crystal streams "with pleasing murmurs creep,"
The reader's threatened (not in vain) with "sleep";
Then, at the last and only couplet fraught
With some unmeaning thing they call a thought,
A needless Alexandrine ends the song
That, like a wounded snake, drags its slow length along.
Leave such to tune their own dull rhymes, and know
What's roundly smooth or languishing slow;
And praise the easy vigor of a line
Where Denham's strength and Waller's sweetness join.
True ease in writing comes from art, not chance,
As those move easiest who have learned to dance.
'Tis not enough no harshness gives offense,

The sound must seem an echo to the sense.
Soft is the strain when Zephyr gently blows,
And the smooth stream in smoother numbers flows;
But when loud surges lash the sounding shore,
The hoarse, rough verse should like the torrent roar.
When Ajax strives some rock's vast weight to throw,
The line too labors, and the words move slow;
Not so when swift Camilla scours the plain,
Flies o'er the unbending corn, and skims along the main.

*1.* Point out instances where sound complements sense.

*2.* Note in the harsh or impeded lines what happens when consonants are "jammed," i.e., when the sound at the end of one word is the same as the sound at the beginning of the next, no matter what the consonant sound is.

*3.* Is there anything unusual about the rhyming words that Pope uses? Is it their position or their composition that makes them stand out? Is it both?

## *THE FORMS OF VERSE*

The so-called forms of verse—lyric, dramatic, narrative—depend for definition on repeated characteristics. If a lyric did not repeat the characteristics of other lyrics more than the characteristics of a dramatic monologue, it wouldn't be a lyric. The same is true of sub-categories of the major forms—ode, sonnet, ballad, dramatic monologue, villanelle, rondeau, etc.

As with other patterns, poets work with and against the established forms. New forms are always being created out of the old. Nobody had ever heard of a lyrical ballad 200 years ago; the form would have been a contradiction in terms, since ballads were narratives. In the 1870s a reviewer finally coined a term for a form that had been very popular for the preceding half century—the dramatic monologue. In our day *Rundscheibe* and "concrete" verse have appeared, and some of the older terms have been so loosened by popular usage and poetic practice (as, for example, when in radio-TV parlance *ballad* means a love song set to a slow beat) that redefinition may be necessary before the terms can be used seriously again.

*Form* is a very loose word. Its use here may suggest that we mean by it *metrical form*. Actually the "forms of verse" are sometimes definable by their metrical form, sometimes not. There is a ballad stanza, but the dramatic monologue has no characteristic metrical form. A sonnet is often said to contain 14 lines, but the earliest sonnet sequence in English was composed of 18-line sonnets, and some of the best in the language have 16 lines. Definitions of forms are approximations of patterns from which the poet departs at will, and often the definition is not metrical.

The advantage of a fixed form is, of course, that the poet employs a ready-made pattern of expectation: the reader expects certain things to happen in a certain order. If they do, he is satisfied. If they don't and a new harmony appears, he may be pleasantly surprised.

The advantage to the reader of knowing something about the fixed forms is obvious: he knows the patterns of expectation. The reader who admires a sonnet without realizing that it is a sonnet will get from the experience of reading the poem enjoyment and satisfaction, but not as much as the reader who knows the form he is dealing with.

We will confine ourselves in this chapter to the most common forms in English: the ballad,* the sonnet,* and the dramatic monologue.* (Oddly enough, ballads and sonnets are not native to English; English seems to have originated only one metrical form: the limerick.) Readers who wish to study more exotic forms can find them in Chapter 8 and the Glossary.

## The Ballad

Ballads are usually categorized as folk ballads or literary ballads; a subcategory of this last is the lyrical ballad. They all (ideally) have in common their metrical form: the ballad stanza, a quatrain (a four-line stanza) composed of alternating lines of iambic tetrameter and trimeter, rhyming abab or abcb. They differ in origin, mode of original presentation, and focus. The folk ballad is the oral product probably of a single author, changed by being passed through the hands of countless performers (e.g., the early English ballad "Lord Randal" becomes "Lord Randolph" in the American East, "James Randolph" in the American South, "Jamie Rambo" in the American West). The literary ballad is the printed product of a single author.

The folk ballad is pure story, unlikely to indulge in neat transitions, complicated motivation, close physical description, or open sentiment. It is stripped-down narrative. The literary ballad is more likely to deal with close analysis and detail; the extreme type is the lyrical ballad, which concentrates on the speaker's reaction to the story rather than the story itself. Notice the paradox: the ballad, supposedly narrative, becomes lyrical.)

Ballads have, despite their changes in focus, tended to develop the same topics: the untimely death of the young, the proud, the beautiful; the ruthless abuse of power; jealousy among the great; the curse of a woman's favor.

Here are examples of the three kinds.

### THE THREE RAVENS

There were three ravens sat on a tree,
*Down a down, hay down, hay down,*
There were three ravens sat on a tree,
*With a down,*

There were three ravens sat on a tree,
They were as black as they might be,
*With a down, derry, derry, derry, down, down.*

The one of them said to his mate,
"Where shall we our breakfast take?

"Down in yonder green field
There lies a knight slain under his shield.

"His hounds they lie down at his feet,
So well they can their master keep.

"His hawks they fly so eagerly,
There's no fowl dare him come nigh."

Down there comes a fallow doe,
As great with young as she might go.

She lift up his bloody head,
And kissed his wounds that were so red.

She got him up upon her back,
And carried him to earthen lake.

She buried him before the prime;
She was dead herself ere evensong time.

God send every gentleman
Such hawks, such hounds, and such a lemman.

*1.* What does the nonsense refrain imply about the way the poem was to be performed? Could the ballad have accompanied a dance?

*2.* A "fallow doe" is a deer distinguished by its pale brown or reddish-yellow color–i.e., by its human skin-color. Why doesn't the poet simply say that a pregnant girl came down to the knight?

*3.* Bearing in mind your answer to question 2, why are the ravens necessary? Notice that the living things in the poem are ravens, hounds, hawks, a doe.

*4.* Is this ballad in ballad stanzas? Notice that the stanzas can be rewritten to conform:

There were three ravens sat on a tree,
    Down a down, hay down, hay down
They were as black as they might be.
    With a down derry, derry, derry, down, down.

Can you hazard a guess about an earlier form of this ballad? About what happened to that earlier form?

*5.* Is there any emotion stated directly in the ballad? From what does the emotion arise?

*6.* Using this ballad as evidence, what does it mean to say that "the folk ballad sings itself"?

The following is a literary ballad:

## LA BELLE DAME SANS MERCI

"O what can ail thee, knight-at-arms,
  Alone and palely loitering?
The sedge has wither'd from the lake,
  And no birds sing.

"O what can ail thee, knight-at-arms,
  So haggard and so woe-begone?
The squirrel's granary is full,
  And the harvest's done.

"I see a lily on thy brow
  With anguish moist and fever dew;
And on thy cheek a fading rose
  Fast withereth too."

"I met a lady in the meads,
  Full beautiful—a faery's child,
Her hair was long, her foot was light,
  And her eyes were wild.

"I made a garland for her head,
  And bracelets too, and fragrant zone;
She look'd at me as she did love,
  And made sweet moan.

"I set her on my pacing steed
  And nothing else saw all day long,
For sidelong would she bend, and sing
  A faery's song.

"She found me roots of relish sweet,
  And honey wild, and manna dew,
And sure in language strange she said—
  'I love thee true.'

"She took me to her elfin grot,
  And there she wept, and sigh'd full sore;
And there I shut her wild wild eyes
  With kisses four.

"And there she lullèd me asleep,
  And there I dream'd—Ah! woe betide!
The latest dream I ever dream'd
  On the cold hill's side.

"I saw pale kings and princes too,
  Pale warriors, death-pale were they all;
They cried—'La Belle Dame sans Merci
  Hath thee in thrall!'

"I saw their starv'd lips in the gloom,
  With horrid warning gapèd wide,
And I awoke and found me here,
  On the cold hill's side.

"And this is why I sojourn here,
  Alone and palely loitering,
Though the sedge is wither'd from the lake,
  And no birds sing."

—JOHN KEATS

*1.* This ballad was composed in April 1819. What elements of the folk ballad does it imitate?

2. How does it differ from the folk ballad?

*a.* Look at the first two stanzas. In each, what do the first two lines deal with? What do the third and fourth lines of each deal with? If we assume three subjects in the poem, the knight, nature, and the lady, which two of those subjects are dealt with in the pairs of lines we have singled out?

*b.* What happens in the third stanza to those two subjects originally kept separate?

*c.* How does the focus of the poem change? Notice the pronouns that begin stanzas 3–11.

*d.* Is there a prologue and an epilogue to this poem?

*e.* This ballad can hardly be called "pure story." What is this beautiful woman without pity?

Here is a lyrical ballad:

## SHE DWELT AMONG THE UNTRODDEN WAYS

She dwelt among the untrodden ways
  Beside the springs of Dove.
A Maid whom there were none to praise
  And very few to love;

A violet by a mossy stone
  Half hidden from the eye!
—Fair as a star, when only one
  Is shining in the sky.

She lived unknown, and few could know
  When Lucy ceased to be;
But she is in her grave, and, oh,
  The difference to me!

—WILLIAM WORDSWORTH

*1.* What elements of the folk ballad does this lyrical ballad imitate?

2. How does this lyrical ballad differ from the folk ballad?

*a.* On what does the poem focus? Look, for example, at the last line.

*b.* Resolve the paradoxes in the poem, remembering the focus. How can a way be "untrodden"? If there were "none to praise" her, how could there be any, much less "very few to love" her? If she lived "unknown," how could any, much less "few" know her death?

*c.* What does a phrase like "ceased to be" (as opposed to *died*) suggest about the speaker's attitude toward the girl?

*d.* What are the characteristics of the violet and the star that are being selected here for comparison with the girl?

*e.* In no way is this pure story; it isn't story at all except by implication. What is the implied story?

## The Sonnet

The sonnet,* says the *Random House Dictionary of the English Language*, is "a poem, properly expressive of a single, complete thought, idea, or sentiment, of 14 lines, usually in iambic pentameter, with rhymes arranged according to one of certain definite schemes, being in the strict or Italian form divided into a major group of 8 lines (the octave) followed by a minor group of 6 lines (the sestet), and in a common English form into three quatrains followed by a couplet." That is an ironclad pattern of expectation. It could hardly be improved upon, except to note that the Italian form (which generally rhymes abba, abba, cde, cde, or some variant of that in the sestet) contains a two-part development suited well to question and answer, cause and effect, then-and-now; and that the English form (which generally rhymes abab, cdcd, efef, gg, a boon to English poets, since English, unlike Romance languages, is rhyme poor) contains a three- or four-part development, suited best to playing three changes on a single theme and summarizing the three in a final couplet. Another way of saying that is that the two forms are *radically* different.

Here is a contemporary sonnet:

## ART REVIEW

Recently displayed at the Times Square Station, a new Vandyke on the face-cream girl.
(Artist unknown. Has promise, but lacks the brilliance Shown by the great masters of the Elevated age)
The latest wood carving in a Whelan telephone booth, titled "O Mortal Fools WA 9-5090," shows two winged hearts above an ace of spades.
(His meaning is not entirely clear, but this man will go far)
A Charcoal nude in the rear of Flatbush Ahearn's Bar & Grill, "Forward to the Brotherhood of Man," has been boldly conceived in the great tradition.
(We need more, much more of this)
Then there is the chalk portrait, on the walls of a waterfront warehouse, of a gentleman wearing a derby hat: "Bleecker Street Mike is a double-crossing rat,"
(Morbid, but powerful. Don't miss)

Know then by these presents, know all men by these signs and omens, by these simple thumbprints on the throat of time,
Know that Pete, the people's artist, is ever watchful,
That Tuxedo Jim has passed among us and was much displeased, as always,
That George the Ghost (no man has ever seen him) and Billy the Bicep boy will neither bend nor break,
That Mr. Harkness of Sunnyside still hopes for the best, and has not lost the human touch,
That Phantom Phil, the master of them all, has come and gone, but will return, and all is well.

—KENNETH FEARING

*1.* Suppose that you have to argue that this is an Italian sonnet, despite the obvious lack of iambic pentameter and any rhyme scheme at all. Argue the case anyway.

*2.* What replaces accentual-syllabic meter in the poem? (Reread the first line aloud as a guide.)

*3.* Two dictions mingle in the octave: the diction of the reporter and the diction of the art critic. Scribblings on walls, graffiti, are treated as serious art objects in the octave. Is that treatment justified by the sestet?

*4.* The tone changes in the sestet: "Know then by these presents" is a phrase from judicial decisions, against which there is very little appeal. What effect does that echo have on what is said in the sestet?

*5.* What are the effects of other echoes in the poem?

*a.* "The Elevated age"—when the El, the elevated trains, were still running in New York.

*b.* "O Mortal Fools"—Puck's slogan; what does it mean when a man says that and then leaves his telephone number?

*c.* "simple thumbprints on the throat of time."

(1) Compare Longfellow: "footprints on the sands of time."

(2) What would a person be killing if he left thumbprints on the throat of time?

*6.* Is the last line ironic or straightforward? Are things "well" so long as we pay serious attention to graffiti?

Here is a stylized English sonnet.

## SONNET 138

When my love swears that she is made of truth,
I do believe her, though I know she lies,
That she might think me some untutored youth,
Unlearnéd in the world's false subtleties.
Thus vainly thinking that she thinks me young,
Although she knows my days are past the best,
Simply I credit her false-speaking tongue:
On both sides thus is simple truth suppressed.
But wherefore says she not she is unjust?
And wherefore say not I that I am old?

Oh, love's best habit is in seeming trust,
And age in love loves not to have years told.
Therefore I lie with her and she with me,
And in our faults by lies we flattered be.

—WILLIAM SHAKESPEARE

*1.* What words at the beginning of quatrains and the couplet signal the divisions of the thought that correspond with the unit divisions?

*2.* In what way does the couplet not only summarize what has gone before but add another aspect? (What word is being played upon for its multiple meanings?)

The following is an example of what happens when sonnet forms marry. John Keats wrote both English and Italian sonnets; he found both unsuited to his purposes but out of the two created a new stanza form in which he wrote his odes. Here is the first stanza of his "Ode on a Grecian Urn":

1

Thou still unravished bride of quietness,
Thou foster child of silence and slow time,
Sylvan historian, who canst thus express
A flowery tale more sweetly than our rhyme:
What leaf-fringed legend haunts about thy shape
Of deities or mortals, or of both,
In Tempe or the dales of Arcady?
What men or gods are these? What maidens loath?
What mad pursuit? What struggle to escape?
What pipes and timbrels? What wild ecstasy?

*1.* What did he borrow from each form?

*2.* How did he combine them? Look at the second stanza also:

2

Heard melodies are sweet, but those unheard
Are sweeter; therefore, ye soft pipes, play on;
Not the sensual ear, but, more endeared,
Pipe to the spirit ditties of no tone:
Fair youth, beneath the trees, thou canst not leave
Thy song, nor ever can those trees be bare;
Bold Lover, never, never canst thou kiss,
Though winning near the goal–yet, do not grieve;
She cannot fade, though thou hast not thy bliss,
Forever wilt thou love, and she be fair!

Here is the first sonnet of a sequence of fifty, first published in 1862.

## SONNET 1

By this he knew she wept with waking eyes:
That, at his hand's light quiver by her head,
The strange low sobs that shook their common bed
Were called into her with sharp surprise,
And strangled mute, like little gaping snakes,
Dreadfully venomous to him. She lay
Stone-still, and the long darkness flowed away
With muffled pulses. Then, as midnight makes
Her giant heart of Memory and Tears
Drink the pale drug of silence, and so beat
Sleep's heavy measure, they from head to feet
Were moveless, looking through their dead black years,
By vain regret scrawled over the blank wall.
Like sculptured effigies they might be seen
Upon their marriage-tomb, the sword between;
Each wishing for the sword that severs all.

—GEORGE MEREDITH

*1.* The "sonnet" has 16 lines. What, then, makes it a sonnet?

*2.* Is the pattern of development closer to the Italian or the English? Or is it a compromise?

*3.* What are the husband and wife, now strangers, being compared to as they lie stiffly beside each other?

*4.* What is "the sword that severs all"?

## The Dramatic Monologue

The dramatic monologue has no distinguishing metrical form. Traditionally it has tended to blank verse, possibly because of the voice-like quality of that meter. But what makes the dramatic monologue distinctive is its focus: it concentrates on the character of mind of a single speaker who is not the poet and who is speaking at a moment just before or after a crisis in his life, in a specific dramatic situation in which conflict emerges. A listener is almost always implied; although the listener never speaks, his presence conditions the utterance of the speaker.

Here is the best-known dramatic monologue in English:

### MY LAST DUCHESS

FERRARA

That's my last Duchess painted on the wall,
Looking as if she were alive. I call
That piece a wonder, now: Frà Pandolf's hands
Worked busily a day, and there she stands.
Will't please you sit and look at her? I said
"Frà Pandolf" by design, for never read
Strangers like you that pictured countenance,
The depth and passion of its earnest glance,
But to myself they turned (since none puts by
The curtain I have drawn for you, but I)

And seemed as they would ask me, if they durst,
How such a glance came there; so, not the first
Are you to turn and ask thus. Sir, 'twas not
Her husband's presence only, called that spot
Of joy into the Duchess' cheek; perhaps
Frà Pandolf chanced to say, "Her mantle laps
Over my lady's wrist too much," or "Paint
Must never hope to reproduce the faint
Half-flush that dies along her throat": such stuff
Was courtesy, she thought, and cause enough
For calling up that spot of joy. She had
A heart—how shall I say?—too soon made glad,
Too easily impressed: she liked whate'er
She looked on, and her looks went everywhere.
Sir, 'twas all one! My favour at her breast,
The dropping of the daylight in the West,
The bough of cherries some officious fool
Broke in the orchard for her, the white mule
She rode with round the terrace—all and each
Would draw from her alike the approving speech,
Or blush, at least. She thanked men,—good! but thanked
Somehow—I know not how—as if she ranked
My gift of a nine-hundred-years-old name
With anybody's gift. Who'd stoop to blame
This sort of trifling? Even had you skill
In speech—(which I have not)—to make your will
Quite clear to such an one, and say, "Just this
Or that in you disgusts me; here you miss,
Or there exceed the mark"—and if she let
Herself be lessoned so, nor plainly set
Her wits to yours, forsooth, and made excuse,
—E'en then would be some stooping; and I choose
Never to stoop. Oh sir, she smiled, no doubt,
Whene'er I passed her; but who passed without

Much the same smile? This grew; I gave commands;
Then all smiles stopped together. There she stands
As if alive. Will't please you rise? We'll meet
The company below, then. I repeat,
The Count your master's known munificence
Is ample warrant that no just pretence
Of mine for dowry will be disallowed;
Though his fair daughter's self, as I avowed
At starting, is my object. Nay, we'll go
Together down, sir. Notice Neptune, though,
Taming a sea-horse, thought a rarity,
Which Claus of Innsbruck cast in bronze for me!

—ROBERT BROWNING

*1.* Consider the verse form: couplets that sound like blank verse. Why would a poet adapt the couplet in that fashion if he were writing a dramatic monologue?

*2.* What has been done to the lines to muffle the rhymes?

*3.* This monologue has often been read as the unconscious revelation of an egomaniac. That assumes that the speaker (who is probably the Duke of Ferrara) does not realize that he is revealing his ruthlessness. What in the poem might indicate that he is fully aware of what he is saying, that he means to reveal that ruthlessness?

*4.* Bearing in mind your answer to question 3, what details in the poem suggest that the Duke is being contrasted in his pride and sophistication to the late Duchess's openness and innocence? Would this support your answer to question 4?

*5.* One word in the first line breaks the diction: *last.* What does it suggest? The latest one in a series? The final one of a series? Does your answer here affect your answers to 3 and 4?

*6.* It is probably ultimately undiscoverable whether the Duke had his last Duchess put away somewhere or killed. Why is it unnecessary to be able to answer that question exactly to understand what the Duke is saying, by implication, to the emissary?

7. Dukes outrank Counts. What is the Duke saying to the Count through his emissary?

*FOR DISCUSSION.*

## THOMAS RYMER

True Thomas lay oer yon grassy bank,
  And he beheld a ladie gay,
A ladie that was brisk and bold,
  Come riding oer the fernie brae.

Her skirt was of the grass-green silk,
  Her mantel of the velvet fine,
And ilka tett of her horse's mane
  Hung fifty silver bells and nine.

True Thomas he took off his hat,
  And bowed him low down till his knee:
"All hail, thou mighty Queen of Heaven!
  For your peer on earth I never did see."

"O no, O no, True Thomas," she says,
  "That name does not belong to me;
I am but the queen of fair Elfland,
  And I'm come here for to visit thee.

"But ye maun go wi me now, Thomas,
  True Thomas, ye maun go wi me,
For ye maun serve me seven years,
  Thro weel or wae as may chance to be."

She turned about her milk-white steed,
  And took True Thomas up behind,
And aye wheneer her bridle rang,
  The steed flew swifter than the wind.

For forty days and forty nights
  He wade thro red blude to the knee,
And he saw neither sun nor moon,
  But heard the roaring of the sea.

O they rade on, and further on,
  Until they came to a garden green:
"Light down, light down, ye ladie free,
  Some of that fruit let me pull to thee."

"O no, O no, True Thomas," she says,
  "That fruit maun not be touched by thee,
For a' the plagues that are in hell
  Light on the fruit of this countrie.

"But I have a loaf here in my lap,
  Likewise a bottle of claret wine,
And now ere we go farther on,
  We'll rest a while, and ye may dine."

When he had eaten and drunk his fill,
  "Lay down your head upon my knee,"
The lady sayd, "ere we climb yon hill,
  And I will show you fairlies three.

"O see not ye yon narrow road,
  So thick beset wi thorns and briers?
That is the path of righteousness,
  Tho after it but a few enquires.

"And see not ye that braid braid road,
  That lies across yon lillie leven?
That is the path of wickedness,
  Tho some call it the road to heaven.

"And see not ye that bonny road,
  Which winds about the fernie brae?
That is the road to fair Elfland,
  Where you and I this night maun gae.

"But Thomas, ye maun hold your tongue,
  Whatever you may hear or see,
For gin ae word you should chance to speak,
  You will neer get back to your ain countrie."

He has gotten a coat of the even cloth,
  And a pair of shoes of velvet green,
And till seven years were past and gone
  True Thomas on earth was never seen.

*1.* Compare this folk ballad with the literary ballad, "La Belle Dame Sans Merci," earlier in this chapter.

*a.* What differences are there in the two stories that are told?

*b.* What differences are there in the technique of telling the stories?

*c.* What differences are there in the total shape of the poem? Consider, for example, beginnings and endings.

*2.* Does reading this earlier version, so to speak, of Keats' poem help you to decide what the beautiful lady represents in Keats' poem? What significance does Thomas Rymer's last name have?

## THE WINDHOVER

### TO CHRIST OUR LORD

I caught this morning morning's minion, kingdom of daylight's
    dauphin, dapple-dawn-drawn Falcon, in his riding
  Of the rolling level underneath him steady air, and striding
High there, how he rung upon the rein of a wimpling wing
In his ecstasy! then off, off forth on swing,
  As a skate's heel sweeps smooth on a bow-bend: the hurl and
    gliding
  Rebuffed the big wind. My heart in hiding
Stirred for a bird,—the achieve of, the mastery of the thing!

Brute beauty and valor and act, oh, air, pride, plume, here
Buckle! AND the fire that breaks from thee then, a billion
Times told lovelier, more dangerous, O my chevalier!

No wonder of it: shéer plód makes plow down sillion
Shine, and blue-bleak embers, ah my dear,
Fall, gall themselves, and gash gold-vermilion.

—GERARD MANLEY HOPKINS

*1.* This is an unusual sonnet, but still a sonnet. The difficulties in understanding the sonnet center on individual words. It is not, for example, clear whether "Buckle!" means "fold up and therefore disappear" or "attach these qualities to me, as with armor," and the image of the knight that runs through the poem does not entirely clarify the choice. A correlative problem is "O my chevalier!" Christ, who figures in the epigraph ("To Christ Our Lord") was and is often represented as the king or the perfect knight. The kestrel hawk (the windhover) is also one who rides, fights and wins in the poem; he is even said to ride the currents and to ring "upon the rein." In what sense may what the bird does be said to be what Christ did? In what way are the two possible meanings of "Buckle!" not contradictory?

*2.* The most important aspect of the poem is the resemblances it states. The speaker's heart is said to be in hiding. He sees the hawk conquer the elements. He alludes to Christ. Then he says, in a moment of revelation, that simply plodding along behind a plow horse, or the collapse of burnt-out wood as it sends up its last lovely shower of sparks, is as beautiful as what the hawk was doing—presumably because they all witness to some central idea of mastery, beauty, and duty. What is that central idea?

*3.* If the resemblances sound forced, consider what color likenesses are to be found in a hawk seen against a dappled dawn, the shine of the earth in a newly-turned furrow, and the blue-black embers as they collapse.

## AMERICA

Although she feeds me bread of bitterness,
And sinks into my throat her tiger's tooth,
Stealing my breath of life, I will confess

I love this cultured hell that tests my youth!
Her vigor flows like tides into my blood,
Giving me strength erect against her hate.
Her bigness sweeps my being like a flood.
Yet as a rebel fronts a king in state,
I stand within her walls with not a shred
Of terror, malice, not a word of jeer.
Darkly I gaze into the days ahead,
And see her might and granite wonders there,
Beneath the touch of time's unerring hand,
Like priceless treasures sinking in the sand.

—CLAUDE MC KAY

Here is a comment on the poem:

The *I* or *me* of a sonnet is not necessarily the poet. The speaker of this poem is, as he says, a "youth." Where he finds threats, hate, and impossible odds, he also finds a challenge, a test for his manhood: the vigor of the female America only makes him *erect* against her *hate*. She bites his neck, but it is not clear who is raping whom. The figures are somewhat mixed, appropriately. America is variously a mother (feeding the speaker with the Biblical bitter herbs), a tiger, a vampire (drawing blood and injecting by the bite a "cultured hell," a "vigor," into his blood), a king (a king?)—in other words, a dangerous, deadly, immensely attractive, exciting entity, sexual, bisexual, asexual.

The last quatrain gives the story away. "Darkly I gaze" echoes St. Paul's remarks about how when he was a child he gazed into a glass darkly and he spoke as a child, but when he matured, he saw and spoke as an adult. The last two lines are pathetic, given the character of the speaker. He obviously knows nothing of "time's unerring hand," or, for that matter, of time's erring hand. He is unconscious of time. conscious only of the hot stirring in his blood that makes him challenge the world and its history. He will lose.

"Darkly I gaze" may have another significance in the poem. The poet, Claude McKay, was black. Reread the comment above and then say whether you agree with it or not.

## NEGRO HERO

I had to kick their law into their teeth in order to save them.
However I have heard that sometimes you have to deal
Devilishly with drowning men in order to swim them to shore.
Or they will haul themselves and you to the trash and the fish
beneath.
(When I think of this, I do not worry about a few
Chipped teeth.)

It is good I gave glory, It is good I put gold on their name.
Or there would have been spikes in the afterward hands.
But let us speak only of my success and the pictures in the
Caucasian dailies
As well as the Negro weeklies. For I am gem.
(They are not concerned that it was hardly The Enemy my
fight was against
But them.)

It was a tall time. And of course my blood was
Boiling about in my head and straining and howling and singing
me on.
Of course I was rolled on wheels of my boy itch to get at
the gun.
Of course all the delicate rehearsal shots of my childhood
massed in mirage before me.
Of course I was child
And my first swallow of the liquor of battle bleeding black
air dying and demon noise
Made me wild.

It was kinder than that, though, and I showed like a banner
my kindness.

I loved. And a man will guard when he loves.
Their white-gowned democracy was my fair lady.
With her knife lying cold, straight, in the softness of her sweet-flowing sleeve.
But for the sake of the dear smiling mouth and the stuttered promise I toyed with my life.
I threw back!—I would not remember
Entirely the knife.

Still—am I good enough to die for them, is my blood bright enough to be spilled,
Was my constant back-question—are they clear
On this? Or do I intrude even now?
Am I clean enough to kill for them, do they wish me to kill for
them or is my place while death licks his lips and strides to them
In the galley still?

(In a southern city a white man said
Indeed, I'd rather be dead;
Indeed, I'd rather be shot in the head
Or ridden to waste on the back of a flood
Than saved by the drop of a black man's blood.)

Naturally, the important thing is, I helped to save them, them and a part of their democracy.
Even if I had to kick their law into their teeth in order to do that for them.
And I am feeling well and settled in myself because I believe it was a good job,
Despite this possible horror: that they might prefer the
Preservation of their law in all its sick dignity and their knives
To the continuation of their creed
And their lives.

—GWENDOLYN BROOKS

This is a poem that seems to communicate quickly and completely because of the natural flow of its language. Test the fullness of your understanding of the poem by answering these questions:

*1.* A parallel is being drawn between the speaker and another person by the use of

kick the law into their teeth in order to save them
drowning men
I gave glory
spikes in the afterward hands
For I am gem
creed

Who is the person? Reread the last four lines and draw the parallel more exactly.

*2.* The most-often repeated phrase in the poem is "their law"; it occurs three times. This "law" is opposed to "creed" and "lives" but yoked with "knives." What is this law? If you have trouble answering, answer question 3 first.

*3.* "I had to kick their law into their teeth" is an odd phrase. It sounds more or less like

I kicked his teeth in
I threw it in their teeth
The law has teeth in it
The law is an eye for an eye and a tooth for a tooth
Throw the lie in his teeth

You have heard it said, "An eye for an eye, and a tooth for a tooth." . . . Another law I give you: "You shall love one another as I have loved you."

I kicked the habit, in the teeth of . . .

All of those phrases have overtones. Some of them may be quite unconnected with the poem. Sort out what is usable and reasonable.

## HYMN TO PROSERPINE

AFTER THE PROCLAMATION IN ROME OF THE CHRISTIAN FAITH

VICISTI, GALILÆE

I have lived long enough, having seen one thing, that love
 hath an end;

Goddess and maiden and queen, be near me now and befriend.
Thou art more than the day or the morrow, the seasons that laugh or that weep;
For these give joy and sorrow; but thou, Proserpina, sleep.
Sweet is the treading of wine, and sweet the feet of the dove;
But a goodlier gift is thine than foam of the grapes or love.
Yea, is not even Apollo, with hair and harpstring of gold,
A bitter God to follow, a beautiful God to behold?
I am sick of singing: the bays burn deep and chafe: I am fain
To rest a little from praise and grievous pleasure and pain.
For the Gods we know not of, who give us our daily breath,
We know they are cruel as love or life, and lovely as death.
O Gods dethroned and deceased, cast forth, wiped out in a day!
From your wrath is the world released, redeemed from your chains, men say.
New Gods are crowned in the city; their flowers have broken your rods;
They are merciful, clothed with pity, the young compassionate Gods.
But for me their new device is barren, the days are bare;
Things long past over suffice, and men forgotten that were.
Time and the Gods are at strife; ye dwell in the midst thereof,
Draining a little life from the barren breasts of love.
I say to you, cease, take rest; yea, I say to you all, be at peace,
Till the bitter milk of her breast and the barren bosom shall cease.
Wilt thou yet take all, Galilean? but these thou shalt not take,

The laurel, the palms and the pæan, the breast of the nymphs in the brake;
Breasts more soft than a dove's, that tremble with tenderer breath;
And all the wings of the Loves, and all the joy before death;
All the feet of the hours that sound as a single lyre,
Dropped and deep in the flowers, with strings that flicker like fire,
More than these wilt thou give, things fairer than all these things?
Nay, for a little we live, and life hath mutable wings.
A little while and we die; shall life not thrive as it may?
For no man under the sky lives twice, outliving his day.
And grief is a grievous thing, and a man hath enough of his tears:
Why should he labor, and bring fresh grief to blacken his years?
Thou hast conquered, O pale Galilean; the world has grown gray from thy breath;
We have drunken of things Lethean, and fed on the fulness of death.
Laurel is green for a season, and love is sweet for a day;
But love grows bitter with treason, and laurel outlives not May.
Sleep, shall we sleep after all? for the world is not sweet in the end;
For the old faiths loosen and fall, the new years ruin and rend.
Fate is a sea without shore, and the soul is a rock that abides;
But her ears are vexed with the roar and her face with the foam of the tides.
O lips that the live blood faints in, the leavings of rack and rods!

O ghastly glories of saints, dead limbs of gibbeted Gods!
Though all men abase them before you in spirit, and all knees bend,
I kneel not neither adore you, but standing, look to the end.
All delicate days and pleasant, all spirits and sorrows are cast
Far out with the foam of the present that sweeps to the surf of the past:
Where beyond the extreme sea-wall, and between the remote sea-gates,
Waste water washes, and tall ships founder, and deep death waits:
Where, mighty with deepening sides, clad about with the seas as with wings,
And impelled of invisible tides, fulfilled of unspeakable things,
White-eyed and poisonous-finned, shark-toothed and serpentine-curled,
Rolls, under the whitening wind of the future, the wave of the world.
The depths stand naked in sunder behind it, the storms flee away;
In the hollow before it the thunder is taken and snared as a prey;
In its sides is the north-wind bound; and its salt is of all men's tears;
With light of ruin, and sound of changes, and pulse of years:
With travail of day after day, and with trouble of hour upon hour;
And bitter as blood is the spray; and the crests are as fangs that devour:
And its vapor and storm of its steam as the sighing of spirits to be;

And its noise as the noise in a dream; and its depth as the
roots of the sea:
And the height of its head as the height of the utmost
stars of the air:
And the ends of the earth at the might thereof tremble,
and time is made bare.
Will ye bridle the deep sea with reins, will ye chasten the
high sea with rods?
Will ye take her to chain her with chains, who is older
than all ye Gods?
All ye as a wind shall go by, as a fire shall ye pass and be
past;
Ye are Gods, and behold, ye shall die, and the waves be
upon you at last.
In the darkness of time, in the deeps of the years, in the
changes of things,
Ye shall sleep as a slain man sleeps, and the world shall
forget you for kings.
Though the feet of thine high priests tread where thy lords
and our forefathers trod,
Though these that were Gods are dead, and thou being
dead art a God,
Though before thee the throned Cytherean be fallen, and
hidden her head,
Yet thy kingdom shall pass, Galilean, thy dead shall go
down to thee dead.
Of the maiden thy mother men sing as a goddess with grace
clad around;
Thou art throned where another was king; where another
was queen she is crowned.
Yea, once we had sight of another: but now she is queen,
say these.
Not as thine, not as thine was our mother, a blossom of
flowering seas,

Clothed round with the world's desire as with raiment, and fair as the foam,
And fleeter than kindled fire, and a goddess and mother of Rome.
For thine came pale and a maiden, and sister to sorrow; but ours,
Her deep hair heavily laden with odor, and color of flowers,
White rose of the rose-white water, a silver splendor, a flame,
Bent down into us that besought her, and earth grew sweet with her name.
For thine came weeping, a slave among slaves, and rejected; but she
Came flushed from the full-flushed wave, and imperial, her foot on the sea.
And the wonderful waters knew her, the winds and the viewless ways,
And the roses grew rosier, and bluer the sea-blue stream of the bays.
Ye are fallen, our lords, by what token? we wist that ye should not fall.
Ye were all so fair that are broken; and one more fair than ye all.
But I turn to her still, having seen she shall surely abide in the end;
Goddess and maiden and queen, be near me now and befriend.
O daughter of earth, of my mother, her crown and blossom of birth,
I am also, I also thy brother; I go as I came unto earth.
In the night where thine eyes are as moons are in heaven, the night where thou art,

Where the silence is more than all tunes, where sleep overflows from the heart,
Where the poppies are sweet as the rose in our world, and the red rose is white,
And the wind falls faint as it blows with the fume of the flowers of the night,
And the murmur of spirits that sleep in the shadow of Gods from afar
Grows dim in thine ears and deep as the deep dim soul of a star,
In the sweet low light of thy face, under heavens untrod by the sun,
Let my soul with their souls find place, and forget what is done and undone.
Thou art more than the God who number the days of our temporal breath;
For these give labor and slumber; but thou, Proserpina, death.
Therefore now at thy feet I abide for a season in silence. I know
I shall die as my fathers died, and sleep as they sleep; even so.
For the glass of the years is brittle wherein we gaze for a span;
A little soul for a little bears up this corpse which is man.
So long I endure, no longer; and laugh not again, neither weep.
For there is no God found stronger than death; and death is a sleep

—A. C. SWINBURNE

*1.* A dramatic monologue that probably requires some special information. The words *Vicisti, Galilæe* are the dying words of the Emperor Julian, sometimes called "The Apostate" because he first embraced Christianity, then rejected it. Is there anything in the poem that would lead you to believe that the speaker is someone other than Julian?

2. Three women are mentioned repeatedly and contrasted in the poem, either by name or by their legendary qualities: Venus, Mary, and Proserpine. It is crucial to understanding the poem to know that Proserpine, as the goddess of the seasons and the underworld, is also the goddess of flux and change.

*a.* What was once the speaker's view of Venus and what she stood for?

*b.* What is the speaker's view of Mary?

*c.* Why does he eventually take comfort in worshipping Proserpine? What private and public satisfaction does he get from believing in her?

## THE BLESSED DAMOZEL

The blessed Damozel leaned out
  From the gold bar of Heaven;
Her eyes were deeper than the depth
  Of waters stilled at even;
She had three lilies in her hand,
  And the stars in her hair were seven.

Her robe, ungirt from clasp to hem,
  No wrought flowers did adorn,
But a white rose of Mary's gift,
  For service meetly worn;
Her hair that lay along her back,
  Was yellow like ripe corn.

Herseemed she scarce had been a day
  One of God's choristers;
The wonder was not yet quite gone
  From that still look of hers;
Albeit, to them she left, her day
  Had counted as ten years.

(To one it is ten years of years:
. . . Yet now, here in this place,
Surely she leaned o'er me,—her hair
Fell all about my face. . . .
Nothing: the autumn-fall of leaves.
The whole year sets apace.)

It was the rampart of God's house
That she was standing on;
By God built over the sheer depth
In which is Space begun;
So high, that looking downward thence,
She scarce could see the sun.

It lies in Heaven, across the flood
Of ether, as a bridge.
Beneath, the tides of day and night
With flame and darkness ridge
The void, as low as where this earth
Spins like a fretful midge.

Around her, lovers, newly met
'Mid deathless love's acclaims,
Spoke evermore among themselves,
Their heart-remembered names;
And the souls, mounting up to God,
Went by her like thin flames.

And still she bowed herself, and stooped
Out of the circling charm;
Until her bosom must have made
The bar she leaned on warm,
And the lilies lay as if asleep
Along her bended arm.

From the fixed place of Heaven, she saw
  Time, like a pulse, shake fierce
Through all the worlds. Her gaze still strove,
  Within the gulf to pierce
Its path; and now she spoke as when
  The stars sang in their spheres.

The sun was gone now; the curled moon
  Was like a little feather
Fluttering far down the gulf; and now
  She spoke through the still weather.
Her voice was like the voice the stars
  Had when they sang together.

(Ah sweet! Even now in that bird's song,
  Strove not her accents there,
Fain to be hearkened? When those bells
  Possessed the mid-day air,
Strove not her steps to reach my side
  Down all the echoing stair?)

"I wish that he were come to me,
  For he will come," she said.
"Have I not prayed in Heaven? on earth
  Lord, Lord, has he not prayed?
Are not two prayers a perfect strength?
  And shall I feel afraid?

"When round his head the aureole clings,
  And he is clothed in white,
I'll take his hand and go with him
  To the deep wells of light;
We will step down as to a stream,
  And bathe there in God's sight.

"We two will stand beside that shrine,
  Occult, withheld, untrod,
Whose lamps are stirred continually
  With prayer sent up to God;
And see our old prayers granted, melt
  Each like a little cloud.

"We two will lie i' the shadow of
  That living mystic tree
Within whose secret growth the Dove
  Is sometimes felt to be,
While every leaf that His plumes touch
  Saith His Name audibly.

"And I myself will teach to him
  I myself, lying so,
The songs I sing here; which his voice
  Shall pause in, hushed and slow,
And find some knowledge at each pause,
  Or some new thing to know."

(Alas! we two, we two, thou say'st!
  Yea, one wast thou with me
That once of old. But shall God lift
  To endless unity
The soul whose likeness with thy soul
  Was but its love for thee?)

"We two," she said, "will seek the groves
  Where the lady Mary is,
With her five handmaidens, whose names
  Are five sweet symphonies:—
Cecily, Gertrude, Magdalen,
  Margaret and Rosalys.

"Circlewise sit they, with bound locks
  And foreheads garlanded;
Into the fine cloth white like flame,
  Weaving the golden thread,
To fashion the birth-robes for them
  Who are just born, being dead.

"He shall fear, haply, and be dumb:
  Then will I lay my cheek
To his, and tell about our love,
  Not once abashed or weak:
And the dear Mother will approve
  My pride, and let me speak.

"Herself shall bring us, hand in hand,
  To Him round whom all souls
Kneel, the clear-ranged unnumbered heads
  Bowed with their aureoles:
And angels, meeting us, shall sing
  To their citherns and citoles.

"There will I ask of Christ the Lord
  Thus much for him and me:—
Only to live as once on earth
  With Love,—only to be,
As then awhile, for ever now
  Together, I and he."

She gazed, and listened, and then said,
  Less sad of speech than mild,—
"All this is when he comes." She ceased.
  The light thrilled towards her, filled
With angels, in strong level lapse.
  Her eyes prayed, and she smiled.

(I saw her smile.) But soon their path
Was vague in distant spheres.
And then she cast her arms along
The golden barriers,
And laid her face between her hands,
And wept. (I heard her tears.)

—DANTE GABRIEL ROSSETTI

*1.* This poem can be read, with some difficulty, as a lyric instead of as a dramatic monologue. Let us take the easier course and assume that it is a dramatic monologue.

*a.* Who is the speaker?

*b.* What is the situation?

*c.* How does the combination of speaker and situation explain the strange way in which abstract and supernatural details (souls, prayers, angels) are rendered as concrete, visual objects (flames, clouds, a lady and her handmaidens)?

*2.* Does the use of parentheses in the poem have some significance?

*FOR STUDY.*

## MOOD

I think an impulse stronger than my mind
May some day grasp a knife, unloose a vial,
Or with a little leaden ball unbind
The cords that tie me to the rank and file.
My hands grow quarrelsome with bitterness,
And darkly bent upon the final fray;
Night with its stars upon a grave seems less
Indecent than the too complacent day.
God knows I would be kind, let live, speak fair,
Requite an honest debt with more than just,
And love for Christ's dear sake these shapes that wear

A pride that had its genesis in dust,–
The meek are promised much in a book I know
But one grows weary turning cheek to blow.

—COUNTEE CULLEN

## KARMA

Christmas was in the air and all was well
With him, but for a few confusing flaws
In divers of God's images. Because
A friend of his would neither buy nor sell,
Was he to answer for the axe that fell?
He pondered; and the reason for it was,
Partly, a slowly freezing Santa Claus
Upon the corner, with his beard and bell,

Acknowledging an improvident surprise,
He magnified a fancy that he wished
The friend whom he had wrecked were here again.
Not sure of that, he found a compromise;
And from the fullness of his heart he fished
A dime for Jesus who had died for man.

—EDWIN ARLINGTON ROBINSON

## SINCE THERE'S NO HELP

Since there's no help, come let us kiss and part;
Nay, I have done, you get no more of me,
And I am glad, yea, glad with all my heart
That thus so cleanly I myself can free;
Shake hands forever, cancel all our vows,
And when we meet at any time again,

Be it not seen in either of our brows
That we one jot of former love retain.
Now at the last gasp of Love's latest breath,
When, his pulse failing, Passion speechless lies,
When Faith is kneeling by his bed of death,
And Innocence is closing up his eyes,
Now, if thou wouldst, when all have given him over,
From death to life thou mightst him yet recover.

—MICHAEL DRAYTON

## SONNET 29

When, in disgrace with fortune and men's eyes,
I all alone beweep my outcast state,
And trouble deaf heaven with my bootless cries,
And look upon myself, and curse my fate,
Wishing me like to one more rich in hope,
Featured like him, like him with friends possessed,
Desiring this man's art and that man's scope,
With what I most enjoy contented least;
Yet in these thoughts myself almost despising,
Haply I think on thee—and then my state,
Like to the lark at break of day arising
From sullen earth, sings hymns at heaven's gate;
For thy sweet love remembered such wealth brings
That then I scorn to change my state with kings.

—WILLIAM SHAKESPEARE

## OZYMANDIAS

I met a traveler from an antique land
Who said: Two vast and trunkless legs of stone
Stand in the desert . . . Near them, on the sand,

Half sunk, a shattered visage lies, whose frown,
And wrinkled lip, and sneer of cold command,
Tell that its sculptor well those passions read
Which yet survive, stamped on these lifeless things,
The hand that mocked them, and the heart that fed:
And on the pedestal these words appear:
"My name is Ozymandias, king of kings:
Look on my works, ye Mighty, and despair!"
Nothing beside remains. Round the decay
Of that colossal wreck, boundless and bare
The lone and level sands stretch far away.

—P. B. SHELLEY

## O WHERE ARE YOU GOING?

"O where are you going?" said reader to rider,
"That valley is fatal when furnaces burn,
Yonder's the midden whose odors will madden,
That gap is the grave where the tall return."

"O do you imagine," said fearer to farer,
"That dusk will delay on your path to the pass,
Your diligent looking discover the lacking
Your footsteps feel from granite to grass?"

"O what was that bird," said horror to hearer,
"Did you see that shape in the twisted trees?
Behind you swiftly the figure comes softly,
The spot on your skin is a shocking disease?"

"Out of this house"—said rider to reader,
"Yours never will"—said farer to fearer,
"They're looking for you"—said hearer to horror,
As he left them there, as he left them there.

W. H. AUDEN

*1.* A poem about poets and other adventurous people. The alliterative patterns are so strong as to distract the reader—as indeed the *reader* in the poem is distracted from listening to what the speaker says. Does this justify the strong alliteration?

*2.* What is the homonym for *rider?*

*3.* What things do "riders" and "writers" have in common, according to the poem?

*4.* What makes *rider* a synonym for *writer, farer,* and *horror?*

*5.* What is the *reader/ fearer/ hearer* afraid of? (A *midden,* incidentally, is a dunghill, a manure pile.) What is the *dusk* that is so ominous to him?

*6.* Who was it that was associated with a bird, hung on a "twisted tree," and cured people who had on their "skin . . . a shocking disease"?

*7.* The *rider/ writer/ farer/ horror* says to the *reader/ fearer/ hearer,* "Out of this house . . . / Yours never will." Out of what house? Never will what?

*8.* "They're looking for you" is a phrase that "sane" men speak to lunatics, or others that they take to be lunatics. What justifies the phrase here?

*9.* In the last line, the *reader/ fearer/ hearer* leaves *them,* not *him,* there. Who are *them?*

One, two
Button my shoe;
Three, four,
Shut the door;
Five, six
Pick up sticks . . . .

*1.* Lines designed to teach children how to count. Why are the lines this short? Compare "Jack and Jill/ Went up the hill/ To fetch a pail of water," a poem appropriate to slightly older children. What would a child do with a line as long as the following, assuming it was intended for oral presentation?

Like a wounded snake, drags its slow length along.

## CARGOES

Quinquireme of Nineveh from distant Ophir,
Rowing home to haven in sunny Palestine,
With a cargo of ivory,
And apes and peacocks,
Sandalwood, cedarwood, and sweet white wine.

Stately Spanish galleon coming from the Isthmus,
Dipping through the Tropics by the palm-green shores,
With a cargo of diamonds,
Emeralds, amethysts,
Topazes, and cinnamon, and gold moidores.

Dirty British coaster with a salt-cake smoke stack,
Butting through the Channel in the mad March days,
With a cargo of Tyne coal,
Road-rails, pig-lead,
Firewood, iron-ware, and cheap tin trays.

—JOHN MASEFIELD

*1.* The combination of sounds pleasant to the ear is called euphony; the combination of sounds unpleasant to the ear is called cacaphony. How much of the effect of this poem depends on those two devices?

*2.* Does a difference in stress patterns reinforce the effect of vowel and consonant sounds here?

## gee i like to think of dead

gee i like to think of dead it means nearer because deeper
firmer since darker than little round water at one end of
the well      it's too cool to be crooked and it's too firm
to be hard but it's sharp and thick and it loves,      every
old thing falls in rosebugs and jackknives and kittens and

pennies they all sit there looking at each other having the fastest time because they've never met before

dead's more even than how many ways of sitting on your head your unnatural hair has in the morning

dead's clever too like POF goes the alarm off and the little striker having the best time tickling away everybody's brain so everybody just puts out their finger and they stuff the poor thing all full of fingers

dead has a smile like the nicest man you've never met who maybe winks at you in a streetcar and you pretend you don't but really you do see and you are My how glad he winked and hope he'll do it again

or if it talks about you somewhere behind your back it makes your neck feel pleasant and stoopid   and if dead says may i have this one and was never introduced you say Yes because you know you want it to dance with you and it wants to and it can dance and Whocares

dead's fine like hands do you see that water flowerpots in windows but they live higher in their house than you so that's all you see but you don't want to

dead's happy like the way underclothes All so differently solemn and inti and sitting on one string

dead never says my dear,Time for your musiclesson and you like music and to have somebody play who can but you know you never can and why have to?

dead's nice like a dance where you danced simple hours and you take all your prickley-clothes off and squeeze-into-largeness without one word   and you lie still as anything   in largeness and this largeness begins to give you,the dance all over again and you,feel all again all over the way men you liked made you feel when they touched you(but that's not all)because largeness tells you so you can feel what you made,men feel when,you touched,them

dead's sorry like a thistlefluff-thing which goes landing away all by himself on somebody's roof or something where who-ever-heard-of-growing and nobody expects you to anyway

dead says come with me he says(andwhyevernot)into the round well and see the kitten and the penny and the jackknife and the rosebug

and you say Sure you say (like that) sure i'll come with you you say for i like kittens i do and jackknives i do and pennies i do and rosebugs i do

—e. e. cummings

## THE LOVE SONG OF J. ALFRED PRUFROCK

*S'io credesse che mia risposta fosse*
*A persona che mai tornasse al mondo,*
*Questa fiamma staria senza piu scosse.*
*Ma perciocche giammai di questo fondo*
*Non torno vivo alcun, s'i' odo il vero,*
*Senza tema d'infamia ti rispondo.*[1]

Let us go then, you and I,
When the evening is spread out against the sky

---

[1]"If I thought
My answer made to one who ever might
Return again up to the living world
This fiery tongue would motionless remain.
But since no living soul has ever left
This pit of Hell, if I hear true report,
I dare to answer without fear of shame."
Dante, *Inferno*, Canto xxvii.

Like a patient etherized upon a table;
Let us go, through certain half-deserted streets,
The muttering retreats
Of restless nights in one-night cheap hotels
And sawdust restaurants with oyster-shells:
Streets that follow like a tedious argument
Of insidious intent
To lead you to an overwhelming question. . . .
Oh, do not ask, "What is it?"
Let us go and make our visit.

In the room the women come and go
Talking of Michelangelo.

The yellow fog that rubs its back upon the window-panes,
The yellow smoke that rubs its muzzle on the window-panes,
Licked its tongue into the corners of the evening,
Lingered upon the pools that stand in drains,
Let fall upon its back the soot that falls from chimneys,
Slipped by the terrace, made a sudden leap,
And seeing that it was a soft October night,
Curled once about the house, and fell asleep.

And indeed there will be time
For the yellow smoke that slides along the street,
Rubbing its back upon the window-panes;
There will be time, there will be time
To prepare a face to meet the faces that you meet;
There will be time to murder and create,
And time for all the works and days of hands
That lift and drop a question on your plate;
Time for you and time for me,
And time yet for a hundred indecisions,
And for a hundred visions and revisions,
Before the taking of a toast and tea.

In the room the women come and go
Talking of Michelangelo.

And indeed there will be time
To wonder, "Do I dare?" and, "Do I dare?"
Time to turn back and descend the stair,
With a bald spot in the middle of my hair–
(They will say: "How his hair is growing thin!")
My morning coat, my collar mounting firmly to the chin,
My necktie rich and modest, but asserted by a simple pin–
(They will say: "But how his arms and legs are thin!")
Do I dare
Disturb the universe?
In a minute there is time
For decisions and revisions which a minute will reverse.

For I have known them all already, known them all:
Have known the evenings, mornings, afternoons,
I have measured out my life with coffee spoons;
I know the voices dying with a dying fall
Beneath the music from a farther room.
  So how should I presume?

And I have known the eyes already, known them all–
The eyes that fix you in a formulated phrase,
And when I am formulated, sprawling on a pin,
When I am pinned and wriggling on the wall,
Then how should I begin
To spit out all the butt-ends of my days and ways?
  And how should I presume?

And I have known the arms already, known them all–
Arms that are braceleted and white and bare
(But in the lamplight, downed with light brown hair!)
Is it perfume from a dress
That makes me so digress?

Arms that lie along a table, or wrap about a shawl,
  And should I then presume?
  And how should I begin?

. . . .

Shall I say, I have gone at dusk through narrow streets
And watched the smoke that rises from the pipes
Of lonely men in shirt-sleeves, leaning out of windows? ...

I should have been a pair of ragged claws
Scuttling across the floors of silent seas.

. . . .

And the afternoon, the evening, sleeps so peacefully!
Smoothed by long fingers,
Asleep . . . tired . . . or it malingers,
Stretched on the floor, here beside you and me.
Should I, after tea and cakes and ices,
Have the strength to force the moment to its crisis?
But though I have wept and fasted, wept and prayed,
Though I have seen my head (grown slightly bald) brought
    in upon a platter,
I am no prophet—and here's no great matter;
I have seen the moment of my greatness flicker,
And I have seen the eternal Footman hold my coat,
    and snicker,
And in short, I was afraid.

And would it have been worth it, after all,
After the cups, the marmalade, the tea,
Among the porcelain, among some talk of you and me,
Would it have been worth while,
To have bitten off the matter with a smile,
To have squeezed the universe into a ball
To roll it toward some overwhelming question,
To say: "I am Lazarus, come from the dead,
Come back to tell you all, I shall tell you all"—
If one, settling a pillow by her head,

Should say: "That is not what I meant at all;
That is not it, at all."

And would it have been worth it, after all,
Would it have been worth while,
After the sunsets and the dooryards and the sprinkled streets,
After the novels, after the teacups, after the skirts that trail along the floor—
And this, and so much more?—
It is impossible to say just what I mean!
But as if a magic lantern threw the nerves in patterns on a screen:
Would it have been worth while
If one, settling a pillow or throwing off a shawl,
And turning toward the window, should say:
"That is not it at all,
That is not what I meant, at all."

. . . .

No! I am not Prince Hamlet, nor was meant to be;
Am an attendant lord, one that will do
To swell a progress, start a scene or two,
Advise the prince; no doubt, an easy tool,
Deferential, glad to be of use,
Politic, cautious, and meticulous;
Full of high sentence, but a bit obtuse;
At times, indeed, almost ridiculous—
Almost, at times, the Fool.

I grow old. . . . I grow old. . . .
I shall wear the bottoms of my trousers rolled.

Shall I part my hair behind? Do I dare to eat a peach?
I shall wear white flannel trousers, and walk upon the beach.
I have heard the mermaids singing, each to each.

I do not think that they will sing to me.

I have seen them riding seaward on the waves
Combing the white hair of the waves blown back
When the wind blows the water white and black.

We have lingered in the chambers of the sea
By sea-girls wreathed with seaweed red and brown
Till human voices wake us, and we drown.

—T. S. ELIOT

## THE WIFE OF USHER'S WELL

1

There lived a wife at Usher's Well,
  And a wealthy wife was she;
She had three stout and stalwart sons,
  And sent them o'er the sea.

2

They hadna been a week from her,
  A week but barely ane,
Whan word came to the carlin wife
  That her three sons were gane.

3

They hadna been a week from her,
  A week but barely three,
Whan word came to the carlin wife
  That her sons she'd never see.

4

"I wish the wind may never cease,
  Nor fashes in the flood,
Till my three sons come hame to me,
  In earthly flesh and blood."

5

It fell about the Martinmass,
  When lights are lang and mirk,
The carlin wife's three sons came hame,
  And their hats were o' the birk.

6

It neither grew in syke nor ditch,
  Nor yet in any sheugh;
But at the gates o' Paradise,
  That birk grew fair eneugh.

7

"Blow up the fire, my maidens,
  Bring water from the well;
For a' my house shall feast this night,
  Since my three sons are well."

8

And she has made to them a bed,
  She's made it large and wide,
And she's ta'en her mantle her about,
  Sat down at the bed-side.

9

Up then crew the red, red cock,
  And up and crew the gray;
The eldest to the youngest said,
  " 'T is time we were away."

10

The cock he hadna crawed but once,
  And clapped his wings at a',
When the youngest to the eldest said,
  "Brother, we must awa'.

11

"The cock doth craw, the day doth daw,
  The channerin' worm doth chide;
Gin we be missed out o' our place,
  A sair pain we maun bide.

12

"Fare ye weel, my mother dear!
  Fareweel to barn and byre!
And fare ye weel, the bonny lass,
  That kindles my mother's fire!"

## THE DEMON LOVER

1

"O where have you been, my long, long love,
  This long seven years and mair?"
"O I'm come to seek my former vows
  Ye granted me before."

2

"O hold your tongue of your former vows,
  For they will breed sad strife;
O hold your tongue of your former vows,
  For I am become a wife."

3

He turned him right and round about,
  And the tear blinded his ee:
"I wad never hae trodden on Irish ground,
  If it had not been for thee.

4

"I might hae had a king's daughter,
Far, far beyond the sea;
I might have had a king's daughter,
Had it not been for love o thee."

5

"If ye might have had a king's daughter,
Yer sel ye had to blame;
Ye might have taken the king's daughter,
For ye kend that I was nane.

6

"If I was to leave my husband dear,
And my two babes also,
O what have you to take me to,
If with you I should go?"

7

"I hae seven ships upon the sea—
The eighth brought me to land—
With four-and-twenty bold mariners,
And music on every hand."

8

She has taken up her two little babes,
Kiss'd them báith cheek and chin:
"O fair ye weel, my ain two babes,
For I'll never see you again."

9

She set her foot upon the ship,
No mariners could she behold;
But the sails were o the taffetie,
And the masts o the beaten gold.

10

They had not sailed a league, a league,
  A league but barely three,
When dismal grew his countenance,
  And drumlie grew his ee.

11

They had not sailed a league, a league,
  A league but barely three,
Until she espied his cloven foot,
  And she wept right bitterlie.

12

"O hold your tongue of your weeping," says he,
  "Of your weeping now let me be;
I will shew you how the lilies grow
  On the banks of Italy."

13

"O what hills are yon, yon pleasant hills,
  That the sun shines sweetly on?"
"O yon are the hills of heaven," he said,
  "Where you will never win."

14

"O whaten mountain is yon," she said,
  "All so dreary wi frost and snow?"
"O yon is the mountain of hell," he cried,
  "Where you and I will go."

15

He strack the tap-mast wi his hand,
  The fore-mast wi his knee,
And he brake that gallant ship in twain,
  And sank her in the sea.

## THE BALLAD OF CHOCOLATE MABBIE

It was Mabbie without the grammar school gates.
And Mabbie was all of seven.
And Mabbie was cut from a chocolate bar.
And Mabbie thought life was heaven.

The grammar school gates were the pearly gates,
For Willie Boone went to school.
When she sat by him in history class
Was only her eyes were cool.

It was Mabbie without the grammar school gates
Waiting for Willie Boone.
Half hour after the closing bell!
He would surely be coming soon.

Oh, warm is the waiting for joys, my dears!
And it cannot be too long.
Oh, pity the little poor chocolate lips
That carry the bubble of song!

Out came the saucily bold Willie Boone.
It was woe for our Mabbie now.
He wore like a jewel a lemon-hued lynx
With sand-waves loving her brow.

It was Mabbie alone by the grammar school gates.
Yet chocolate companions had she:
Mabbie on Mabbie with hush in the heart.
Mabbie on Mabbie to be.

—GWENDOLYN BROOKS

## THE TWA CORBIES

1

As I was walking all alane,
I heard twa corbies making a mane;

The tane unto the t'other say,
"Where sall we gang and dine to-day?"

2

"In behint yon auld fail dike,
I wot there lies a new slain knight;
And naebody kens that he lies there,
But his hawk, his hound, and lady fair.

3

"His hound is to the hunting gane,
His hawk to fetch the wild-fowl hame,
His lady's ta'en another mate,
So we may mak our dinner sweet.

4

"Ye'll sit on his white hause-bane,
And I'll pike out his bonny blue een;
Wi' ae lock o' his gowden hair
We'll theek our nest when it grows bare.

5

"Mony a one for him makes mane,
But nane sall ken where he is gane;
O'er his white banes, when they are bare,
The wind sall blaw for evermair."

## EDWARD

"Why dois your brand sae drap wi bluid,
Edward, Edward,
Why dois your brand sae drap wi bluid,
And why sae sad gang yee O?"

"O I hae killed my hauke sae guid,
Mither, mither,
O I hae killed my hauke sae guid,
And I had nae mair bot hee O."

"Your haukis bluid was nevir sae reid,
Edward, Edward,
Your haukis bluid was nevir sae reid,
My deir son I tell thee O."
"O I hae killed my reid-roan steid,
Mither, mither,
O I hae killed my reid-roan steid,
That erst was sae fair and frie O."

"Your steid was auld, and ye hae gat mair,
Edward, Edward,
Your steid was auld, and ye hae gat mair,
Sum other dule ye drie O."
"O I hae killed my fadir deir,
Mither, mither,
O I hae killed my fadir deir,
Alas, and wae is mee O!"

"And whatten penance wul ye drie for that,
Edward, Edward?
And whatten penance will ye drie for that?
My deir son, now tell me O."
"Ile set my feit in yonder boat,
Mither, mither,
Ile set my feit in yonder boat,
And Ile fare ovir the sea O."

"And what wul ye doe wi your towirs and your ha,
Edward, Edward?
And what wul ye doe wi your towirs and your ha,
That were sae fair to see O?"

"Ile let thame stand tul they doun fa,
Mither, mither,
Ile let thame stand tul they doun fa,
For here nevir mair maun I bee O."

"And what wul ye leive to your bairns and your wife,
Edward, Edward?
And what wul ye leive to your bairns and your wife,
Whan ye gang ovir the sea O?"
"The warldis room, late them beg thrae life,
Mither, mither,
The warldis room, late them beg thrae life,
For thame nevir mair wul I see O."

"And what wul ye leive to your ain mither deir,
Edward, Edward?
And what wul ye leive to your ain mither deir?
My deir son, now tell me O."
"The curse of hell frae me sall ye beir,
Mither, mither,
The curse of hell frae me sall ye beir,
Sic counseils ye gave to me O."

# 7

# *Patterns of Reference*

No poem begins from zero. Many poems contain references to past events, to something that happened and has been remembered. These events are "repeated" in poems by allusion* (a reference to an event or person, real or fictitious), paraphrase* (a rewording), quotation* (exact reproduction), or parody* (an imitation of a style).

Many poems, then, require that the reader bring specific information to the poems. When that information is not readily available (how often it is not is suggested by the abundance of footnotes in textbook anthologies), the poem will seem obscure or it will become for the reader a quite different poem from what it once was or still is to other readers.

## Occasional Poems

"Occasional" poems (poems written on and for a specific event) tend especially to suffer this last fate. Often they have shed their information, so to speak, and have become something other than what they were.

Here are two examples:

Little Jack Horner
Sat in a corner
Eating his Christmas pie.
He stuck in his thumb
And pulled out a plum
And said, "What a good boy am I."

*1.* What kind of poem do you take this to be? For what audience do you assume it was written?
*2.* Does it change the poem to add the following information? When Henry VIII was sacking the monasteries, his lieutenant was John Horner, who kept part of the spoils for himself.

Georgie Porgie, puddin' and pie,
Kissed the girls and made them cry.
When the boys came out to play,
Georgie Porgie ran away.

*1.* What kind of poem do you take this to be? For what audience do you assume it was written? (Recall that it is used as a rope-skipping rhyme.)
*2.* Does it change the poem to point out that the original "Georgie" was George IV, King of England from 1820 to 1830, who was reputed to be a sexual sadist, a glutton, a retarded adolescent who threw temper tantrums when asked to face serious problems?

Of course, the kind of event and its degree of accessibility to the reader varies enormously from poem to poem. If the event repeated in the poem is part of the general cultural heritage of the race, the information is likely there, in the reader, as in the following first lines of poems that range in date from 100 B.C. to the present. Identify as many of the allusions as you can:

(1) Batter my heart, three-personed God
(2) By the waters of Babylon, there we sat down
(3) Borgia, thou once wert almost too august
(4) Helen, thy beauty is to me
(5) I weep for Adonais–he is dead!
(6) Pile the bodies high at Austerlitz and Waterloo
(7) Your mind and you are our Sargasso Sea

But information about an event may be much more restricted. For example:

At the round earth's imagined corners

*1.* This is the first line of a seventeenth-century poem. The reference is to maps of the period, which projected the earth as a flat surface. Why would this information be restricted?

St. Agnes' Eve–Ah, bitter chill it was!

*1.* This is a preparatory reference to the legend that on St. Agnes' Eve a virgin can, through a prescribed ritual, see her husband-to-be in a dream. Why would this information be restricted?

It little profits that an idle king

*1.* This is the first line of a dramatic monologue dealing with Ulysses. The line paraphrases another from the Bible: "What shall it profit a man if he gain the whole world and lose his own soul?" Why would this information be restricted?

Swallow, my sister, O sister swallow

*1.* This is a reference to Ovid's story of Philomela and Procne. Why would this information be restricted?

To-day, this insect, and the world I breathe

*1.* This is a paraphrase, almost a parody, of the first line of the *Aeneid:* "Of arms and the man I sing." Why would this information be restricted?

2. Look back over the preceding five examples. Is it the nature of the information itself, the way in which it is used, or both that imposes the restrictions?

Why do poets repeat events in their poems? Reference to a previous event, whether it is allusion, paraphrase, quotation, or parody, is a kind of shorthand:

(1) it can immediately place the subject dealt with in the poem in a cultural context; the reader sees that the subject of the poem is another in a series of similar events or, on the other hand, a unique event.

(2) it can supply, efficiently and economically, a tone, an attitude, a point of view, because past events have not only a denotation (a factual designation) but a connotation (an emotional overtone).

Even a proper name (which can be considered an event—a real or fictitious person lived under that name: he was an event in history) has this double weight of meaning.

Here is a stanza containing one name:

I sometimes think that never blows so red
The rose as where some buried Caesar bled;
    That every Hyacinth the Garden wears
Dropt in her Lap from some once lovely Head.

—EDWARD FITZGERALD

*1. Caesar.* Denotation: title of the Roman emperors from Augustus to Hadrian. More particularly, Julius Caesar (100–44 B.C.), killed in a conspiracy by Brutus, et al.

Connotation: strength, power, wisdom, ruthlessness,

tragedy; more particularly, a man cut off at the height of his power and glory.

Is the stanza drawing more heavily on the denotation or the connotation? Answering the two questions that follow will help you decide.

2. *Hyacinth.* One of two flowers in the poem, Hyacinth gets its name from the mythical Hyacinthus, a handsome, promising youth, killed at the height of his promise and beauty by Apollo. The flower is said to have sprung up where Hyacinthus' blood fell. The other flower is the rose. What qualities of the rose are being drawn upon in the poem? How do selected overtones of *Caesar* and *Hyacinth* determine your answer here?

3. Is there a minimum amount of outside information required to understand the stanza?

References can be grouped in series so that each group or pattern becomes a sort of condensed catalog; each pattern contributes part of the poem's total meaning. Here is an example:

poem, Or Beauty hurts Mr. Vinal

take it from me kiddo
believe me
my country, 'tis of

you, land of the Cluett
Shirt Boston Garter and Spearmint
Girl With The Wrigley Eyes (of you
land of the Arrow Ide
and Earl &
Wilson
Collars) of you i
sing:land of Abraham Lincoln and Lydia E. Pinkham,
land above all of Just Add Hot Water And Serve—
from every B. V. D.

let freedom ring

amen. i do however protest, anent the un
-spontaneous and otherwise scented merde which
greets one (Everywhere Why) as divine poesy per
that and this radically defunct periodical. i would
suggest that certain ideas gestures
rhymes, like Gillette Razor Blades
having been used and reused
to the mystical moment of dullness emphatically are
Not To Be Resharpened. (Case in point

if we are to believe these gently O sweetly
melancholy trillers amid the thrillers
these crepuscular violinists among my and your
skyscrapers–Helen & Cleopatra were Just Too Lovely,
The Snail's On The Thorn enter Morn and God's
In His andsoforth

do you get me?) according
to such supposedly indigenous
throstles Art is O World O Life
a formula: example, Turn Your Shirttails Into
Drawers and If It Isn't An Eastman It Isn't A
Kodak therefore my friends let
us now sing each and all fortissimo A-
mer
i

ca, I
love,
You. And there're a
hun-dred-mil-lion-oth-ers, like
all of you successfully if
delicately gelded (or spaded)
gentlemen (and ladies)– pretty

littleliverpill-
hearted-Nujolneeding-There's-A-Reason
americans (who tensetendoned and with
upward vacant eyes, painfully
perpetually crouched, quivering, upon the
sternly allotted sandpile
—how silently
emit a tiny violetflavoured nuisance: Odor?

ono.
comes out like a ribbon lies flat on the brush

—e. e. cummings

*1.* Assume that there are four groups of references:

*a.* to America's professed ideals (exemplified in the parodied patriotic songs)

*b.* to American commercial slogans

*c.* to excrement ("from every B. V. D.," "scented merde," "emit a tiny violetflavoured nuisance")

*d.* to imported, outworn, second-rate art (bad Browning: "The Snail's On The Thorn"; bad Shelley: "O World O Life")

What is the relationship between those groups? The answer to that question can be made easier by answering the following questions:

*2.* What does it say about a people's ideals if their heroes are Abraham Lincoln and Lydia Pinkham, two quite different kinds of emancipators?

*3.* What is it that squats on a sandbox-toilet in the fashion the poet describes?

*4.* What is the relation of the two references in the conclusion of the poem?

*a.* "Odor?/ ono" is a pun on the name of a once well-known deodorant, Odorono.

*b.* "comes out like a ribbon lies flat on the brush" was the slogan for a popular toothpaste.

*5.* What is the poet saying about the relationship of art and commercialism in our society, considering the linking of pop culture with toothpaste and excrement almost simultaneously? What are Americans, metaphorically, putting into their mouths?

*6.* How much specific information would you judge the reader has to bring to this poem to understand it simply at the level of the broad statement it makes?

In a poem, an esoteric reference (what we have called "highly restricted" information), if it is introduced without somehow being explained by the poem itself, often not only puzzles but offends readers who don't possess the information. If a reference wholly new to the reader is introduced, it can be distracting and even threatening. The measure of this phenomenon is that readers often return with pleasure to esoteric poems they rejected on first meeting; the external "events" are now a comfortable part of their consciousness. Let's try to illustrate at least half that point:

## THE MOTHER OF GOD

The threefold terror of love; a fallen flare
Through the hollow of an ear;
Wings beating about the room;
The terror of all terrors that I bore
The Heavens in my womb.

Had I not found content among the shows
Every common woman knows,
Chimney corner, garden walk,
Or rocky cistern where we tread the clothes
And gather all the talk?

What is this flesh I purchased with my pains,
This fallen star my milk sustains,
This love that makes my heart's blood stop
Or strikes a sudden chill into my bones
And bids my hair stand up?

—W. B. YEATS

*1.* This poem is a highly unorthodox but very human presentation of Mary, the Mother of God. Note that the first stanza of the poem is built on a series of repeated oppositions:

| | |
|---|---|
| terror | love |
| fallen flare (i.e., star) | hollow of an ear (stars do not usually enter the ear) |
| wings | room (birds do not generally fly about rooms) |
| Heaven | womb |

The first column might be called "supernatural"; the second, "natural." Which of those columns, either in content or mood, dominates the second stanza?

*2.* What happens to the content and mood of those two columns in the third stanza?

*3.* Can you say at this point how Mary in this poem views the birth of her Son? Is the "Word made flesh" for her a paradox or an unhappy contradiction? Does she understand what has happened to her?

*4.* To this point, we have avoided the repeated events. "The threefold terror of love" suggests the Trinity. "Heavens in my womb" is the Son. "Wings beating about the room" can be either the angel in the Annunciation story or the dove, symbol of the Holy Spirit, or both. But many readers are going to be puzzled by "a fallen flare/ Through the hollow of an ear." Many medieval artists represented the impregnation of Mary as a shaft of light from the heavens striking her ear, thus at one stroke harmonizing the absence of intercourse, the grace from on high, and that aspect of the Annunciation story that represents Mary's knowledge of her conception as coming from a heavenly messenger who speaks to her.

As objectively as possible, try to say what effect the preceding piece of esoteric information has on your attitude toward the poem.

## THE SECOND COMING

Turning and turning in the widening gyre
The falcon cannot hear the falconer;

Things fall apart; the center cannot hold;
Mere anarchy is loosed upon the world,
The blood-dimmed tide is loosed, and everywhere
The ceremony of innocence is drowned;
The best lack all conviction, while the worst
Are full of passionate intensity.

Surely some revelation is at hand;
Surely the Second Coming is at hand.
The Second Coming! Hardly are those words out
When a vast image out of *Spiritus Mundi*
Troubles my sight: somewhere in sands of the desert
A shape with lion body and the head of a man,
A gaze blank and pitiless as the sun
Is moving its slow thighs, while all about it
Reel shadows of the indignant desert birds.

The darkness drops again; but now I know
That twenty centuries of stony sleep
Were vexed to nightmare by a rocking cradle,
And what rough beast, its hour come round at last,
Slouches towards Bethlehem to be born?

—W. B. YEATS

1. The ultimate repetition of event occurs when a theory must be understood in order to explain a practice; hence, this poem. Yeats held the theory that history moves in cycles of expansion and consolidation; in roughly twenty-century cycles civilizations moved from coherence to anarchy and then back to coherence, and so on. His symbol for that process was the gyre, a cone or expanding spiral, which could then be inverted. Another way to say the same thing, in terms of this poem, is that in twenty centuries Christ will have produced the anti-Christ.

In what way is what the falcon does as it rises in its gyre to strike comparable to this theory of history? How is its rise to striking position analogous to the theory of history, including the idea that things fall apart, i.e., what is the supposed relationship of falcon to falconer?

2. What is "mere" about "anarchy"?

3. Does the "blood-dimmed tide" mean some sort of force whose judgment is dimmed by blood, lust, etc., or a force whose blood (bravery, courage, tradition, etc.) is dimmed by time, or some combination of the two? How do you know?

4. What is the "ceremony of innocence"? Look up the two nouns in a dictionary if you have trouble. What is the ceremony drowned *in*?

5. The *Spiritus Mundi* is the collective mind of man, informed by history, the Great Memory, the Collective Unconscious, etc. What the *Spiritus Mundi* sees is a sphinx. What are the overtones of *sphinx?* Why then is it appropriate that the poem ends with a question mark?

An ill-managed reference can destroy a poem. Here is an example by Herman Melville:

## THE APPARITION

THE PARTHENON UPLIFTED ON ITS ROCK
FIRST CHALLENGING THE VIEW ON THE APPROACH TO ATHENS

Abrupt the supernatural Cross,
  Vivid in startled air,
Smote the Emperor Constantine
And turned his soul's allegiance there.

With other power appealing down,
  Trophy of Adam's best!
If cynic minds you scarce convert,
You try them, shake them, or molest.

Diogenes, that honest heart,
  Lived ere your date began;
Thee had he seen, he might have swerved
In mood nor barked so much at Man.

Melville is apparently contrasting the real and solid achievement of Greece, symbolized by the Parthenon, with the Roman Emperor Constantine's turning to Christianity and turning the Empire with him, because he thought he saw a cross in the sky.

*1.* Diogenes, who was a cynic philosopher, is reputed to have searched the world for an honest man without finding one. Melville says that if Diogenes could have seen the Parthenon (and what it symbolized) he might have changed his mind. How do you react to that?

*2.* Does it change your reaction to discover that Melville was wrong when he said that Diogenes lived before the building of the Parthenon?

*3.* Generalize on what happens when learned references turn out to be ignorant.

*FOR DISCUSSION.*

## A HISTORY OF ENGLAND, ABRIDGED

The death of Kings grows shabbier:

Charles went under the axe protesting;
German George, with reason, died raving;
The Sixth got something
In the lungs; abdicated Edward is the darling
of the go-go girls.

Charles, if and when,
Come to some good end.

England needs you.

*1.* This is both a catalog poem and an occasional poem. The following gives a gloss on the first five lines of the poem; you are asked to explain the last three.

Line 1: the thesis

Line 2: Charles I was beheaded in the Puritan revolution following the English Civil War.

Line 3: George III, the third King of England in the Hanoverian line, died insane after losing, among other things, the American colonies.

Line 4: George VI, the father of Elizabeth II, died of a lung disease.

Line 5: Edward, the present Duke of Windsor, lives the life of a *bon vivant* and has been photographed with Playboy Bunnies and go-go girls. He abdicated his throne to marry a divorcée.

Lines 6 and 7: Who is Charles?

Line 8: What recruiting phrase used in both the U.S. and England is being parodied here?

2. What is the difference between using topical references in an occasional poem and topical references in a poem whose theme is more far-reaching? Compare, for example, this poem with "poem, Or Beauty hurts Mr. Vinal," found earlier in this chapter.

## FOR SIR ISAAC NEWTON

Nature and Nature's laws lay hid in Night:
God said, *Let* Newton be! and all was Light.

—ALEXANDER POPE

*1.* What two references are built into this couplet?

*2.* Would the couplet be read the same way by readers born before Einstein and those born after?

## HOMAGE

They said to him, "It is a very good thing that you have
done, yes, both good and great, proving this other
passage to the Indies. Marvelous," they said. "Very.
But where, Señor, is the gold?"

They said: "We like it, we admire it very much, don't
misunderstand us, in fact we think it's almost great.
But isn't there, well, a little too much of this Prince

of Denmark? After all, there is no one quite like
you in your lighter vein."
"Astonishing," they said. "Who would have thought you
had it in you, Orville?" They said, "Wilbur, this
machine of yours is amazing, if it works, and perhaps
some day we can use it to distribute eggs, or to
advertise."

And they were good people, too. Decent people.
They did not beat their wives. They went to church.
And they kept the law.

—KENNETH FEARING

*1.* Who is the man referred to in verse paragraph 1? In verse paragraph 2? Who are the men in verse paragraph 3?

*2.* What is being said about the values of the common man?

## ANNIVERSARIES

Great Leo roared at my birth,
The windowpanes were lit
With stars' applausive light,
And I have heard that the earth
As far away as Japan
Was shaken again and again
The morning I came forth.
Many drew round me then,
Admiring. Beside my bed
The tall aunts prophesied,
And cousins from afar,
Predicting a great career.

At ten there came an hour
When, waking out of ether
Into an autumn weather
Inexpressibly dear,

I was wheeled superb in a chair
Past vacant lots in bloom
With goldenrod and with broom,
In secret proud of the scar
Dividing me from life,
Which I could admire like one
Come down from Mars or the moon,
Standing a little off.

By seventeen I had guessed
That the "really great loneliness"
Of James's governess
Might account for the ghost
On the other side of the lake.
Oh, all that year was lost
Somewhere among the black
Keys of Chopin! I sat
All afternoon after school,
Fingering his ripe heart,
While boys outside in the dirt
Kicked, up and down, their ball.

Thirty today, I saw
The trees flare briefly like
The candles upon a cake
As the sun went down the sky,
A momentary flash,
Yet there was time to wish
Before the light could die,
If I had known what to wish,
As once I must have known,
Bending above the clean,
Candlelit tablecloth
To blow them out with a breath.

—DONALD JUSTICE

*1.* The theme of this poem is probably discernible without a gloss on its central allusion, but it is only complete if the allusion is recognized and assimilated. "That the 'really great loneliness'/ Of James's governess/ Might account for the ghost/ On the other side of the lake" is an allusion to Henry James' novella *The Turn of the Screw.* The governess who narrates the story may actually be seeing ghosts and perceiving objective evil. On the other hand, she may be simply projecting her own repressed desires on two innocent children. The governess, who is in love with her employer, has spent a loveless, companionless life. How does that fit into the poem?

*2.* Is there possibly another allusion in the poem? With what other character in literature do you associate the belief that he is destined to great things, is prophesied to be all-powerful, is said to be immortal (unless one odd thing happens), realizes that it is all nonsense when he sees the trees begin to move, and acknowledges his illusion by saying, "Out, out brief candle .... "?

## ON HIS BLINDNESS

When I consider how my light is spent
  Ere half my days in this dark world and wide,
  And that one talent which is death to hide
  Lodged with me useless, though my soul more bent
To serve therewith my Maker, and present
  My true account, lest he returning chide,
  Doth God exact day-labor, light denied?
  I fondly ask. But Patience, to prevent
That murmur, soon replies, God doth not need
  Either man's work or his own gifts. Who best
  Bear his mild yoke, they serve him best. His state
Is kingly: Thousands at his bidding speed,
  And post o'er land and ocean without rest;
  They also serve who only stand and wait.

—JOHN MILTON

*1.* The allusion is to the Parable of the Talents (MATTHEW 25:14–30) in which the one servant who hid instead of using or investing the single talent (a coin) given him by his lord was cast "into outer darkness." How does the reference to a double darkness make the allusion even more appropriate and poignant?

*2.* The allusion generates the major metaphor in the octave. Explain how these phrases flow out of the allusion:

> . . . my light is spent
> Lodged with me . . .
> . . . present/ My true account . . .
> Doth God exact day-labor . . .

*3.* What is developed as the central metaphor of the sestet? Does it spring from the parable too?

*4.* How has Milton changed the form of the Italian sonnet to make it less a division into two parts (8/6) than a continuous unit?

## THE RITE

"Now you must die," the young one said,
"and all your art be overthrown."
The old one only bowed his head
as if those words had been his own.
And with no pity in his eyes
The young man acted out his part
and put him to the sacrifice
and drank his blood and ate his heart.

—DUDLEY RANDALL

*1.* This poem is a mixture of cultural references. Every generation in its youth reacts against the values and art of the preceding generation; paradoxically, however, only the presence of the old explains the form and content of the new. The phrase "all your art be overthrown" is therefore both accurate and inaccurate. What, then, does "The old one only bowed his head/ as if those words had been his own" mean? Were they his own once?

*2.* In some primitive cultures, and in some not so primitive, a conqueror drank the blood and ate the heart of the one he hated or the one he had defeated. But he did it so that he might incorporate into himself the best qualities of the enemy. What, then, will the young man's art have in it, so far as this poem implies?

*3.* In some ancient fertility rites, the old king was slain by the new king, who was in turn, usually a year later, killed by the next king. What is the difference between king 1, king 2, king 3, etc., or, as in this poem, poet 1, poet 2, etc.? Are we seeing change or sameness?

*4.* Does the poem suggest something about words like *change, renewal, progress?*

## MEMORIES OF WEST STREET AND LEPKE

Only teaching on Tuesdays, book-worming
in pajamas fresh from the washer each morning,
I hog a whole house on Boston's
"hardly passionate Marlborough Street,"
where even the man
scavenging filth in the back alley trash cans,
has two children, a beach wagon, a helpmate,
and is a "young Republican."
I have a nine months' daughter,
young enough to be my granddaughter.
Like the sun she rises in her flame-flamingo infants' wear.

These are the tranquillized *Fifties*,
and I am forty. Ought I to regret my seedtime?
I was a fire-breathing Catholic C.O.,
and made my manic statement,
telling off the state and president, and then
sat waiting sentence in the bull pen
beside a Negro boy with curlicues
of marijuana in his hair.

Given a year,
I walked on the roof of the West Street Jail, a short
enclosure like my school soccer court,
and saw the Hudson River once a day
through sooty clothesline entanglements
and bleaching khaki tenements.

Strolling, I yammered metaphysics with Abramowitz,
a jaundice-yellow ("it's really tan")
and fly-weight pacifist,
so vegetarian,
he wore rope shoes and preferred fallen fruit.
He tried to convert Bioff and Brown,
the Hollywood pimps, to his diet.
Hairy, muscular, suburban,
wearing chocolate double-breasted suits,
they blew their tops and beat him black and blue.

I was so out of things, I'd never heard
of the Jehovah's Witnesses.
"Are you a C.O.?" I asked a fellow jailbird.
"No," he answered, "I'm a J.W."
He taught me the "hospital tuck,"
and pointed out the T shirted back
of *Murder Incorporated's* Czar Lepke,
there piling towels on a rack,
or dawdling off to his little segregated cell full
of things forbidden the common man:
a portable radio, a dresser, two toy American
flags tied together with a ribbon of Easter palm.
Flabby, bald, lobotomized,
he drifted in a sheepish calm,
where no agonizing reappraisal
jarred his concentration on the electric chair—
hanging like an oasis in his air
of lost connections . . . .

—ROBERT LOWELL

*1.* This is a heavily referenced poem in which the allusions and the specific descriptions coalesce to characterize the speaker.

*a.* "'hardly passionate Marlborough Street'": Henry James said that an example of extreme understatement would be that Marlborough Street was hardly passionate.

*b.* "C.O.": conscientious objector (What is a fire-breathing Catholic C.O."?—a contradiction?)
*c.* "West Street Jail": a jail in New York where prisoners are held before they are sent to state or federal prisons
*d.* "Lepke": Lou (Lepke) Buchalter, a kingpin of Murder, Inc., executed in 1944

In what way are most of the major characters in the poem "hardly passionate"?

2. The speaker says, "I was so out of things." Is he also "hardly passionate"? Consider his present existence: teaching one day a week, reading in pajamas the rest of the time, alone in a house on a "hardly passionate street."

## NOSTALGIA—NOW THREEPENCE OFF

Where are they now, the heroes of furry-paged books and comics brighter than life which packed my inklined desk in days when BOP meant Boy's Own Paper, where are they anyway?

Where is Percy F. Westerman? Where are H. L. Gee and Arthur Mee? Where is Edgar Rice (The Warlord of Mars) Burroughs, the Bumper Fun Book and the Wag's Handbook? Where is the Wonder Book of Reptiles? Where the hell is Little Arthur?

Where are the Beacon Readers? Did Ro-ver that tireless hound, devour his mon-o-syll-ab-ic-all-y correct family? Did Little Black Sambo and Epaminondas dig the last sit-in?

Did Peter Rabbit get his when myxomatosis came round the second time, did the Flopsy Bunnies stiffen to a standstill, grow bug-eyed, fly-covered and then disintegrate?

Where is G. A. Henty and his historical lads—Wolfgang the Hittite, Armpit the Young Viking, Cyril who lived in Sodom? Where are their uncorrupted bodies and Empire-building brains, England needs them, the Sunday Times says so.

There is news from the Struwelpeter mob. Johnny-Head-in-Air spends his days reporting flying saucers, the telephone receiver never cools from the heat of his hand. Little Harriet, who played with matches, still burns, but not with fire. The Scissorman is everywhere.

Babar the Elephant turned the jungle into a garden city. But things went wrong. John and Susan, Titty and Roger became unaccountably afraid of water, sold their dinghies, all married each other, live in a bombed-out cinema on surgical spirits and weeds of all kinds.

Snow White was in the News of the World—Virgin Lived With Seven Midgets, Court Told. And in the psychiatric ward an old woman dribbles as she mumbles about a family of human bears, they ate porridge, yes Miss Goldilocks of course they did.

Hans Brinker vainly whirled his silver skates round his head as the jackboots of Emil and the Detectives invaded his Resistance cellar.

Some failed. Desperate Dan and Meddlesome Matty and Strang the Terrible and Korky the Cat killed themselves with free gifts in a back room at the Peter Pan Club because they were impotent, like us. Their audience, the senile chums of Red Circle School, still wearing for reasons of loyalty and lust the tatters of their uniforms, voted that exhibition a super wheeze.

Some succeeded. Tom Sawyer's heart has cooled, his ingenuity flowers at Cape Canaveral.

But they are all trodden on, the old familiar faces, so at the rising of the sun and the going down of the ditto I remember I remember the house where I was taught to play up play up and play the game though nobody told me what the game was, but we know now don't we, we know now, but lives of great men all remind us we can make our lives sublime and departing leave behind us arseprints on the sands of time, but the tide's come up, the castles are washed down, where are they now, where are they, where are the deep shelters? There are no deep shelters. Biggles may drop it, Worrals of the Wraf may press the button. So Billy and Bessie Bunter, prepare for the last and cosmic Yarooh and throw away the Man-Tan. The sky will soon be full of suns.

—ADRIAN MITCHELL

*1.* Here is a catalog of allusions. Some may escape American readers, although there are enough English and American allusions to indicate the tenor of the reference; in some instances the poem partially explains its own reference, as with the Beacon Readers. The catalog is composed of "children's literature," fantasy that bears no resemblance to the reality children will face when they suddenly mature.

A second catalog of realities is implied in the comments on fantasies. What are those realities?

*2.* The allusions/ paraphrases/ parodies that may escape the reader are built into the climax of the poem. They are different from the earlier references because they all have a moral character; they are all directive and, to some extent, coercive. We select two as examples:

> *a.* "so at/ the rising of the sun and the going down of the ditto I re-/member I remember the house where I was. . . ." Compare that passage with the following poem by Thomas Hood:

## I REMEMBER, I REMEMBER

I remember, I remember,
The house where I was born,
The little window where the sun
Came peeping in at morn;
He never came a wink too soon,

Nor brought too long a day,
But now, I often wish the night
Had borne my breath away!

I remember, I remember,
The roses, red and white,
The violets, and the lily-cups,
Those flowers made of light!
The lilacs where the robin built,
And where my brother set
The laburnum on his birthday,—
The tree is living yet!

I remember, I remember,
Where I was used to swing,
And thought the air must rush as fresh
To swallows on the wing;
My spirit flew in feathers then,
That is so heavy now,
And summer pools could hardly cool
The fever on my brow!

I remember, I remember,
The fir trees dark and high;
I used to think their slender tops
Were close against the sky:
It was a childish ignorance,
But now 'tis little joy
To know I'm farther off from heaven
Than when I was a boy.

2. (Continued):

*b.* "but / lives of great men all remind us we can make our lives sublime / and departing leave behind us arseprints on the sands of time...." Compare that with the next poem, which is by Henry Wadsworth Longfellow. What is Longfellow saying about the moral direction he received?

## A PSALM OF LIFE

Tell me not, in mournful numbers,
  Life is but an empty dream!—
For the soul is dead that slumbers,
  And things are not what they seem.

Life is real! Life is earnest!
  And the grave is not its goal;
Dust thou art, to dust returnest,
  Was not spoken of the soul.

Not enjoyment, and not sorrow,
  Is our destined end or way;
But to act, that each to-morrow
  Finds us farther than to-day.

Art is long, and Time is fleeting,
  And our hearts, though stout and brave,
Still, like muffled drums, are beating
  Funeral marches to the grave.

In the world's broad field of battle,
  In the bivouac of Life,
Be not like dumb, driven cattle!
  Be a hero in the strife!

Trust no Future, howe'er pleasant!
  Let the dead Past bury its dead!
Act,—act in the living Present!
  Heart within, and God o'erhead!

Lives of great men all remind us
  We can make our lives sublime,
And, departing, leave behind us
  Footprints on the sands of time;

Footprints, that perhaps another,
Sailing o'er life's solemn main,
A forlorn and shipwrecked brother,
Seeing, shall take heart again.

Let us, then, be up and doing,
With a heart for any fate;
Still achieving, still pursuing,
Learn to labor and to wait.

*3.* Explain the last sentence in Longfellow's poem.

## MR. EDWARDS AND THE SPIDER

I saw the spiders marching through the air,
Swimming from tree to tree that mildewed day
In latter August when the hay
Came creaking to the barn. But where
The wind is westerly,
Where gnarled November makes the spiders fly,
Into the apparitions of the sky,
They purpose nothing but their ease and die
Urgently beating east to sunrise and the sea;

What are we in the hands of the great God?
It was in vain you set up thorn and briar
In battle array against the fire
And treason crackling in your blood;
For the wild thorns grow tame
And will do nothing to oppose the flame;
Your lacerations tell the losing game
You play against a sickness past your cure.
How will the hands be strong? How will the heart endure?

A very little thing, a little worm,
Or hourglass-blazoned spider, it is said,
Can kill a tiger. Will the dead
Hold up his mirror and affirm
To the four winds the smell
And flash of his authority? It's well
If God who holds you to the pit of hell,
Much as one holds a spider, will destroy,
Baffle and dissipate your soul. As a small boy

On Windsor Marsh, I saw the spider die
When thrown into the bowels of fierce fire:
There's no long struggle, no desire
To get up on its feet and fly—
It stretches out its feet
And dies. This is the sinner's last retreat;
Yes, and no strength exerted on the heat
Then sinews the abolished will, when sick
And full of burning, it will whistle on a brick.

But who can plumb the sinking of that soul?
Josiah Hawley, picture yourself cast
Into a brick-kiln where the blast
Fans your quick vitals to a coal—
If measured by a glass,
How long would it seem burning! Let there pass
A minute, ten, ten trillion, but the blaze
Is infinite, eternal: this is death,
To die and know it. This is the Black Widow, death.

—ROBERT LOWELL

*1.* Jonathan Edwards, the eighteenth-century American preacher and theologian, at age 11 wrote a treatise on flying spiders in which he emphasized the harmony he saw in the spider's "Pleasure and Recreation," since it proved to him that God provided not only the necessities of life but the means of pleasure for all His creatures. In his late thirties Edwards preached two sermons that included references to the spider: "The Future Punishment of the Wicked Unavoidable and Intolerable" and "Sinners in the Hands of an Angry God." In both sermons he portrayed humans as being at the mercy of spiders and as spiders themselves, hanging over the flames of hell.

Most of the poem is either quotation from or paraphrase of material from these three sources. But it is a dramatic monologue, composed as if it were a composite sermon.

What is Jonathan Edwards' view of human life?

*2.* Josiah Hawley is a composite of two people: Edwards' uncle, who committed suicide, and Edwards' cousin, who succeeded in having Edwards deposed from his pulpit. What do they seem to have in common, given Edwards' theology and his view of himself?

## SCOFFERS

Mock on, mock on, Voltaire, Rousseau,
Mock on, mock on; 'tis all in vain;
You throw the sand against the wind,
And the wind blows it back again.

And every sand becomes a gem,
Reflected in the beams divine;
Blown back, they blind the mocking eye,
But still in Israel's paths they shine.

The atoms of Democritus
And Newton's particles of light
Are sands upon the Red Sea shore
Where Israel's tents do shine so bright.

—WILLIAM BLAKE

*1.* Here, the meaning depends on the allusions. What do Voltaire and Rousseau have in common?

*2.* Identify the "atoms of Democritus" and "Newton's particles of light."

*3.* Sand and wind appear and reappear in the poem. Why are they important in the poem? What is the allusion in "upon the Red Sea shore"?

## LINES PRINTED UNDER THE ENGRAVED PORTRAIT OF MILTON, 1688

Three poets, in three distant ages born,
Greece, Italy, and England did adorn.
The first in loftiness of thoughts surpassed,
The next in majesty, in both the last.
The force of Nature could no farther go;
To make a third she joined the former two.

—JOHN DRYDEN

*1.* Identify the allusions in the preceding poem. Who are the three poets?

## SURVEY OF LITERATURE

In all the good Greek of Plato
I lack my roast beef and potato.

A better man was Aristotle
Pulling steady on the bottle.

I dip my hat to Chaucer
Swilling soup from his saucer,

And to Master Shakespeare
Who wrote big on small beer.

The abstemious Wordsworth
Subsisted on a curd's-worth.

But a slick one was Tennyson,
Putting gravy on his venison.

What these men had to eat and drink
Is what we say and what we think.

The flatulence of Milton
Came out of wry Stilton.

Sing a song for Percy Shelley,
Drowned in pale lemon jelly,

And for precious John Keats,
Dripping blood of pickled beets.

Then there was poor Willie Blake,
He foundered on sweet cake.

God have mercy on the sinner
Who must write with no dinner,

No gravy and no grub,
No pewter and no pub,

No belly and no bowels,
Only consonants and vowels.

—JOHN CROWE RANSOM

*1.* Here are two catalogs in a single poem. List the poets that the speaker seems most to approve of; then list the ones that he thinks less of.

*2.* The "biographical" details are either imaginary or only metaphorically true (e.g., Keats did die of tubercular hemorrhages and Shelley was drowned, although not in pale lemon jelly). What "diets" does the speaker approve of and what do they stand for?

*3.* What does the "approved" list of poets have as a common denominator? What does the lesser group have? How does the final couplet distinguish the two groups?

*FOR STUDY.*

## ON NOT WRITING AN ELEGY

My friend told me about kids in a coffee house
who laughed and celebrated the killing. Another friend
didn't care, sick at his own divorce,
drinking martinis with a delicate hand,
saying he couldn't care when I said I cried
like everybody. Still, I am the vain one,
a bullet in my shoulder, six seconds to go
before another burns in my head. Trying
to write about the thing, I always end
by feeling I have been shot. My brain, my spine
gone, and with time winding foolishly,
I am raced, tabled, cleaned out, boxed, flown,
carried and lowered in. I have had this done
on a shiny day with my wife and bodyguards
and everyone there to cry out, and I have cried
without trying and without a clear thought.
This death has had me where I cannot write
or hate or love, numb as a coined face
fallen where all flames have only to burn
down. Lost where I must only lose my place,
I mourn the glories of our blood and state.

—RICHARD FROST

*1.* Compare the last line of the preceding poem ("I mourn the glories of our blood and state") with the following by James Shirley:

## THE CONTENTION OF AJAX AND ULYSSES

The glories of our blood and state
    Are shadows, not substantial things;

There is no armor against Fate;
  Death lays his icy hand on kings:
    Sceptre and crown
    Must tumble down,
And in the dust be equal made
With the poor crooked scythe and spade.

## I-FEEL-LIKE-I'M-FIXING-TO-DIE-RAG

Come on, all of you big strong men,
Uncle Sam needs your help again.
He's got himself in a terrible jam
Way down yonder in Viet Nam.
So put down your books and pick up your guns,
We're going to have a whole lot of fun.

CHORUS
  And it's one-two-three
  What're we fighting for?
  Don't ask me,
  I don't give a damn;
  Next stop is Viet Nam.
  And it's five-six-seven,
  Open up the Pearly Gates.
  Now ain't no time to wonder why.
  Whoopee! We're all gonna die.

Well, come on, generals, let's move fast,
Your big chance has come at last.
Gotta go out and get those Reds,
The only good Commie is one that's dead;
And you know that peace can only be won
When they blow them all to kingdom come.

CHORUS
  And it's one-two-three,
  What're we fighting for?

Don't ask me,
I don't give a damn;
Next stop is Viet Nam.
And it's five-six-seven,
Open up the Pearly Gates.
Well, ain't no time to wonder why.
Whoopee! We're all gonna die.

Well, come on, Wall Street, don't move slow,
Why, man, this war is a go-go-go!
There's plenty good money to be made
By supplying the Army with the tools of the trade.
Just hope and pray that if they drop the bomb,
They drop it on the Viet Cong.

Chorus
And it's one-two-three,
What're we fighting for?
Don't ask me,
I don't give a damn;
Next stop is Viet Nam.
And it's five-six-seven,
Open up the Pearly Gates.
Well, ain't no time to wonder why.
Whoopee! We're all gonna die.

Well, come on, mothers, throughout the land,
Pack your boys off to Viet Nam
Come on, fathers, don't hesitate,
Send them off before it's too late;
Be the first one on the block
To have your boy come home in a box.

Chorus
And it's one-two-three,
What're we fighting for?
Don't ask me,
I don't give a damn;

Next stop is Viet Nam.
And it's five-six-seven,
Open up the Pearly Gates.
Well, ain't no time to wonder why.
Whoopee! We're all gonna die.

—JOE MC DONALD

*1.* Compare the preceding with this college cheer, old style:
One-two-three-four
Who are we cheering for?
Five-six-seven-eight
Who do we appreciate?

*2.* Now, compare it with these "patriotic" slogans, old style:
*a.* Uncle Sam needs you.
*b.* Be the first one on the block to own a ______.
*c.* Theirs not to reason why
Theirs but to do or die.
*d.* The only good Indian is a dead Indian.

## ON HIS DECEASED WIFE

Methought I saw my late espouséd saint
Brought to me like Alcestis from the grave,
Whom Jove's great son to her glad husband gave,
Rescued from Death by force, though pale and faint.
Mine, as whom washed from spot of child-bed taint
Purification in the Old Law did save,
And such, as yet once more I trust to have
Full sight of her in heaven without restraint,
Came vested all in white, pure as her mind.
Her face was veiled; yet to my fancied sight
Love, sweetness, goodness, in her person shined
So clear as in no face with more delight.
But O, as to embrace me she inclined,
I waked, she fled, and day brought back my night.

—JOHN MILTON

*1.* Consider the following in terms of Milton's poem:
*a.* "espouséd saint": Milton's second wife, Katherine Woodstock, whom he had never seen (because he went blind six years before their marriage) and who died less than two years after their marriage
*b.* "Alcestis": the wife of Admetus, brought back from the dead by Hercules
*c.* "Purification": see LEVITICUS 12

## THE GIFT OF FIRE

IN MEMORY OF NORMAN MORRISON, WHO BURNED HIMSELF TO DEATH IN FRONT OF THE PENTAGON ON NOVEMBER 2, 1965

In a time of damnation
when the world needed a Savior,
when the dead gathered routinely,
comic-strip flat and blurred,

he took the god at his promise
and set himself on fire,
skin, brain, sex, smile

so we should see, really see
by that unbearable light
the flower of the single face,
the intricate moth of consciousness:

but he lived in the land of the one-eyed
where the blind is king.

—LISEL MUELLER

## JOURNEY OF THE MAGI

"A cold coming we had of it,
Just the worst time of the year
For a journey, and such a long journey:

The ways deep and the weather sharp,
The very dead of winter."
And the camels galled, sore-footed, refractory,
Lying down in the melting snow.
There were times we regretted
The summer palaces on slopes, the terraces,
And the silken girls bringing sherbet.
Then the camel men cursing and grumbling
And running away, and wanting their liquor and women,
And the night-fires going out, and the lack of shelters,
And the cities hostile and the towns unfriendly
And the villages dirty and charging high prices:
A hard time we had of it.
At the end we preferred to travel all night,
Sleeping in snatches,
With the voices singing in our ears, saying
That this was all folly.

Then at dawn we came down to a temperate valley,
Wet, below the snow line, smelling of vegetation;
With a running stream and a water-mill beating the darkness,
And three trees on the low sky,
And an old white horse galloped away in the meadow.
Then we came to a tavern with vine-leaves over the lintel,
Six hands at an open door dicing for pieces of silver,
And feet kicking the empty wine-skins.
But there was no information, and so we continued
And arrived at evening, not a moment too soon
Finding the place; it was (you may say) satisfactory.

All this was a long time ago, I remember,
And I would do it again, but set down
This set down
This: were we led all that way for
Birth or Death? There was a Birth, certainly,
We had evidence and no doubt. I had seen birth and death,
But had thought they were different; this Birth was

Hard and bitter agony for us, like Death, our death.
We returned to our places, these Kingdoms,
But no longer at ease here, in the old dispensation,
With an alien people clutching their gods.
I should be glad of another death.

—T. S. ELIOT

## THE U.S. SAILOR WITH THE JAPANESE SKULL

Bald-bare, bone-bare, and ivory yellow: skull
Carried by a thus two-headed U.S. sailor
Who got it from a Japanese soldier killed
At Guadalcanal in the ever-present war: our

Bluejacket, I mean, aged 20, in August strolled
Among the little bodies on the sand and hunted
Souvenirs: teeth, tags, diaries, boots; but bolder still
Hacked off his head and under a leopard tree skinned it:

Peeled with a lifting knife the jaw and cheeks, bared
The nose, ripped off the black-haired scalp and gutted
The dead eyes to these thoughtful hollows: a scarred
But bloodless job, unless it be said brains bleed.

Then, his ship underway, dragged this aft in a net
Many days and nights—the cold bone tumbling
Beneath the foaming wake, weed-worn and salt-cut
Rolling safe among fish and washed with Pacific;

Till on a warm and level-keeled day hauled in
Held to the sun and the sailor, back to a gun-rest,
Scrubbed the cured skull with lye, perfecting this:
Not foreign as he saw it first: death's familiar cast.

Bodiless, fleshless, nameless, it and the sun
Offend each other in strange fascination

As though one of the two were mocked; but nothing is in
This head, or it fills with what another imagines

As: here were love and hate and the will to deal
Death or to kneel before it, death emperor,
Recorded orders without reasons, bomb-blast, still
A child's morning, remembered moonlight on Fujiyama:

All scoured out now by the keeper of this skull
Made elemental, historic, parentless by our
Sailor boy who thinks of home, voyages laden, will
Not say, "Alas! I did not know him at all."

—WINFIELD TOWNLEY SCOTT

*1.* Consider the last stanza and compare to Hamlet, who returns home from a voyage, finds a gravedigger tossing out the skull of a former friend while digging the grave of Hamlet's sweetheart, and says, "Alas, poor Yorick! I knew him, Horatio . . . ."

2. "The keeper of this skull/ Made elemental, historic, parentless . . . . " Who is the "keeper"? The Japanese soldier? The American sailor? Both?

## THE EMANCIPATORS

When you ground the lenses and the moons swam free
From that great wanderer; when the apple shone
Like a sea-shell through your prism, voyager;
When, dancing in pure flame, the Roman mercy,
Your doctrines blew like ashes from your bones;

Did you think, for an instant, past the numerals
Jellied in Latin like bacteria in broth,
Snatched for by holy Europe like a sign?
Past sombre tables inched out with the lives
Forgotten or clapped for by the wigged Societies?

You guessed this? The earth's face altering with iron,
The smoke ranged like a wall against the day?

—The equations metamorphose into use: the free
Drag their slight bones from tenements to vote
To die with their children in your factories.

Man is born in chains, and everywhere we see him dead.
On your earth they sell nothing but our lives.
You knew that what you died for was our deaths?
You learned, those years, that what men wish is Trade?
It was you who understood; it is we who change.

—RANDALL JARRELL

*1.* Consider the following:
*a.* In stanza 1 the three men referred to by mentioning their discoveries are Galileo, Newton, and Bruno.
*b.* Line 16 alludes to Rousseau's *The Social Contract,* in which he says, "Man is born free, but everywhere he is in chains."

## ULYSSES

It little profits that an idle king,
By this still hearth, among these barren crags,
Matched with an aged wife, I mete and dole
Unequal laws unto a savage race,
That hoard, and sleep, and feed, and know not me.
I cannot rest from travel: I will drink
Life to the lees; all times I have enjoyed
Greatly, have suffered greatly, both with those
That loved me, and alone; on shore, and when
Through scudding drifts the rainy Hyades
Vext the dim sea: I am become a name;
For always roaming with a hungry heart
Much have I seen and known; cities of men
And manners, climates, councils, governments,
Myself not least, but honoured of them all;
And drunk delight of battle with my peers,

Far on the ringing plains of windy Troy.
I am a part of all that I have met;
Yet all experience is an arch wherethrough
Gleams that untravelled world, whose margin fades
For ever and for ever when I move.
How dull it is to pause, to make an end,
To rust unburnished, not to shine in use!
As though to breathe were life. Life piled on life
Were all too little, and of one to me
Little remains; but every hour is saved
From that eternal silence, something more,
A bringer of new things; and vile it were
For some three suns to store and hoard myself,
And this grey spirit yearning in desire
To follow knowledge like a sinking star,
Beyond the utmost bound of human thought.
This is my son, mine own Telemachus,
To whom I leave the sceptre and the isle–
Well-loved of me, discerning to fulfil
This labour, by slow prudence to make mild
A rugged people, and through soft degrees
Subdue them to the useful and the good.
Most blameless is he, centered in the sphere
Of common duties, decent not to fail
In offices of tenderness, and pay
Meet adoration to my household gods,
When I am gone. He works his work, I mine.
There lies the port; the vessel puffs her sail:
There gloom the dark broad seas. My mariners,
Souls that have toiled, and wrought, and thought with me–
That ever with a frolic welcome took
The thunder and the sunshine, and opposed
Free hearts, free foreheads–you and I are old;
Old age hath yet his honour and his toil:

Death closes all; but something ere the end,
Some work of noble note, may yet be done,
Not unbecoming men that strove with Gods.
The lights begin to twinkle from the rocks:
The long day wanes: the slow moon climbs: the deep
Moans round with many voices. Come, my friends,
'Tis not too late to seek a newer world.
Push off, and sitting well in order smite
The sounding furrows; for my purpose holds
To sail beyond the sunset, and the baths
Of all the western stars, until I die.
It may be that the gulfs will wash us down:
It may be we shall touch the Happy Isles,
And see the great Achilles, whom we knew.
Though much is taken, much abides; and though
We are not now that strength which in old days
Moved earth and heaven; that which we are, we are;
One equal temper of heroic hearts,
Made weak by time and fate, but strong in will
To strive, to seek, to find, and not to yield.

—ALFRED, LORD TENNYSON

*1.* Compare line 1 to "What shall it profit a man, if he shall gain the whole world and lose his own soul?" (MARK)

*2.* Compare lines 6 and 7 to "The wine of life is drawn, and the mere lees/ Is left this vault to brag of." (*Macbeth*, II, iii, 91–92)

*3.* Compare line 23 to "Perseverance, dear my lord,/ Keeps honor bright; to have done is to hang/ Quite out of fashion, like a rusty mail/ In monumental mockery." (*Troilus and Cressida*, III, iii, 150–153; spoken by Ulysses to Achilles)

*4.* Compare line 43 to "He does His will, I mine." (Shelley, *The Cenci*, IV, i, 38; spoken by the Cenci of God, as the Cenci curses his child)

*5.* Compare line 70 to "And courage never to submit or yield." (*Paradise Lost*, I, 108; spoken by Satan)

## QUATRAIN

Jack, eating rotten cheese, did say,
Like Samson I my thousands slay;
I vow, quoth Roger, so you do.
And with the self-same weapon too.

—BENJAMIN FRANKLIN

## HOPE

THE SPIRIT KILLETH, BUT
THE LETTER GIVETH LIFE.

The week is dealt out like a hand
That children pick up card by card.
One keeps getting the same hand.
One keeps getting the same card.

But twice a day—except on Saturday—
But every day—except on Sunday—
The wheel stops, there is a crack in Time:
With a hiss of soles, a rattle of tin,
My own gray Daemon pauses on the stair,
My own bald Fortune lifts me by the hair.

*Woe's me! woe's me! In Folly's mailbox*
*Still laughs the postcard, Hope:*
*Your uncle in Australia*
*Has died and you are Pope.*
*For many a soul has entertained*
*A Mailman unawares—*
*And as you cry, Impossible,*
*A step is on the stairs.*

One keeps getting the same dream
Delayed, marked *Postage Due*,
The bill that one has paid

Delayed, marked *Payment Due*—
Twice a day, in a rotting mailbox,
The white grubs are new:
And Faith, once more, is mine
Faithfully, but Charity
Writes hopefully about a new
Asylum—but Hope is as good as new.

*Woe's me! woe's me! In Folly's mailbox*
*Still laughs the postcard, Hope:*
*Your uncle in Australia*
*Has died and you are Pope.*
*For many a soul has entertained*
*A Mailman unawares—*
*And as you cry, Impossible,*
*A step is on the stairs.*

—RANDALL JARRELL

*1.* Consider the following in terms of comparable lines within the preceding poem:

*a.* "The letter killeth but the spirit giveth life." (St. Paul)
*b.* "So faith, hope, and love abide, these three; but the greatest of these is love." (St. Paul)
*c.* "Be not forgetful to entertain strangers: for thereby some have entertained angels unawares." (St. Paul)

## POETRY

I, too, dislike it: there are things that are important beyond
all this fiddle.
Reading it, however, with a perfect contempt for it, one
discovers in
it after all, a place for the genuine.
Hands that can grasp, eyes
that can dilate, hair that can rise
if it must, these things are important not because a

high-sounding interpretation can be put upon them but
because they are
useful. When they become so derivative as to become
unintelligible,
the same thing may be said for all of us, that we
do not admire what
we cannot understand: the bat
holding on upside down or in quest of something to

eat, elephants pushing, a wild horse taking a roll, a tireless
wolf under
a tree, the immovable critic twitching his skin like a
horse that feels a flea, the base-
ball fan, the statistician—
nor is it valid
to discriminate against 'business documents and

school-books'; all these phenomena are important. One
must make a distinction
however: when dragged into prominence by half poets.
the result is not poetry,
nor till the poets among us can be
literalists of
the imagination'—above
insolence and triviality and can present

for inspection, imaginary gardens with real toads in them,
shall we have
it. In the meantime, if you demand on the one hand,
the raw material of poetry in
all its rawness and
that which is on the other hand
genuine, then you are interested in poetry.

—MARIANNE MOORE

*1.* Consider the following in terms of the preceding poem:
*a.* "Where the boundary between prose and poetry lies, I shall never be able to understand.... Poetry is verse: prose is not verse. Or else poetry is everything with the exception of business documents and school books." (Leo Tolstoy, *Diary*)
*b.* "Too literal realist of the imagination, as others are of nature" (W. B. Yeats, *William Blake and the Imagination*)

# A Note on Parody

Parody is a repetition, an imitation, of the style of an author or a poem for purposes of ridicule. At its best, parody is literary criticism; at less than its best it becomes burlesque or travesty by making the original seem to say what its author never would have said about a subject that he never wrote about. We saw parody at work earlier in poems by Kenneth Fearing and Adrian Mitchell (pp. 237-238, 244-246). But parody as the structural principle of an entire poem is somewhat different; the difference may be seen in the parodies that follow.

Over a century ago Jane Taylor wrote a poem entitled "The Star"; the first stanza went like this:

Twinkle, twinkle, little star!
How I wonder what you are!
Up above the world so high,
Like a diamond in the sky.

Lewis Carroll parodied the stanza:

Twinkle, twinkle, little bat!
How I wonder what you're at!
Up above the world you fly,
Like a tea tray in the sky.

That is parody. Miss Taylor did not write about bats, but she did write about an object in the sky that she understood but professed not to understand "poetically," and she compared it to an object more familiar. Lewis Carroll did the same; there is, after all, as much resemblance between a bat and a tea tray as between a star and a diamond.

Twinkle, twinkle, little star!
I don't wonder what you are,
For by spectroscopic ken,
I know that you are hydrogen.

Another parody, author unknown. The point to be observed is that this poem and the Carroll poem attack the same absurdity in Miss Taylor's poem: assumed naïveté.

## A. E. HOUSMAN

When lads have done with labor
in Shropshire, one will cry,
"Let's go and kill a neighbor,"
and t'other answers "Aye!"

So this one kills his cousins,
and that one kills his dad;
and, as they hang by dozens
at Ludlow, lad by lad,

each of them one-and-twenty,
all of them murderers,
the hangman mutters: "Plenty
even for Housman's verse."

—HUMBERT WOLFE

*1.* Compare this parody with the Housman poems in this text; then say what aspects of Housman's poems are being singled out for ridicule.

2. What aspects of Housman's style are reproduced in the parody?

## HE LIVED AMIDST TH' UNTRODDEN WAYS

He lived amidst th' untrodden ways
To Rydal Lake that lead;
A bard whom there were none to praise,
And very few to read.

Behind a cloud his mystic sense,
Deep hidden, who can spy?
Bright as the night when not a star
Is shining in the sky.

Unread his works—his "Milk White Doe"
With dust is dark and dim;
It's still in Longman's shop, and oh!
The difference to him!

—HARTLEY COLERIDGE

*1.* What poet and what poem in this text is being parodied?

*2.* Rydal Lake was the home of this poet. The "Milk White Doe" was one of his unsuccessful works. "Longman's" was his publisher. Does someone have to tell you that to enable you to understand the poem?

Here is the same poet parodied again:

## A SONNET

Two voices are there: one is of the deep;
It learns the storm-cloud's thunderous melody,
Now roars, now murmurs with the changing sea,
Now bird-like pipes, now closes soft in sleep:
And one is of an old half-witted sheep
Which bleats articulate monotony,

And indicates that two and one are three,
That grass is green, lakes damp, and mountains steep:
And, Wordsworth, both are thine: at certain times
Forth from the heart of thy melodious rhymes,
The form and pressure of high thoughts will burst:
At other times—good Lord! I'd rather be
Quite unacquainted with the ABC
Than write such hopeless rubbish as thy worst.

—J. K. STEPHEN

*1.* Compare this poem with "The World is Too Much With Us" in this text. What parts of it are parodied?

*2.* What habits of diction and syntax are particularly parodied here?

## BREAKFAST WITH GERARD MANLEY HOPKINS

"Delicious heart-of-the-corn, fresh-from-the-oven flakes are sparkled and spangled with sugar for a can't-be-resisted flavor."

—Legend on a packet
of breakfast cereal

Serious over my cereals I broke one breakfast my fast
With something-to-read-searching retinas retained by print on a packet;
Sprung rhythm sprang, and I found (the mind fact-mining at last)
An influence Father-Hopkins-fathered on the copy-writing racket.

Parenthesis-proud, bracket-bold, happiest with hyphens
The writers stagger intoxicated by terms, adjective-unsteadied—
Describing in graceless phrases fizzling like soda syphons
All things crisp, crunchy, malted, tangy, sugared and shredded.

Far too, yes, too early we are urged to be purged, to savor
Salt, malt and phosphates in English twisted and torn,
As, sparkled and spangled with sugar for a can't-be-resisted flavor,
Come fresh-from-the-oven flakes direct from the heart of the corn.

—ANTHONY BRODE

*1.* This is a double parody. What aspects of Hopkins' style and the style of advertising copy are being parodied?

*2.* *Satire* is sometimes said to be "the isolation and exaggeration of a central absurdity in a person, a practice, or an argument." What is the relationship of parody to satire?

## THE DOVER BITCH
## A CRITICISM OF LIFE

So there stood Matthew Arnold and this girl
With the cliffs of England crumbling away behind them,
And he said to her, "Try to be true to me,
And I'll do the same for you, for things are bad
All over, etc., etc."
Well now, I knew this girl. It's true she had read
Sophocles in a fairly good translation
And caught that bitter allusion to the sea,
But all the time he was talking she had in mind
The notion of what his whiskers would feel like
On the back of her neck. She told me later on
That after a while she got to looking out
At the lights across the channel, and really felt sad,
Thinking of all the wine and enormous beds
And blandishments in French and the perfumes.
And then she got really angry. To have been brought
All the way down from London, and then be addressed
As a sort of mournful cosmic last resort

Is really tough on a girl, and she was pretty.
Anyway, she watched him pace the room
And finger his watch-chain and seem to sweat a bit,
And then she said one or two unprintable things.
But you mustn't judge her by that. What I mean to say is,
She's really all right. I still see her once in a while
And she always treats me right. We have a drink
And I give her a good time, and perhaps it's a year
Before I see her again, but there she is.
Running to fat, but dependable as they come.
And sometimes I bring her a bottle of *Nuit d'Amour*.

—ANTHONY HECHT

*1.* Compare with "Dover Beach," pp. 98-99.

# 8

# *Rigid Patterns: Fixed Forms and Pattern Poems*

There do exist forms of verse in which no variation from a pattern is permissible without disgrace. These are the absolutely fixed forms. They are poems that syllable by syllable, line by line, and rhyme by rhyme must fit a rigid pattern.

Like most things since the French Revolution that have had to fit a predetermined pattern, these forms have gotten themselves a series of bad names: light verse, *vers de société*, French verse (with overtones of *dandified* and *depraved*). In fact, the fixed forms are Japanese, Irish, and French. Perhaps the bad names owe more to their origin than to their precision.

Prominent among the rigid patterns are the haiku,* limerick,* villanelle,* triolet,* and ballade.*

The haiku is a poem composed of 17 syllables divided into three lines of five, seven, and five syllables.

Blossoms on the pear;
a woman in the moonlight
reads a letter there.

## The Haiku

The haiku is difficult to render in English not only because of the limited number of syllables and the strict arrangement, but also because the haiku communicates almost entirely by its images and primarily by visual images. The poet who is writing in English can be expected to have in mind the perfection Japanese poets are capable of in this form. English words, of course, make images; but they are not, so to speak, images in themselves. Japanese, even when rendered in the haiku in the Roman alphabet, still retains the overtones of its ideogrammatic and pictographic character. When a poet writing in English writes *man*, he is, at least psychologically, competing with a Japanese poet who can write *otoko* and rely on the picture of a man standing behind it:  . If the poet writes *rain*, he is competing with a word, *ame*, and a picture of a person with a hat standing in rain, roughly something like this:  . Haiku is not an easy form in English, but none of the fixed forms are.

## The Limerick

The limerick is written in children's meter: five lines rhyming aabba, with lines 1, 2, and 5 in anapestic trimeter and lines 3 and 4 in anapestic dimeter. The line and stanza length never get beyond a child's breathing capacity. This may seem to indicate that the limerick is confined to children's or childlike mentality; what may be called the "obscene tradition of the limerick" would seem to support that view. That is not, of course, true. On the other hand, there are no "heavy limericks," although limericks have been written by and about "heavy" people. Here is a limerick by Oliver Wendell Holmes:

The Reverend Henry Ward Beecher
Called a hen a most elegant creature.

The hen, pleased with that,
Laid an egg in his hat—
And thus did the hen reward Beecher.

The subject matter of the limerick is absurdity, whether in people, custom, or language—or all three at the same time:

There was a young lady of Me.,
Who was of her beauty quite ve.,
But a freckle or two
Later on came in view,
And drove the young lady inse.

### The Villanelle

The king of the fixed forms is the villanelle because, although French, it has never been accused of "lightness." The villanelle is a poem of 19 lines and six stanzas (five tercets and a quatrain), in which the first and third lines of the initial tercet recur alternately at the end of all following tercets and come together at the end of the closing quatrain. Here is a villanelle:

#### DO NOT GO GENTLE INTO THAT GOOD NIGHT

Do not go gentle into that good night,
Old age should burn and rave at close of day;
Rage, rage against the dying of the light.

Though wise men at their end know dark is right,
Because their words had forked no lightning they
Do not go gentle into that good night.

Good men, the last wave by, crying how bright
Their frail deeds might have danced in a green bay,
Rage, rage against the dying of the light.

Wild men who caught and sang the sun in flight,
And learn, too late, they grieved it on its way,
Do not go gentle into that good night.

Grave men, near death, who see with blinding sight
Blind eyes could blaze like meteors and be gay,
Rage, rage against the dying of the light.

And you, my father, there on the sad height,
Curse, bless, me now with your fierce tears, I pray.
Do not go gentle into that good night.
Rage, rage against the dying of the light.

—DYLAN THOMAS

## The Triolet

The queen of the fixed forms is the triolet—two quatrains with a total of two rhymes, the first line repeating as the fourth and seventh and the second line repeating as the eighth.

Here is a triolet by Austin Dobson:

I intended an Ode
And it turned to a Sonnet.
It began *a la mode*,
I intended an Ode;
But Rose crossed the road
In her latest new bonnet;
I intended an Ode,
And it turned to a Sonnet.

*1.* Since the triolet is neither "Ode" nor "Sonnet," Dobson must be playing on the implications of those words in terms of subject matter and tone. What is Dobson saying about his reaction to Rose by talking of odes and sonnets?

*2.* If you read the poem aloud, how do you find yourself changing intonation and emphasis as the refrains recur?

## The Ballade

Probably the most difficult fixed form that has had significant currency in English is the ballade. It consists of three eight- or 10-line stanzas and a four- or five-line envoy or conclusion. Only three rhymes are permitted; each stanza uses the same rhymes, and the rhyme scheme must be ababbcbc. In addition, the last line of three stanzas and the envoi must be identical.

Here is a ballade:

BALLADE OF HELL AND OF MRS. ROEBUCK

I

I'm going out to dine at Gray's
With Bertie, Morden, Charles and Kit,
And Manderly who never pays,
And Jame who wins in spite of it,
And Algernon who won't admit
The truth about his curious hair
And teeth that very nearly fit:—
And Mrs. Roebuck will be there.

II

And then to-morrow someone says
That someone else has made a hit
In one of Mister Twister's plays.
And off we go to yawn at it;
And when it's petered out we quit
For number 20, Taunton Square,
And smoke, and drink, and dance a bit:—
And Mrs. Roebuck will be there.

III

And so through each declining phase
Of emptied effort, jaded wit,

And day by day of London days
Obscurely, more obscurely, lit;
Until the uncertain shadows slit
Announcing to the shuddering air
A Darkening, and the end of it:—
And Mrs. Roebuck will be there.

ENVOI

Prince, on their iron thrones they sit,
Impassible to our despair,
The dreadful Guardians of the Pit:—
And Mrs. Roebuck will be there.

—HILAIRE BELLOC

*1.* What does Mrs. Roebuck symbolize in the poem?
*2.* Who is the "Prince" of the envoi?
*3.* Comment on the suitability of form to tone here. Why is the deadening repetition of "And Mrs. Roebuck will be there" so effective?

It may well be that one day these forms will capitulate to the principle that governs this book: poets work with and against a pattern of expectation. At one time, a long time ago, another absolutely fixed form was the *rondeau.** Chaucer got to it, varied it, and produced the *roundel;* Swinburne got hold of it and created the *rondel.* Anyone these days who says he can tell absolutely the difference between a rondeau, roundel, and rondel is simply showing off.

Of the fixed forms that have had significant currency in English, these three abide.

## Pattern Poems

Pattern poems* are also fixed forms—but fixed by the object they attempt to represent. Pattern poems (sometimes called "shaped verse") are the stepchildren of poetry. They are attempts to make verse a graphic art. Thus pattern poets may belong in the same class as Dr. Johnson's talking dog:

the surprising thing is not that they do it badly but that they do it at all. George Herbert wrote a poem entitled "Easter Wings," which in print approximates the shape of wings, and a poem entitled "The Altar," which approximates the shape of an altar.

## EASTER WINGS

Lord, who createdst man in wealth and store,
Though foolishly he lost the same,
Decaying more and more
Till he became
Most poor;
With thee
Oh, let me rise
As larks, harmoniously,
And sing this day thy victories;
Then shall the fall further the flight in me.

My tender age in sorrow did begin;
And still with sicknesses and shame
Thou didst so punish sin,
That I became
Most thin.
With thee
Let me combine,
And feel this day thy victory;
For if I imp my wing on thine,
Affliction shall advance the flight in me.

Dylan Thomas' "Vision and Prayer" juxtaposes stanzas shaped like diamonds and hourglasses. Poems have been written that are shaped like Christmas trees and goblets; inevitably they are entitled "Christmas Tree" and "Goblet."

### THE ALTAR

A broken ALTAR, Lord, thy servant rears,
Made of a heart; and cemented with tears;
Whose parts are as thy hand did frame;
No workman's tool hath touched the same.
A HEART alone
Is such a stone,
As nothing but
Thy power doth cut.
Wherefore each part
Of my hard heart
Meets in this frame
To praise thy name;
That if I chance to hold my peace,
These stones to praise thee may not cease.
Oh, let thy blessed SACRIFICE be mine,
And sanctify this ALTAR to be thine.

The fact is that the medium of poetry is language, not color or line; a child with a crayon can draw a better altar than an adult can with the printed word. Pattern poems attempt to repeat what can't be repeated without damage to the essential element. There are some things that cannot be repeated by the printed word.

## The Rock Lyric

Another thing that cannot be repeated or represented adequately by the printed word is the contemporary rock lyric. It is the fashion today to reprint these lyrics in poetry anthologies. That is a disservice to the composer and to the reader. A good rock lyric is a delicate adjustment—no matter what its volume in performance—of words and music. "Eleanor Rigby," for example, on the printed page is a very thin "poem." But it never was a poem. It is half of a union of words and music. In this text we have given way to the temptation to print a rock lyric only once—"I-Feel-Like-I'm-Fixing-To-Die-Rag"—

and there only because the power of the words quite overwhelms the pedestrian musical accompaniment; the music is, in that instance, background music.

The more dominant the music in a "poem" designed for oral performance, the less dense the language, the less complex the statement and theme. The music that scholars have been able to recover as accompaniment of traditional ballads, for example, is largely mood music, background music, and sometimes only a rhythmic approximation of the metrical beat imbedded in the poem. Thus, the practice of indiscriminately printing lyrics of popular songs makes a travesty of the art form. Rock lyrics are not an art form; rock performances are.

## Visual Forms

There *are* poems that require visual presentation. We have seen earlier examples by Edwin Morgan and Frank Weschler (pp. 161–164). Geometric verse, in which the poem may be read from left to right or from top to bottom, is similar, as in this poem by Sir Walter Raleigh:

### IN THE GRACE OF WIT, OF TONGUE AND FACE

| | | |
|---|---|---|
| Your face | Your tongue | Your wit |
| So fair | So sweet | So sharp |
| First bent | Then drew | So hit |
| Mine eye | Mine ear | My heart |
| | | |
| Mine eye | Mine ear | My heart |
| To like | To learn | To love |
| Your face | Your tongue | Your wit |
| Doth lead | Doth teach | Doth move |
| | | |
| Your face | Your tongue | Your wit |
| With beams | With sound | With art |
| Doth blind | Doth charm | Doth rule |
| Mine eye | Mine ear | My heart |

| | | |
|---|---|---|
| Mine eye | My ear | My heart |
| With life | With hope | With skill |
| Your face | Your tongue | Your wit |
| Doth feed | Doth feast | Doth fill |
| | | |
| Oh face | O tongue | O wit |
| With frowns | With cheeks | With smart |
| Wrong not | Vex not | Wound not |
| Mine eye | My ear | My heart |
| | | |
| This eye | This ear | This heart |
| Shall joy | Shall bend | Shall swear |
| Your face | Your tongue | Your wits |
| To serve | To trust | To fear |

But there is a middle ground: poems that by their presentation on the page give directions to an oral reader and yet have the density of the more traditional poem.

Buffalo Bill's
defunct
who used to
ride a watersmooth-silver
stallion
and break onetwothreefourfive pigeonsjustlikethat
Jesus
he was a handsome man
and what i want to know is
How do you like your blueeyed boy
Mister Death

—e. e. cummings

*1.* Read the poem aloud. Where do you pause? What word do you give greatest emphasis to? Why?

*2.* Jeremy Bentham, the prophet of Utilitarianism, was once asked whether he knew the difference between poetry and prose;

he replied that he did: in prose, the right-hand margin was even; in poetry, uneven. What shape on the page do you expect from a poem? Does this poem break your pattern of expectation?

*3.* Having considered the performance that the typography requires, now consider the density of the language.

*a.* *defunct* is a word used of institutions, not of people.

*b.* Buffalo Bill was not originally famous for shooting clay pigeons; he was famous for killing buffalo. He broke clay pigeons and rode a white stallion only in his traveling Wild West Show, a circus.

*c.* What is it that is "defunct" in the poem?

## IN THE FUNERAL PALLOR

with-
olding all sent-
iment till ar-
rangemen
have fini-
shed steal-
ing the feel-
ing with new sow-
ing and then sew-
ing and so-so-
ing the poor man-
gled used car-
cass, we look with-
out shrink-
ing and if any-
one cries it is be-
cause the finished product
smells
like
it
is
dead

—ANN LONGLEY

*1.* What special effects are produced by the unusual typography in this poem? Read the units as they are printed. What unusual words and phrases appear?

## SOMETIME DURING ETERNITY

Sometime during eternity
some guys show up
and one of them
who shows up real late
is a kind of carpenter
from some square-type place
like Galilee
and he starts wailing
and claiming he is hep
to who made heaven
and earth
and that the cat
who really laid it on us
is his Dad
And moreover
he adds
It's all writ down
on some scroll-type parchments
which some henchmen
leave lying around the Dead Sea somewheres
a long time ago
and which you won't even find
for a coupla thousand years or so
or at least for
nineteen hundred and fortyseven
of them
to be exact
and even then
nobody really believes them
or me
for that matter

You're hot
they tell him
And they cool him
They stretch him on the Tree to cool
And everybody after that
is always making models
of this Tree
with Him hung up
and always crooning His name
and calling Him to come down
and sit in
on their combo
as if he is *the* king cat
who's got to blow
or they can't quite make it
Only he don't come down
from his Tree
Him just hang there
on His Tree
looking real Petered out
and real cool
and also
according to a roundup
of late world news
from the usual unreliable sources
real dead

—LAWRENCE FERLINGHETTI

*1.* What is gained by the unusual placement of the words on the page?

*2.* The dialect of the poem is from the 1950s: "beatnik" dialect based on the jargon of the jazz musician. What double effects, double meanings does this produce? See, for example, *wailing*, *cool*, *blow*.

*3.* Can you account for the strange shift in syntax, "Him just hang there"? Notice that subject becomes object.

*4.* Who are the "some guys" if Christ is one of them, but one who "shows up real late"?

*5.* Is "square-type place like Galilee" a flippant remark or consistent with the attitude found in the Gospels?

*6.* What two references are wrapped up in the phrase "real Petered out"?

7. Considering the phrase "usual unreliable sources," does the poem end on a note of hope or despair?

# *Glossary*

**accent:** intensity of emphasis on a syllable; stress.

**accentual verse:** verse whose pattern is governed by the number of stresses in a line. See pp. 155–56.

**accentual-syllabic verse:** verse scanned by counting accents (stresses) and syllables; the most common type of verse in English, it utilizes classical terms (iamb, trochee, etc.; monometer, dimeter, etc.) to describe its components.

**allegory:** a work or section of a work that personifies or otherwise makes concrete entities out of abstractions in order to represent one thing in the guise of another.

**alliteration:** repetition of consonant sound. When the alliterating consonants are the initial sounds of several words, alliteration is sometimes called head rhyme. See pp. 168–70.

**allusion:** a reference, usually indirect, to a historical or fictional person, place or event.

**ambiguity:** the presence of alternative or complementary meanings in a work.

**analogy:** an extended metaphor; an extension of a comparison of two things on the grounds that if they can be said to resemble each other in one particular, they will resemble each other in others. See pp. 77–79.

**anapest:** in accentual syllabic prosody, a foot composed of two unstressed syllables and one stressed syllable.

**assonance:** the repetition of stressed vowel sounds without agreement of neighboring consonant sounds.

**ballad:** originally, a simple narrative song, normally in four-line stanzas that rhymed abcb, the first and third lines containing approximately four iambic feet; the second and fourth, three iambic feet. But folk, literary, and lyrical ballads differ widely. See pp. 172–77.

**ballade:** a poem consisting of three stanzas of eight (or 10) lines and an envoi (a concluding stanza) of four (or five) lines. The last line of each stanza and of the envoi is identical.

**blank verse:** unrhymed iambic pentameter.

**cadence:** a recurring stress pattern that cannot be analyzed into iambs, trochees, etc., or measured into monometer, dimeter, etc.

**catalog:** poems consisting of a repetitive series of images, metaphors, similes, or allusions bound together by a common idea or feeling.

**cesura:** an internal pause in a line that does not affect the metrical count.

**common measure:** the ballad stanza rigidly regularized into an abab rhyme scheme; also called the **hymnal stanza.**

**compensation:** a pause that is to be counted as a syllable in the metrical pattern, often because of the isochronic principle that dictates that the interval between major stresses tends to remain the same. See p. 160.

**conceit:** an elaborate, often far-fetched image or metaphor.

**connotation:** the overtones of a word; meanings contained in a word or image that point to attitudes and emotional reactions rather than to objective definition.

**consonance:** the repetition of final consonant sounds.

**couplet:** two lines of verse that belong together because they complete a rhyme or a thought or both.

**dactyl:** in accentual-syllabic prosody, a three-syllable foot in which the first syllable is stressed and the second and third are unstressed.

**denotation:** the objective meaning of a word; a definition that strips away the overtones of a word.

**dirge:** a lament, without meditation. See **elegy** and pp. 102–3.

**doggerel:** badly written verse, whether by intention or ignorance.

**dramatic monologue:** a poem "spoken" by a single speaker in which, often unintentionally, he reveals his character to a listener or listeners whose presence we know only through signs the speaker gives us.

**elegy:** a lament that includes meditation. See **dirge** and pp. 138–48.

**end-stopped line:** a line with a strong pause at the end produced by punctuation or rhyme.

**English sonnet:** a poem generally in 14 lines, composed of three quatrains and a couplet; also called the **Shakespearean sonnet.** See pp. 177, 179.

**enjambment:** the device used when one line runs over without pause into another because of the sense of the line, lack of punctuation, or absence of rhyme.

**epic:** a narrative poem dealing with the heroic adventures of one central character.

**epigram:** a short, witty poem, rarely more than three lines long.

**epitaph:** a short poem suitable for inscription on a gravestone.

**feminine ending:** an unstressed syllable at the end of a line.

**figurative language:** the language of comparison; the term includes metaphor, simile, analogy, irony, paradox, and allegory.

**foot:** the basic unit of measurement in accentual-syllabic prosody. A foot includes one stressed syllable and a varying number of unstressed syllables. There are four basic foot patterns in English:

iambic ∪ |
trochaic | ∪
anapestic ∪ ∪ |
dactylic | ∪ ∪

The spondaic foot ( || ) is commonly cited, but it is extremely rare.

The number of feet in a line are named:

1. monometer
2. dimeter
3. trimeter
4. tetrameter
5. pentameter
6. hexameter
7. heptameter
8. octameter

**form:** a general term for the contour of a poem, including its metrical pattern. A subdivision of form is **structure,** the arrangement of images, metaphors, and symbols in a poem.

**free verse:** unmetered poetry. See p. 155.

**haiku:** a poem of 17 syllables in three lines. The first line contains five syllables; the second, seven; the third, five. See pp. 274–75.

**heroic couplet:** two lines of iambic pentameter rhyming together and usually containing a single thought.

**homonym:** a word with the same pronunciation as another but with a different meaning and usually a different spelling, as in *bare* and *bear.*

**iamb:** in accentual-syllabic prosody, a two-syllable foot in which the first syllable is unstressed and the second is stressed.

**image:** the representation in language of a sense experience.

**inversion:** the breaking of a normal pattern by reversing the usual order of elements.

**irony:** a statement or situation that contains within it a contrast to its apparent meaning. See pp. 36, 85–86.

**Italian sonnet:** generally a 14-line poem composed of an octave (the first eight lines) and a sestet (the concluding six lines). The octave normally rhymes abba abba; the sestet may rhyme in any number of ways. Also called the **Petrarchan sonnet.** See p. 177.

**light verse:** verse generally rigid in form but playful in its themes. The term includes limericks, parodies, and many occasional poems.

**limerick:** a five-line poem rhyming aabba; lines 1, 2, and 5 usually contain three stresses, and lines 3 and 4 have two stresses. See pp. 275–76.

**lyric:** a poem designed for oral performance, with or without musical accompaniment, and concentrated thematically on personal feeling.

**metaphor:** a figure of speech likening one thing to a different thing by speaking of the one as the other, as in "All the world's a stage" or "God fashioned the ship of the world carefully" or "The ancient pulse of germ and birth/ Was shrunken hard and dry."

**meter:** the pattern that results when rhythm is organized into a regular, recurring beat that can be analyzed into units. Meter is the regularized ideal, and in that sense it is an abstraction; the poet departs at will from the metrical pattern. See pp. 154–66.

**occasional poem:** a poem written to commemorate a particular event.

**octave:** usually, the first eight lines of an Italian sonnet; rarely, any poem in eight lines.

**ode:** a lyric poem usually addressed to some person or thing. Originally the ode was lofty in tone and elaborate in design. Most twentieth-century odes, however, have tended toward simplicity of tone and design, perhaps as an ironic commentary on the world view that the older form of the ode implied.

**onomatopoeia:** the use of words that imitate the natural sound made by or associated with the thing named, as in *buzz, bang, clank*, and *whine*.

**paradox:** a statement that seems contradictory but may be true. See pp. 7–8, 50–51, 89–90.

**paraphrase:** a rewording of something already said or written in order to restate the thought or meaning of the original.

**parody:** a composition imitating the style of another author or work for purposes of ridicule.

**pastoral:** a poem of shepherds and the idyllic country life, although the theme of the poem may be extremely sophisticated.

**pattern poem:** a fixed form of poetry that attempts to make verse a graphic art.

**prosody:** the science of verse structure dealing with such components as stress, rhyme, alliteration, assonance, consonance, and meter. For prosodic systems used in English verse, see pp. 154–166.

**pun:** a word that may have two or more meanings because of the similarity of sound. *One man's Mede is another man's Persian.*

**quantitative verse:** classical, i.e., Latin and Greek, verse, in which the dominant metrical element is the quantity or duration of sounds. See p. 157.

**quotation:** the exact reproduction of a passage from another work or from speech.

**refrain:** a phrase or line repeated at the end of each section of a poem. **Incremental refrains** add to their meaning in each repetition either by introducing a change of diction or, into the stanza itself, information that sheds new light on the refrain. See pp. 32–35.

**rhyme:** the repetition of similar vowel and consonant sounds.

The repetition usually but by no means always comes at regular intervals. Rhymes can be categorized by several different means:

1. by the position of the rhyme:
   a. **end rhyme,** in which the final vowel and consonant sounds in a line recur in succeeding lines: "That's my last Duchess painted on the wall,/ Looking as if she were alive. I call"
   b. **internal rhyme,** in which a combination of vowel and consonant sounds repeats within a line: "Ah, distinctly I remember it was in the bleak December."
   c. **head** (or **initial**) **rhyme,** in which the last sounds of one line rhyme with the first sounds of the next: "The sunlight on the garden/ Hardens and grows cold."
2. by the strength of the rhyme:
   a. **full rhyme,** in which both the recurring vowel and consonant sounds are identical: top/stop
   b. **light rhyme,** in which the vowel sounds take different degrees of stress: be/hilly
   c. **slant rhyme,** in which the vowel sounds are similar but not identical: steel/hill
   d. **eye rhyme,** in which the rhyming syllables appear identical only to the eye: sties/properties
3. by the coincidence of rhyme and stress:
   a. **masculine rhyme,** in which the final syllable of each rhyming word is stressed: disturb/perturb
   b. **feminine rhyme,** in which the final syllable of each rhyming word is unstressed: sleeping/peeping
4. by the number of rhyming syllables. Theoretically, one may rhyme any number of syllables. The

practical limit in English seems to be four, as when Byron used quadruple rhyme in coupling *ladies intellectual* with *henpeck'd you-all.*

So-called **historical rhyme** is not a kind of rhyme but an accident of history; it occurs when pronunciation changes and full rhyme is reduced to light, slant, or eye rhyme. To Alexander Pope and his readers, for example, *join* and *divine* made a full rhyme.

**rhythm:** a recurrence of beats or stresses in a discernible but not necessarily rigidly regular pattern.

**rondeau:** a fixed form of verse running on two alternating rhymes. It usually consists of five quatrains in which the lines of the first quatrain are used consecutively to end each of the remaining four quatrains which are in turn sometimes followed by an envoi of four lines that terminates with the opening words of the poem.

**scansion:** the metrical analysis of lines and stanzas. See p. 159.

**sestet:** the last six lines of an Italian sonnet.

**simile:** a figure of speech that compares two different items by linking them with *like, as*, and *then.*

**sonnet:** a poem on a single subject, traditionally in 14 lines. **English** or **Shakespearean sonnets** traditionally contain three quatrains and a couplet, rhyming abab cdcd efef gg. **Italian** or **Petrarchan sonnets** traditionally contain an octave (the first eight lines) and a sestet (the final six lines); the octave rhymes abba abba, and the sestet rhymes cdcded or cdecde or cdedce, although some Italian sonnets use a concluding couplet rhyme. The **Spenserian sonnet,** an English form but rarer in English than the Italian or traditional English form, combines features of both the others, rhyming abab bcbc cdcd ee. For a full set of examples, see pp. 177–82, 187–89.

**spondee:** in accentual-syllabic prosody, a foot composed of two stressed syllables (very rare in English).

**stanza:** a group of lines with a rhyme scheme that is repeated.

When groups of lines do not rhyme, as in blank verse and most free verse, the groups are usually called **verse paragraphs.**

Stanzas sometimes take their names from the number of lines they contain, sometimes from their originator, sometimes from their most popular practitioner. The shortest stanza in English is the **couplet,** two lines rhyming together. Couplets that complete a single thought in each two-line unit and are written in pentameter are called **heroic couplets** because of their use in heroic (epic) verse and, more remotely, because of the use of iambic pentameter, rhymed and unrhymed, in heroic verse. Couplets may be **open** or **closed;** that is, the second line may run its sense over into the third line (the first line of the succeeding couplet), or may complete its sense in the second line. The first is open, the second closed; by definition, heroic couplets are closed. For open couplets, see "My Last Duchess," pp. 182–84.

**Tercets** are three-line stanzas. If they rhyme aba bcb cdc, and so on, they are said to be **terza rima.** If they rhyme aaa bbb ccc, and so on, they are called **triplets.**

**Quatrains,** probably the most popular stanza in English, contain four lines. Quatrains have myriad rhyme schemes, e.g.:

1. the ballad stanza, which rhymes abcb or abab and traditionally alternates tetrameter and trimeter lines; the abab quatrain in strict iambic meter is often called the **hymnal stanza.**
2. the In Memoriam stanza, containing four iambic lines rhyming abba cddc, and so on; named for Tennyson's use of it in *In Memoriam*, although he did not originate the form.
3. the Rubaiyat stanza, having four pentameter lines rhyming aaba; named for Edward Fitzgerald's use of it in his "The Rubaiyat of Omar Khayyam."

*Rubaiyat* itself means "quatrains."

Five- and six-line stanzas are common, but no one pattern has so asserted itself as to gain an established name. The best known seven-line stanza is **rhyme royal,** called "royal" because James I used it, although Chaucer imported it into English. The rhyme royal stanza rhymes ababbcc and is usually composed of pentameter lines.

Notable among eight-line stanzas are

1. **ottava rima,** having eight pentameter lines rhyming abababcc.
2. the **Spenserian stanza,** rhyming ababbcbc; the first seven lines are in iambic pentameter, the last in iambic hexameter.

Stanzas longer than eight lines are uncommon in English.

**stress:** intensity of emphasis on a syllable; accent.

**symbol:** a word or image that stands for itself and another thing as well, as the cross is a symbol of Christianity. The symbol is commonly an object that stands for something abstract. See pp. 81–84, 90–96.

**syntax:** the combination of grammar and rhetoric to make the best use of both in order to write effective, coherent, balanced sentences; or, the order of words.

**terza rima:** a series of three-line stanzas with an interlocked rhyme scheme: aba bcb cdc, and so on.

**tone:** the implied aspect of a composition that indicates the attitude of the poet or speaker toward the theme of the poem and the reader.

**triolet:** a poem composed of two quatrains using two rhymes only, arranged in an abaaabab pattern. The first line is repeated as the fourth and seventh lines. The second line repeats as the eighth. See p. 277.

**trochee:** in accentual-syllabic prosody, a foot of two syllables, the first syllable stressed and the second unstressed.

**verse:** poetry in meter; one line of a poem; or, in speaking of hymns, a popular synonym for **stanza.**

**villanelle:** a 19-line poem on two rhymes in six stanzas. The first and third lines of the first stanza recur alternately at the end of the other stanzas; both are repeated at the end of the last stanza, a quatrain.

**voice:** the combination of words, syntax, tone, etc., that characterizes an individual poet or speaker in a poem.

# *Acknowledgments*


Aldine•Atherton, Inc. for "Message Clear" from *The Second Life* by Edwin Morgan, copyright © 1968 by Edwin Morgan and Edinburgh University Press. Reprinted by permission of Aldine•Atherton, Inc.

Kingsley Amis for "Terrible Beauty." First published in *Encounter*. Reprinted by permission of the author.

Atheneum Publishers, Inc. for "The Dover Bitch" from *The Hard Hours* by Anthony E. Hecht. Copyright © 1960 by Anthony E. Hecht. Appeared originally in *Transatlantic Review*. Reprinted by permission of Atheneum Publishers, Inc.

Basic Books, Inc. for "On Not Writing an Elegy" by Richard Frost from *Of Poetry and Power* edited by Erwin A. Blicks and Paul Schwaber, © 1964 by Basic Books, Inc., Publishers, New York.

Bookman Associates for "America" from *Selected Poems of Claude McKay*. Copyright 1953 by Bookman Associates. Reprinted by permission of Bookman Associates and Twayne Publishers.

Broadside Press for "The Rite" and "Black Poet, White Critic" from *Cities Burning* by Dudley Randall. Reprinted by permission of Broadside Press.

Jonathan Cape, Ltd. for "Naming of Parts," "Judging Distances," and "Unarmed Combat" from "Lessons of the War" in *A Map of Verona* by Henry Reed. For "Nostalgia—Now Threepence Off" from *Poems* by Adrian Mitchell. Reprinted by permission of Jonathan Cape, Ltd.

Chatto & Windus for "Ghazal" from *Leaflets* by Adrienne Rich. Reprinted by permission of author and publisher.

J. M. Dent & Sons, Ltd. for "Do not go gentle into that good night" from *Collected Poems of Dylan Thomas*. Reprinted by permission of J. M. Dent & Sons, Ltd. and the Trustees for Copyrights of the late Dylan Thomas.

Doubleday & Company, Inc. for "Highway: Michigan" from *Collected Poems of Theodore Roethke.* Copyright 1940 by Theodore Roethke. Reprinted by permission of Doubleday & Company, Inc.

Faber and Faber Limited for "The Unknown Citizen," "O Where Are You Going?" and "On This Island" from *Collected Shorter Poems 1927-1957* by W. H. Auden. For "Journey of the Magi" and "The Love Song of J. Alfred Prufrock" from *Collected Poems 1909-1962* by T. S. Eliot. Reprinted by permission of Faber and Faber Limited.

Ferrar, Straus & Giroux, Inc. for "Hope" and "The Emancipators" from *The Complete Poems of Randall Jarrell,* copyright © 1945, 1951, 1955, 1969 by Mrs. Randall Jarrell. For "Memories of West Street and Lepke" from *Life Studies* by Robert Lowell, copyright © 1958 by Robert Lowell. Reprinted by permission of Ferrar, Straus & Giroux, Inc.

Joseph Leonard Grucci for "Rhine Burial" from *Time of Hawks* (1955) and *The Invented Will* (1962), Pittsburgh, Pa.: Mayer Press. Reprinted by permission of author and publisher.

Harcourt Brace Jovanovich, Inc. for "Afternoon of a Pawnbroker" and "Art Review" from *Afternoon of a Pawnbroker and Other Poems,* copyright, 1943, by Kenneth Fearing; renewed, 1970, by Bruce Fearing. For "Journey of the Magi" and "The Love Song of J. Alfred Prufrock" from *Collected Poems 1909-1962* by T. S. Eliot, copyright, 1946, by Harcourt Brace Jovanovich, Inc.; copyright © 1963, 1964, by T. S. Eliot. For "Death of a Toad" from *Ceremony and Other Poems* by Richard Wilbur, copyright, 1948, 1949, 1950 by Richard Wilbur. For "Mr. Edwards and the Spider" from *Lord Weary's Castle* by Robert Lowell, copyright, 1946, by Robert Lowell. For "anyone lived in a pretty how town," Copyright 1940, by e. e. cummings; renewed, 1968, by Marian Morehouse Cummings. Reprinted from *Poems 1923-1954* by e. e. cummings. For "Buffalo Bill's defunct," Copyright 1923, 1951 by e. e. cummings. Reprinted from his volume, *Poems 1923-1924.* For "gee I like to think of dead," copyright, 1925, by e. e. cummings. Reprinted from his volume, *Poems, 1923-1954.* For "go (perpe) go," "kumrads die because they're told," and "when muckers, pimps and tratesmen," copyright, 1935, by e. e. cummings; renewed, 1963, by Marion Morehouse Cummings. Reprinted from *Poems 1923-1954.* For "i sing of Olaf," Copyright, 1931, 1959, by e. e. cummings. Reprinted from his volume, *Poems 1923-1954.* For "my sweet old etcetera" and "poem, Or Beauty hurts Mr. Vinal," Copyright, 1926, by Horace Liveright; renewed, 1954, by e. e. cummings. Reprinted from *Poems 1923-1954* by e. e. cummings. All reprinted by permission of Harcourt Brace Jovanovich, Inc.

Harper & Row Publishers, Inc. for "The Ballad of Chocolate Mabbie" and "Negro Hero" from *Selected Poems* by Gwendolyn Brooks. Copyright 1945 by Gwendolyn Brooks Blakely. For "Malcolm X" from *In the Mecca* by Gwendolyn Brooks. Copyright 1967 by Gwendolyn Brooks Blakely. For "Mood" from *On These I Stand* by Countee Cullen. Copyright 1929 by Harper & Row Publishers, Inc.;

renewed 1957 by Ida M. Cullen. All reprinted by permission of Harper & Row Publishers, Inc.

Harvard University Press for "Because I Could Not Stop For Death," "Death is a Dialogue," "I Heard A Fly Buzz When I Died," "I Taste A Liquor Never Brewed," and "Some Things that Fly there be." Reprinted by permission of the publishers and the Trustees of Amherst College from Thomas H. Johnson, Editor, *The Poems of Emily Dickinson,* Cambridge, Mass.: The Belknap Press of Harvard University Press, Copyright, 1951, 1955, by the President and Fellows of Harvard College.

Holt, Rinehart and Winston, Inc. for "Nothing Gold Can Stay" and "Stopping by Woods on a Snowy Evening" from *The Poetry of Robert Frost* edited by Edward Connery Latham. Copyright, 1923 by Holt, Rinehart and Winston, Inc. Copyright, 1951 by Robert Frost. For "Is My Team Ploughing," "Terence, This Is Stupid Stuff," and "To An Athlete Dying Young" from "A Shropshire Lad"—Authorized Edition—from *The Collected Poems of A. E. Housman.* Copyright, 1939, 1940, © 1959 by Holt, Rinehart and Winston, Inc. Copyright © 1967, 1968 by Robert E. Symons. All reprinted by permission of Holt, Rinehart and Winston, Inc.

Houghton Mifflin Company for "You, Andrew Marvell" from *Collected Poems 1917-1952* by Archibald MacLeish.

Indiana University Press for "Boy and Top" (translated by Muriel Rukeyser) from *The Selected Poems of Octavio Paz.* For "Dirge" and "Homage" from *New and Selected Poems* by Kenneth Fearing. All reprinted by permission of Indiana University Press.

Margot Johnson Agency for "Life Cycle of a Common Man" from *New and Selected Poems* (University of Chicago Press, 1960), by Howard Nemerov. Reprinted by permission of the Margot Johnson Agency.

Alfred A. Knopf, Inc. for "Of Modern Poetry" from *The Collected Poems of Wallace Stevens.* Copyright 1942 and renewed 1970 by Holly Stevens Stephenson. Reprinted by permission of Alfred A. Knopf, Inc. For "Bells for John Whiteside's Daughter," copyright 1924 by Alfred A. Knopf, Inc. and renewed 1952 by John Crowe Ransom. Reprinted from *Selected Poems,* Revised edition, by John Crowe Ransom, by permission of Alfred A. Knopf, Inc.

Little Brown and Company for "Careless Love" from *Selected Poems 1928-1958* by Stanley Kunitz. Copyright © 1929, 1930, 1944, 1951, 1953, 1954, 1956, 1957, 1958 by Stanley Kunitz. For "Portrait of the Artist as a Prematurely Old Man" from *Verses from 1929 On* by Ogden Nash. Copyright, 1934, by The Curtis Publishing Company. All reprinted by permission of Atlantic-Little Brown and Company.

Anne M. Longley for "In the Funeral Pallor." Printed by permission of the author.

The Macmillan Company for "The Convergence of the Twain" and "Neutral Tones" from *Collected Poems* by Thomas Hardy. Copyright 1925 by The Macmillan Company. For "Cargoes" from *Poems* by John Masefield. Copyright 1912 by The Macmillan Company, renewed 1940 by John Masefield. For "Poetry" from *Collected Poems* by Marianne Moore, Copyright 1935 by Marianne Moore, renewed 1963 by Marianne Moore and T. S. Eliot; and "What Are

Years?" from *Collected Poems* by Marianne Moore, Copyright 1941 by Marianne Moore, renewed 1969 by Marianne Moore. For "The Dark Hills" from *Collected Poems* by Edwin Arlington Robinson, Copyright 1920 by Edwin Arlington Robinson, renewed 1948 by Ruth Nivison; and "Karma" from *Collected Poems* by Edwin Arlington Robinson, Copyright 1925 by Edwin Arlington Robinson, renewed 1953 by Ruth Nivison and Barbara R. Holt. For "The U. S. Sailor with the Japanese Skull" from *Collected Poems* by Winfield Townley Scott, Copyright 1945 by Winfield Townley Scott. For "For Anne Gregory" and "The Mother of God" from *Collected Poems* by William Butler Yeats, Copyright 1933 by The Macmillan Company, renewed 1961 by Bertha Georgie Yeats; and for "The Second Coming" from *Collected Poems* by William Butler Yeats, Copyright 1924 by The Macmillan Company, renewed 1952 by Bertha Georgie Yeats. All reprinted by permission of The Macmillan Company.

The Macmillan Company of Canada and Macmillan London and Basingstoke for "The Convergence of the Twain" and "Neutral Tones" from *Collected Poems* by Thomas Hardy. Reprinted by permission of the publishers.

The Modern Poetry Association for "The Gift of Fire" by Lisel Mueller. From *Poetry* © 1961 The Modern Poetry Association. Reprinted by permission of Daryl Hine, editor.

Charlotte Mortimer for "The Pioneers." Reprinted by permission of the author.

William Morrow and Company, Inc. for "Love Poem" from *The Iron Pastoral* by John Frederick Nims, copyright © 1947 by John Frederick Nims. Reprinted by permission of William Morrow and Company, Inc.

John Murray Publishers Ltd. for "In Westminster Abbey" from *Collected Poems 1959* by John Betjeman. Reprinted by permission of John Murray Publishers Ltd.

New Directions Publishing Corporation for "Sometime During Eternity" from *A Coney Island of the Mind* by Lawrence Ferlinghetti. Copyright © 1958 by Lawrence Ferlinghetti. For "The Orange Bears" from *Collected Poems* by Kenneth Patchen. Copyright 1949 by New Directions Publishing Corporation. For "The Bathtub" from *Personae* by Ezra Pound. Copyright 1926 by Ezra Pound. For "Do not go gentle into that good night" from *Collected Poems* by Dylan Thomas. Copyright 1952 by Dylan Thomas. For "The Red Wheelbarrow" from *Collected Earlier Poems* and "A Sort of a Song" from *Collected Later Poems* by William Carlos Williams. Copyright 1938 and 1944 by William Carlos Williams. All reprinted by permission of New Directions Publishing Corporation.

W. W. Norton & Company, Inc. for "Ghazal" from *Leaflets* by Adrienne Rich. Copyright © 1969 by W. W. Norton & Company, Inc. Reprinted by permission of the publisher.

Oxford University Press for "Carrion Comfort," "Spring and Fall," "Thou Art Indeed Just, Lord," and "The Windhover" from *Book of Complete Poems* by Gerard Manley Hopkins. Reprinted by permission of Oxford University Press.

A. D. Peters & Company for "Ballad of Hell and of Mrs. Roebuck" by Hilaire Belloc. Reprinted by permission of A. D. Peters & Company.

Random House, Inc. for "The Unknown Citizen." Copyright 1940 and renewed 1968 by W. H. Auden. From *The Collected Shorter Poems 1927-1957* by W. H. Auden. For "O Where Are You Going?" Copyright 1934 and renewed 1962 by W. H. Auden. From *The Collected Shorter Poems 1927-1957* by W. H. Auden. For "On This Island" from *The Collected Shorter Poems 1927-1957* by W. H. Auden. Copyright 1937 and renewed 1965 by W. H. Auden. For fourteen lines from "The Age of Anxiety." Copyright 1946, 1947 by W. H. Auden. From *Collected Longer Poems* by W. H. Auden. For "Time of Disturbance" from *Hungerford and Other Poems* by Robinson Jeffers. Copyright 1951 by Robinson Jeffers. For "Survey of Literature," copyright 1927 by Alfred A. Knopf, Inc. Copyright © 1955 by John Crowe Ransom. Reprinted from *Selected Poems*, Revised edition by John Crowe Ransom. All reprinted by permission of Random House, Inc.

The Ben Roth Agency, Inc. for "Breakfast with Gerard Manley Hopkins" by Anthony Brode. Copyright © *Punch*, London.

The Society of Authors for "Is My Team Ploughing" "Terence, This Is Stupid Stuff," "To An Athlete Dying Young," from *Collected Poems* by A. E. Housman. Reprinted by permission of The Society of Authors and Jonathan Cape, Ltd. For "Cargoes" by John Masefield. Reprinted by permission of The Society of Authors and the literary representative of the Estate of John Masefield.

Tradition Music Co. (BMI) for "I-Feel-Like-I'm-Fixing-To-Die-Rag" by Joe MacDonald. Copyright © 1968 by Tradition Music Co.

The Viking Press, Inc. for "Snake" from *The Complete Poems of D. H. Lawrence*, edited by Vivian de Sola Pinto and Warren Roberts. Copyright 1923; renewed 1951 by Frieda Lawrence. All rights reserved. For "Resume" from *The Portable Dorothy Parker*. Copyright 1926, renewed 1954 by Dorothy Parker. All rights reserved. Reprinted by permission of The Viking Press, Inc.

A. P. Watt & Son for "The Second Coming," "For Anne Gregory," "The Mother of God" from *The Collected Poems of W. B. Yeats*. Reprinted by permission of Mr. M. B. Yeats and Macmillan & Co. Ltd.

Frank Weschler for "I Vow." Printed by permission of the author.

Wesleyan University Press for "Lines for a Dead Poet" from *On the Way to the Island* by David Ferry. Copyright © 1957 by David Ferry. For "Anniversaries" from *The Summer Anniversaries* by Donald Justice. Copyright © 1957, 1960 by Donald Justice. The final stanza was first published in *The New Yorker*. All by permission of Wesleyan University Press.

Anne Wolfe for "A. E. Housman" by Humbert Wolfe. Reprinted by permission of Miss Anne Wolfe.

Yale University Press for "For My People" from *For My People* by Margaret Walker, Copyright 1942, 1968 by Yale University Press.

# Index of Authors, Titles, and First Lines

# *Index of Terms**



*Those terms found in the glossary (pp. 288-298) are not indexed here.